A STRANGE IDEA OF ENTERTAINMENT:
CONVERSATIONS WITH
TOM MCLOUGHLIN

EDITED BY
JOSEPH MADDREY

A STRANGE IDEA OF ENTERTAINMENT:
CONVERSATIONS WITH TOM MCLOUGHLIN
©2014 JOSEPH MADDREY & TOM MCLOUGHLIN

ALL RIGHTS RESERVED.

No part of this book may be reproduced in any form or by any means, electronic, mechanical, digital, photocopying, or recording, except for inclusion of a review, without permission in writing from the publisher.

Published in the USA by:

BEARMANOR MEDIA
P.O. BOX 71426
ALBANY, GEORGIA 31708
www.BearManorMedia.com

ISBN-10: 1-59393-560-9 (alk. paper)
ISBN-13: 978-1-59393-560-3 (alk. paper)

FRONT COVER ILLUSTRATION:
MELISSA BENTLEY (roobentley@gmail.com)

BACK COVER ROCK GOD PHOTO:
GORKA RUIZ DE HEREDIA (www.rhythmandphotos.com)

DESIGN AND LAYOUT: VALERIE THOMPSON

TABLE OF CONTENTS

Foreword by Steven Banks . . . 1

Introduction . . . 5

I. Wonder Years (1950–1970) . . . 9

Growing up at MGM / Dad, the fire-eater / Peter Lorre's wake / Chaplin off the wall / Mom & Vincent Price / Monterey Pop / The southern California version of Mick Jagger / Opening for The Doors / Backing up transsexual strippers / The end of the Sixties / Off to Paris

II. Comedy & Horror (1970s) . . . 33

Marcel Marceau's School of Mime / Mr. Hulot / Convincing Woody Allen that he's funny / Goofing off with Dick Van Dyke / Studying with the stars at Sherwood Oaks / Meeting Frank Capra / Playing the mutant bear / The second fastest gun in the universe / Psychic vampires / A personal ghost story

III. Myths & Monsters (1981–1991) ... 75

The first director's cut / Resurrecting Jason Voorhees / The dying man and his angel / Mysteries from a magic pawn shop / Frank Capra meets Freddy Krueger / Stephen King's greatest hits / Life, death and Indian burial grounds

IV. Men & Women (1991–1995) ... 125

Real-life monsters / The Luminol scene / Alison's legacy / A Radio Shack future / The female version of Taxi Driver / One of God's true children / The battle for ambiguity / Directing Kirk Douglas / Coppola's advice

V. More Myths & Monsters (1995–2000) ... 179

Ghosts and innocents / Arthur Conan Doyle, Harry Houdini and the power of imagination / Yes, Burbank, there is a Santa Claus / "Survival movies" / Exit elves? / Meeting Marlon Brando / A Hawksian love story / The return of The Exorcist / Tone wars

VI. Kids & America (2001–2008) ... 229

Demons from the Id / The murder in heaven / American terrorists / Christmas blues and black humor / Teen noir / Seduction, obsession, addiction / Twenty-first century witch hunting / Reality vs. docudrama / The grindhouse girls

VII. Looking Ahead . . . 291

VIII. Tommy Lives! . . . 303

Filmography . . . 321

Appendix: Jason Lives! . . . 325

Index . . . 347

Dedicated to
GOD
For His Vision
and Humor

FOREWORD

A Toast to My Pal, Thomas Maurice McLoughlin,
on the event of his sixtieth birthday
at Hollywood Forever Cemetery
by Steven Banks

In 1950, the following people were born: Bill Murray, Cybil Shepherd, Mark Spitz, Peter Frampton, Stevie Wonder, Richard Branson, Jay Leno, and Karen Carpenter. Seven of them are still alive. But we don't care about them. We care about Tom McLoughlin.

Who is Tom McLoughlin? Well, if you took a bit of Frank Capra, some Marcel Marceau, Mick Jagger, James Brown, Chaplin, add some Walt Disney, Sherlock Holmes, a little Alfred Hitchcock, Tod Browning, Bobby Sands, Martin Scorsese, tossed in some Keaton, Jacques Tati, John Ford, some Norman Rockwell, some Richard Pryor, Mark Twain, tossed in Truffaut and some other French directors whose names I can't pronounce properly, Stan Laurel & Oliver Hardy, Houdini, Marx Brothers, threw in a couple of Beatles, some Kinks, Orson Welles, Chucko The Birthday Clown, and Snitz Edwards—if you took all of them and mixed them in a big, giant blender . . . it would be really disgusting . . . with all that blood and bone and organs. But if you mixed all of those people together . . . it would be the man we know as Thomas Maurice McLoughlin.

Tom started off as a small child . . .

But, enough about Tom, let's talk about me, Steven Banks

I met Tom on a 7UP commercial in 1978. He got the part. I didn't. They wanted someone older. With longer hair.

Throughout the years, I've done many things with Tom. I've worked with Tom on many projects; I've vacationed with Tom; I've dressed up as a banana with Tom; I've slow danced with Tom in public (and gotten paid for it); dressed up as a woman with Tom and cooked a pig's head (and not gotten paid for it); I've pretended to be a homosexual with Tom so we could hang out in a dressing room and watch the female models walk around with their tops off; I was in *The Black Hole* with Tom (not the bar, the movie); and I've dressed up as a monster and scared children with Tom on numerous occasions. I've been to Disneyland, strip clubs, apple orchards, carnivals, sideshows, and looked at Ike Turner's corpse with Tom. I've enjoyed many parties at Tom's house with his lovely wife, Nancy, his children, Shane and Hannah, and their 347 pets. I've been directed by Tom, in the beginning of *One Dark Night*, as the man carrying a large pole.

One thing's for sure, Tom McLoughlin is cool. Here are the Top Ten Reasons why Tom is the coolest guy I know:

#10. He joined Scientology for a hot woman—the only reason to join Scientology—and then left when he broke up with her.

#9. He once enjoyed medicinal herbs with Jimi Hendrix in the sixties.

#8. His band opened for The Doors.

#7. He kissed Albert Ash on the lips.

#6. He saw, in person, the Monterey Pop Festival, and The Beatles at Dodger Stadium, and Led Zeppelin at The Whiskey.

#5. While entertaining an obnoxious and pretentious woman at a dinner party at his house, he served some of his dog Kelly's feces on a plate and announced to the woman that these were a special dessert called "Kelly's Brownies."

#4. He went to Larry Fine's funeral . . . and if you don't know who Larry Fine is, you were probably born in a cave.

#3. He was propositioned by the great ballet dancer Rudolph Nureyev on three separate occasions . . . and turned him down . . . or so he says.

#2. He is one of the few people who can actually say "Some people call me Maurice" and not be joking.

And the **#1** reason Tom is the coolest guy I know: His wife gave him a birthday party in a cemetery.

But back to me, Steven Banks.
Tommy gave me the greatest birthday gift I have ever received: a personal visit from one of my heroes, the great comedian Wally Boag . . . and if you don't know who Wally Boag is, get out your iPhone4—if you can get service—and Google him. I wanted to bring one of Tom's heroes here tonight, but they're all dead. One of them may be buried here, so at least we're close.

But, seriously . . . on a personal note: if it wasn't for Tom McLoughlin, no one would know what *Home Entertainment Center* or Billy The Mime was and I'd still be doing junior high school assembly shows . . . and addicted to crystal meth.

We are all here tonight because we love Tom or admire Tom or are hoping he will hire us on his next movie—which I wish he would shoot in Los Angeles so I could get a small part.

Now to paraphrase Clarence in *It's a Wonderful Life*: "No man is poor or a failure who has friends."

A toast to my other big brother, Tom McLoughlin, the richest man in town.

Tom's sixtieth birthday party at Hollywood Forever Cemetery.
Photo credit: Bern Agency

INTRODUCTION

I met filmmaker Tom McLoughlin in the spring of 2008. I was searching for interview subjects for a documentary on the history of American horror films, and my friend John Muir recommended Tom. "He knows a lot about classic monster movies," John said. I knew that McLoughlin had directed a respectable Gothic horror film called *One Dark Night* and the best sequel in the *Friday the 13th* series, but I didn't really think of him as a "horror director." Even so, I decided to call.

I talked to Tom one dark night while he was editing *Fab Five: The Texas Cheerleader Scandal*. It turned out to be the first of many long conversations. Horror movies, he explained, had helped him to get through his formative years, growing up across the street from MGM studios. When he was about ten years old, his mother suffered a nervous breakdown. Around the same time, Tom became fascinated with Vincent Price—particularly the maniacal characters he portrayed in Roger Corman's film adaptations of Edgar Allan Poe. On weekdays, he would skip out on classes at St. Timothy's Grade School and take a city bus to Santa Monica for the noontime movies, where he reveled in the artificial madness of Roderick Usher, Nicolas Medina, and the evil Prince Prospero. Around the same time, he discovered the classic Universal monsters on television. After watching *Dracula*, he rode his bike to Holy Cross Cemetery in Culver City and sat beside Bela Lugosi's grave, remembering the dead man's immortal words: "To die . . . to be truly dead . . . that must be glorious."

One week after that first conversation, Tom and I sat down in my Studio City apartment and recorded an interview for *Nightmares in*

Red, White and Blue. We talked for more than two hours, until the tape ran out. Afterwards, I wanted to keep going . . . not just to hear Tom's thoughts on horror movies, but to hear more about his life, which sounded fantastic enough to be its own movie. In the days that followed, I realized that Tom McLoughlin is living proof that Hollywood myths can profoundly shape a person's life, blurring the line between fiction and reality.

Before he was a filmmaker, McLoughlin was a singer in a rock 'n' roll band that played regularly on the Sunset Strip in the late '60s, opening for classic rock bands like The Doors, The Animals, and Chicago Transit Authority. When the music died, he went to Paris and studied mime with the legendary Marcel Marceau. When he returned to Los Angeles, he tried his luck at acting, and slowly worked toward his ultimate goal of becoming a director. Along the way, he crossed paths with countless legends: Woody Allen, Dick Van Dyke, Lucille Ball, Carol Burnett, John Frankenheimer, and Frank Capra, who became a personal mentor. All of this happened before he made his first film.

McLoughlin's life and career are nothing if not eclectic, but his stories—fiction and nonfiction alike—are bound together by an unyielding sense of adventure and whimsy. In *Friday the 13th Part 6: Jason Lives!*, a cemetery caretaker discovers an open grave and an empty coffin. Believing it to be the work of teenage pranksters, he grumbles something about "damn kids"—then promptly breaks the fourth wall, turns to the moviegoing audience and quips, "Some folks have a strange idea of entertainment." It's an amusing self-incrimination.

This book is the outcome of the ten lengthy interviews conducted in the fall of 2008, through which I tried to glean as much as I could about the filmmaker's creative process. I have always believed that true creativity is based on a subtle dialogue between everyday life and art, and McLoughlin's answers consistently reinforced this idea. His movies have drawn heavily on his early childhood influences, from Charlie Chaplin to *Famous Monsters of Filmland*. Likewise, his adult relationships with friends and family have played a major role in his fiction. In 1990, while McLoughlin was directing *Stephen King's Sometimes They Come Back*—a film about letting go of the past and facing the future—his father died and his daughter was born. This was a turning point in his career as well as in his personal life.

Over the course of the following decade, he took his wife Nancy and two young children with him on every shoot. Nancy often appeared in supporting roles, while Shane and Hannah made frequent cameos and helped with production. Each film was a family affair, and the director's real-world experiences as a father and husband continually found their way onscreen, in a succession of films about family dynamics.

In 1993, McLoughlin directed two back-to-back films about mental instability. He describes *A Murder of Innocence*, based on the true story of spree killer Laurie Dann, as a reflection of the "dark side" of his mother's illness. *The Yarn Princess*, a story about single mother with mental deficiencies, is a rumination on the qualities that made his mother such a wonderful caregiver. Similarly, *The Lies Boys Tell* (1994) provided McLoughlin with an opportunity to eulogize his father.

The filmmaker turned his focus toward young children at a time when he was re-experiencing childhood from an adult perspective. He was interested in exploring both the dark side of those formative years, starting with *Journey* and *The Turn of the Screw* (both 1995) and culminating with *The Unsaid* (2001), as well as the light side, in *Fairy Tale: A True Story* (1997) and the surprisingly ethereal *Murder in Greenwich* (2002). As his own children got older and entered high school, so did the characters in his films. In 2004, McLoughlin kicked off a series of Lifetime movies about teenagers struggling to find their places in the world: *She's Too Young* (2004), *Odd Girl Out* (2005), *Cyber Seduction: His Secret Life* (2005), *Not Like Everyone Else* (2006), and *Fab Five: The Texas Cheerleader Scandal* (2008).

On the verge of his fourth decade as a filmmaker, McLoughlin is trending toward more socially-conscious films. *D.C. Sniper: 23 Days of Fear* (2003) and *Not Like Everyone Else* are harrowing reflections of post-9/11 America. *The Staircase Murders* (2007) and *The Wronged Man* (2009) are unsettling depictions of contemporary crime and punishment. As always, the filmmaker's focus remains on the characters because, as his mentor Frank Capra taught him, movies are a people-to-people medium.

The director's first responsibility is to empathize with his characters (even the most reprehensible ones) and to understand their thoughts and motivations. That's how McLoughlin has established personal connections with nearly all of the stories he's told, and that is why he's a filmmaker worth studying. The best filmmakers comprehend our everyday hopes and our fears, our trials and our triumphs, and show them to us through the magic of the movies. That has been—and continues to be—the story of Tom McLoughlin's life.

PART I: WONDER YEARS

Growing up at MGM / Dad, the fire-eater / Peter Lorre's wake / Chaplin on the wall / Mom & Vincent Price / Monterey Pop / The southern California version of Mick Jagger / Opening for The Doors / backing up transsexual strippers / The end of the Sixties / Off to Paris

MGM back lot in 1938 (with arrow pointing to the McLoughlin house)
Photo credit: Marc Wanamaker/Bison Archives

JOSEPH MADDREY: You're a Los Angeles native, born in 1950 in Culver City, which was home to the MGM back lot. That means that *The Wizard of Oz*, *Gone with the Wind*, and Alfred Hitchcock's *Rebecca* were practically filmed in your backyard. What was it like growing up in the dream machine?

TOM MCLOUGHLIN: Technically I was born in Santa Monica, and then grew up in Culver City. In those days, Culver City was a pretty sleepy town. The back lot of MGM extended way up into the Baldwin Hills area where there are now apartments and condos. It was enormous! So it was a great place to go play as a kid.

You were allowed to play there?

Well, it wasn't allowed . . . but there was only maybe one security guard there on the weekends, so you could do a lot of screwing around before you'd get caught.

What about your parents? They let you wander?

Yeah, that was one of the great things about that period. People weren't so paranoid about letting kids run wild. I didn't realize how much things had changed until a few years ago. I was watching some kid walking down the street and I thought, "Why is he out walking by himself?" Then I thought, *I can't believe I'm thinking this way.* When I was growing up, kids would disappear after school for hours and hours and hours. You might get punished if it was dark when you came home, but as long as you got home *just before* dark, you were okay.

The old Hal Roach studios were still around in those days—that's where *Laurel and Hardy* and *The Little Rascals* were shot—and all of those sets were still up. Desilu Productions, which is now called Culver Studios, also had a back lot. Twentieth Century Fox had their back lots there. I went to school at St. Timothy Catholic School on Pico Boulevard, which was two blocks away from the Twentieth Century Fox lots, and my friends knew how to get into those places. So I really did grow up in "movie city."

I accepted the fact that this fantasy world existed side-by-side with the real world. At the time, nobody said, "Wow, you live near the studios?!" I didn't think of it as magical at the time, because I took it all for granted. It's only once those old buildings were torn down that people said, "God, that must have been amazing." And looking back on it, it was.

Tom with best friend Ron Nachtwey and his kid brother Donald, visiting Frankenstein's Monster at the Movie Land Wax Museum

Did growing up in Los Angeles affect the way that you watched movies?

No. Not at all. In fact, because all that stuff was so commonplace to me, I wasn't interested in most of the mainstream American movies. What was interesting to me was the Universal horror movies—because they were set in Europe. When I finally went to England and France years later, and saw all of these landscapes that I knew from movie facades, I had an inclination to walk behind them and look for the slats holding them up. It was a surreal experience. I could suddenly appreciate what a good job the filmmakers did—how they made those facades look like the real thing—and how you could make any part of the world literally exist in your own backyard.

How did your parents come to live in Los Angeles?

My parents were both from Michigan. My father grew up in Kalamazoo and my mother in Detroit, so they were not very far from one another but they didn't meet until they both were working at the same paint store on Pico and Robertson in West L.A. My mother had come out here to be near her brother, because there wasn't much going on for her in Detroit. My dad came out here to attend USC Film School.[1] After film school, it was very hard for him to get a job in the film business because film school wasn't taken seriously in 1949. It was, "Film school? Are you kidding me?" It was a joke . . .

Because none of the great filmmakers at that time had gone to film school?

Right. Cinematographer Conrad Hall was in my father's graduating class and he was the only one—at least that I know of—who went on to a big career. My dad was a very quiet, shy guy, and he didn't really know what to do with his production knowledge. His

---

[1] Maurice "Navarre" McLoughlin was part of the first graduating class at USC, in 1949.

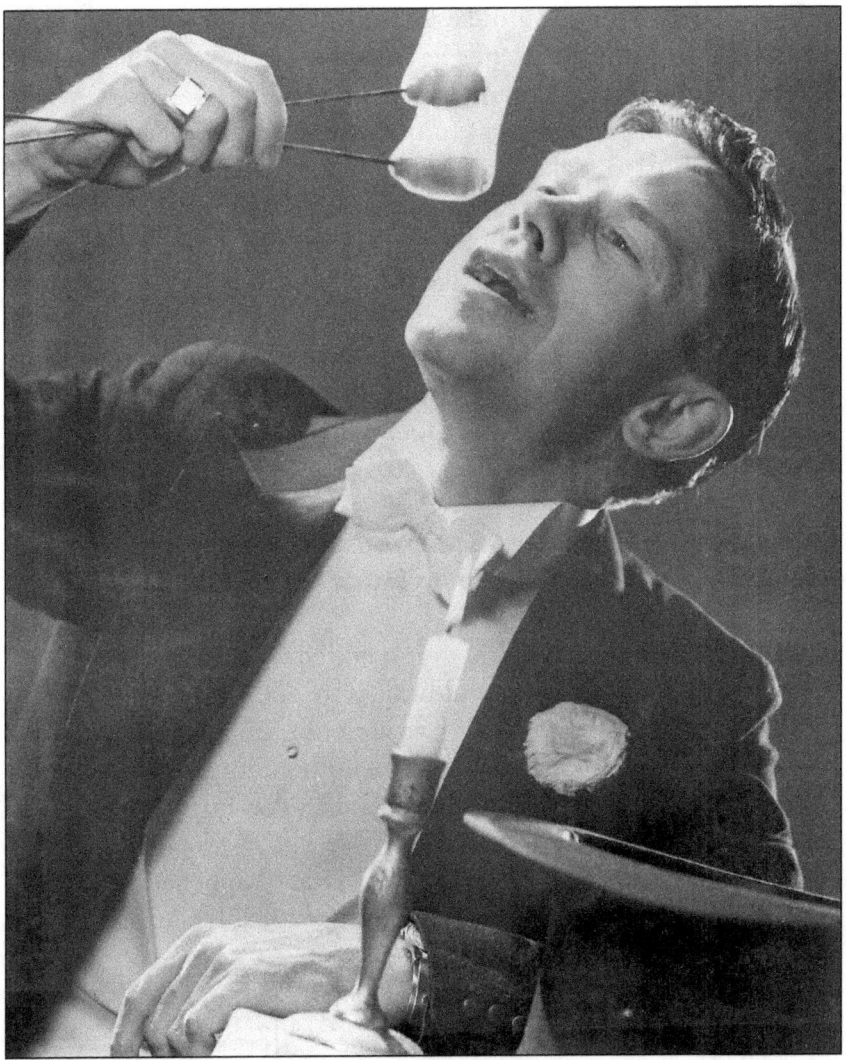

"Navarre, The Man from Mars"

other skill was that he was a magician in vaudeville, so he had that to fall back on. His best income was doing movies where they needed a fire-eater. He was a fire-eater in the famous film noir *Nightmare Alley* [1947], and in the Burt Lancaster [vehicle] *The Flame and the Arrow* [1950]. *Casbah* [1948] with Peter Lorre. *Houdini* [1953], the Tony Curtis–Janet Leigh film. I can't remember all the movies he was in . . . pretty much anything made between the late '40s and about 1960 that had a carnival or a circus in it. His stage name was "Navarre, the Man from Mars."

The very last thing he did was *Americathon* [1979] with John Ritter and Dorothy Stratten. He fell madly in love with Dorothy Stratten, and he was quite upset over her death.[2]

But his lifelong fantasy was to make movies. Since he never got the opportunity to make movies, he kind of lived vicariously through *my* making films. When I was a kid and made these 8mm shorts, he was my coach, my mentor. He'd tell me what shots I was missing. He didn't encourage me to go to film school, because in his experience it hadn't done much good. He basically pushed me to get an industry job. He said, "Do anything you can to get into the business because it's about *showing* them that you can do it. Make the connection so that somebody opens a door for you somewhere."

I've heard people say that the most useful thing about film school is networking. Did he do much networking at USC?

I don't remember my father ever having any close friends. There was nobody that he would call from the old days, nobody that came over to the house. I have a picture of him in my office with this Asian gentleman and they're both editing in 16mm at USC. One time I said, "What happened to that guy? Obviously you two worked closely together . . ." He said, "Yeah, we saw each other for a while and then I don't know what happened to him." He just wasn't good at maintaining connections. He kept very much to himself.

When he passed on, I realized that there were so many things that I didn't know about him because he really didn't talk about things. He was in the service during World War II, but I never heard any stories from his time in the service, and I know there were a lot of traumatic things that occurred. He just wasn't keen on sharing his personal life. And I don't know if that was just part of his generation—that guys from that era just didn't talk as much—or what.

---

[2] Dorothy Stratten was murdered in 1980 by her estranged husband. The crime became the basis for two screen adaptations, the 1981 TV movie *Death of a Centerfold* and the 1983 feature film *Star 80*.

I am fascinated by the fact that he loved to get on stage. He had a stage persona that was completely different. When he was doing magic and fire-eating, he was someone else. Then he would disappear back into this shy little man. In the classic Irish tradition, it was only drinking that would allow him to come out again . . . but that was not the best side of him. That's when all the frustration that was part of not accomplishing his dream [of becoming a filmmaker] came out.

Maurice McLoughlin

He had eight years of college and yet he wasn't doing anything in life that showed he was well educated and capable. He wasn't able to get a better job. I think it was a very frustrating life. He graduated film school when he was about forty, then he met my mom, got married and started a family. After that, he had to maintain the family and that didn't really leave room for the dream.

So your main connection with your father was through the movies?

Absolutely. That was *the* connection. He didn't have the same love of the Universal horror movies—although he had done a movie with Peter Lorre, so he appreciated anything that had Peter Lorre in it. One of my favorites was *The Beast with Five Fingers*. I would watch that over and over again. We had a station in L.A. that played the same movie every night at eight. It was called the Million Dollar Movie. So you could watch the same darn movie five nights in a row. And when they played something you liked, that's what you did!

When Peter Lorre died, my dad said, "Hey, do you want to go down and see Peter Lorre tonight? His body is on display at the mortuary." I said, "Yeah, sure." I guess I was about thirteen.[3] So we went to the mortuary across the street from Hollywood Forever Cemetery, and went into this room with a coffin and a couple of candles. And there in the middle of the room lay Peter Lorre. Nobody else was in there . . . It was a surreal experience. To my dad, it was just respect to a colleague. To me, it was something else. Here was this guy that was so frightening onscreen, that had become such a part of my life. (Whenever I wanted to freak girls out, I'd imitate his voice.) Now here he was. Dead.

My mother definitely thought it was sick and twisted, but to me it was an incredibly bonding experience. Today, my son and I do our own "weird" things—like going ghost hunting. People say, "You took your son ghost hunting?" To me it's great, because we share the same desire to pierce the veil . . . to see what might be on the other side. It's not the usual thing—like going camping or playing baseball—but it's something we share.

You have to do what you're both genuinely interested in, or the connection becomes forced.

Exactly. The other thing that is sort of unique to my childhood was that on Sunday nights, my dad would pull out this old German movie projector that he had taken from the streets of Paris when the United States invaded France [at the end of World War II]. Soldiers grabbed everything they could, and somehow my father managed to get this German movie projector and all these reels of film. He didn't even know what the films were until he got them back to the States.

Most of them were old Charlie Chaplin movies with German subtitles. On Sunday nights, he would pin up an old sheet on the wall, and Mom would make popcorn, and we'd sit on the floor and watch these 16mm prints. None of us could read the subtitles, but with Chaplin you didn't need the subtitles. That was my earliest exposure to pantomime. It showed me how you can tell stories non-verbally. After that, whenever we would put on a school fundraiser or something, I would get my friends together

---

[3] Peter Lorre died on March 23, 1964.

and I would imitate Chaplin. My dad would sort of direct me, because I was not smart enough yet to figure out how to do it on my own . . . but right away I knew that's what I wanted to do.

You said that your father lived vicariously through your film-making . . . What kind of films did he want to make?

That's a good question. I don't know. I would guess anything with an attractive woman in it. [laughs] I remember when he took me to see *Dr. No*, the first James Bond movie. He loved it for his reasons—mainly Ursula Andress—and I loved it for mine. He also had a thing for Bridget Bardot and Marilyn Monroe. I developed an interest in that type of woman partly because of his fascination. He didn't pick out gorgeous women on the street—it was always the women from the movies.

He did have a dark side too. Judging by some of the things he did in his USC days, he was a bit of a surrealist. He liked action films quite a bit . . . suspense and thrillers.

Sounds like a film noir guy.

Yeah, *Laura* made a huge impression on him. We always talked about how that period in cinema, from the late '40s into the early '50s, had a great aesthetic.

Film noir isn't such a big stretch from the monster movies you grew up on . . . They both come from a place of anxiety.

Definitely. My father was supposed to have gone into the priesthood. He went to seminary for maybe two and a half years, and he did a lot of plays during that time period, which fueled his desire for being in show business. I think that was his internal struggle. Since the age of ten, he had wanted to be up on stage, doing magic and things. As much as his mother wanted him to be a priest, he wanted to go into show business. I think he felt incredibly guilty about that. Although he never talked to me about it, my mother sometimes talked about it. My father's parents were deeply disappointed that he chose show business over the priesthood, and I think that had a lot to do with my father's darker side . . . He felt conflicted about where he really belonged in life, and maybe that's why he never made it as a filmmaker. He couldn't fully commit.

When you really want something, you have to endure a lot of pain. You have to learn to *love* the pain. I loved the fact that becoming a filmmaker seemed so impossible. That made me want it all the more. I was willing to put everything else second. Of course, that becomes harder once you have a family. Then you think: *I can't ask them to make the same sacrifices that I'm prepared to make.* That's why a lot of people put the dream on hold. They say, "I've got to put this off for a little while in order to be loyal to the role of a husband and father." What I learned is that expanding your world to include other people doesn't mean you have to surrender your dream . . . You just have to bring other people into the dream with you.

Your mother had a nervous breakdown when you were eleven years old. What was your home life like during that time?

In hindsight I can see the writing on the wall. For weeks, everything was building . . . but at the time I couldn't quite understand what was going on. It seemed like maybe my mother was mad at me, or upset about something I had done. Like any kid at that age, I personalized it. I was thinking: *What did I do wrong?*

I always had a really close bond with my mother. Probably because my dad was so introverted and there was so much that my parents didn't talk about. I think my mother made her biggest emotional investments in me, although I didn't realize that at the time. She talked to me because I was there, and it was important for her to have someone to talk to. I wasn't old enough to understand that she was treating me like an adult . . . or that I was acting like an adult in a lot of ways.

Suddenly, that person that I was so close to was walking around in a—for lack of a better term—"zombie state." She was still in her nightgown when I came home from school. She was afraid to drive; afraid to leave the house. I started to realize something wasn't right, but I thought maybe she just had the flu or something and

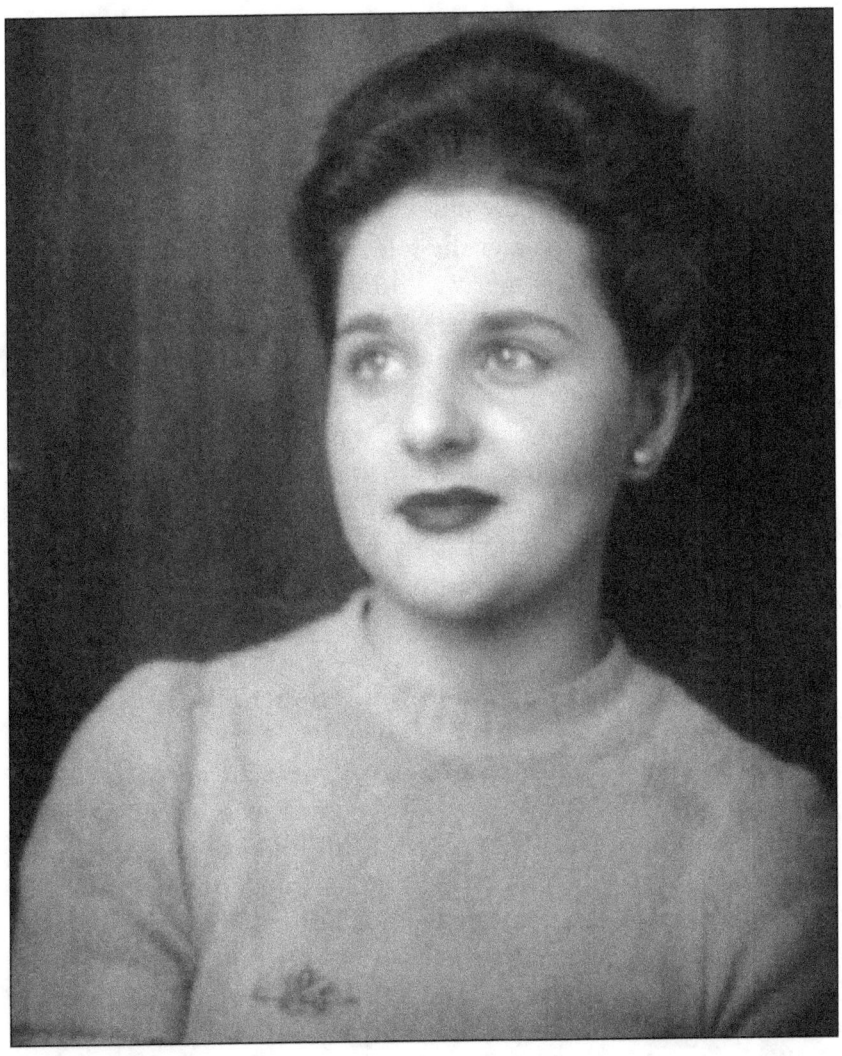

Ethel McLoughlin

she wasn't talking about it. When I came home from school, I obviously wanted to go out and play. I didn't want to think about what was wrong with my mother. I wanted to be a kid . . . But then when there's no dinner, and my parents are arguing all the time, and the arguments start getting more intense and more ugly. I remember going to sleep at night, listening to screaming and yelling that was so disturbing, and trying to block it out. I think it was even worse for my younger sister Kathy and my two younger brothers, Mike and Kevin. We were all so lost and confused.

I remember in those days I was doing my own magic shows. I put a sign in the front yard that had a drawing of a bunny coming out of a top hat, and below that I listed the start times of my magic shows. My mother opened a ketchup bottle and splattered ketchup across the sign. I looked at this sign—all bloody, you know—and I couldn't figure out what that was about. When I asked her about it years later she told me that she thought the magic was going to steal me away from her. She said, "I felt like you were becoming your father—because he loved his magic more than he loved me—and I was so angry that I just wanted to kill the magic." There were so many things that she was trying to piece together in her own mind. She was constantly trying to figure out why she was doing what she was doing. That was how I began to understand that anyone's actions can be interpreted, in another person's mind, as a form of madness. So much of that has crossed over into my work over the years, particularly when I did *Murder of Innocence*.

How did your father respond to your mother's illness?

Did you ever see John Cassavettes's *A Woman Under the Influence*? Gena Rowlands plays this woman who's having a nervous breakdown and Peter Falk is this blue-collar guy. A "*deese, dem, dose*" kind of guy. And he can't understand what the hell is wrong with her. My dad was just like that. He did not know what was going on with her. And over time she slipped further and further away from reality, due to lack of sleep . . . One day I got home from school and my father said, "They took your mother to the hospital." That was when I realized, "Oh she's *really* sick." I was terrified, but I hid it.

You've said that your mother's personality—her warmth as a human being—has also influenced a lot of your films. So your memories aren't all bad . . .

My father gave me a love of the movies and my mother gave me a *love* of people—because the one thing she really knew how to do was to be loving and supportive. No matter what I was doing or what was going on in my life, I knew she would always be loving and supportive. She was never critical of me. She didn't try to tell me how to live my life. She never felt comfortable doing that, because her sense of self was so uncertain, from the moment she was born.

My mother was a twin and her twin sister died at birth. I think there's always something unusual about twins where one doesn't survive—maybe because the other one grows up wondering what it would have been like to have a twin. Whatever the cause, my mother never had a very strong sense of self or security.

To make matters tougher, she got pregnant at sixteen. When my grandmother found out, she said, "We're going to Canada, you're going to have it, and your brother and his wife are going to raise your baby." At the time, she didn't have a really good relationship with her brother—so she had to stand aside all those years and watch her firstborn be raised by her brother and his wife. And she was forbidden to tell her child that she was the real mother. She was sworn to secrecy until my aunt died, and it was only then that she came forward and said she was his birth mother. That happened just a few months before [my mother] died.

So she carried this dark secret for her whole life. It was one of those things that just built and built, until she snapped and she had to be institutionalized. And once you've been labeled as a person with "mental issues," I think it's very hard to get yourself out of that. No matter what happens, you feel like you can't really handle things. You're always afraid that something bad is going to happen . . . so you're constantly thinking, *Who can help me? What kind of medication do I need to go on?*

My father didn't understand the need for medication, because in those days people weren't taking pills for mental illness. Either you were locked up and that was the end of it, or you were supposed to snap out of it and then come back into real life again and carry on as if nothing ever happened . . . but it doesn't work that way.

I guess all of this stuff—my mom's illness and my dad's unfulfilled dreams—created a sense of urgency in me. I thought, *Okay, if I'm going to do something in life, I've got to separate myself from this.* And as soon as I turned sixteen, I got out of there. My girlfriend Amy and I moved into a little house in Hollywood. I still stayed in touch with my parents, but I just couldn't live in their house any longer.

Is that when music became a major influence in your life?

Actually, it started a few years before that. I was twelve in 1962, when the Beatles hit and the whole music scene changed. There was this huge excitement that something new was occurring. Here was something that was unique because it wasn't American and these guys sounded different; they looked different . . . and girls loved them. Girls *screamed* at them. I was *different*, but girls weren't *screaming* at me.

Getting girls to scream was the goal. To achieve that, I was willing to get thrown out of high school; I was willing to get kicked out of restaurants; I was willing to get spit on; I was willing to get beaten up and all of that—so that I could have the rock n roll look with the longer hair and different clothes. I was willing to take the slings and arrows of the establishment to be a part of that.

The first band that I put together was with my longtime friend Ron Natchwey and Henry Mancini's son Chris. I was pretty overwhelmed walking into the world of Henry Mancini, multi-Grammy and Oscar winner, and knowing his kid—who was just as rebellious and crazy as I was, but who had the means to buy amplifiers and guitars and the ability to get into places that I couldn't get into. When we were sixteen, his father gave us was two tickets to the Monterey Pop Festival.[4] Why my parents didn't question it, I don't know. I think they loved the idea that their son was hanging out with Henry Mancini's son. Somehow that

---

[4] The Monterey Pop International Music Festival was the first widely-promoted and heavily-attended rock festival. It took place from June 16 to June 18, 1967, in Monterey, California, and featured career-making performances by Jimi Hendrix, The Who, Janis Joplin and Otis Redding. The festival marked the beginning of the "Summer of Love," and served as a template for the Woodstock Festival two years later.

made it seem okay to them—and they had no idea what we were up to. The sixties music scene really made no sense to them.

We drove his cherry red convertible Mustang up to Monterey, and sat front row center. You can actually see us in the *Monterey Pop* documentary. I'm sitting there with my mouth hanging open—a stoned sixteen-year old watching the most incredible acts. We were all seeing them for the first time: Jimi Hendrix, Janis Joplin, The Who, and then all these other musicians that I never would have been exposed to otherwise—from Hugh Masakela to Ravi Shankar, Simon & Garfunkel, The Mamas and the Papas, Otis Redding.

That festival was very different, I think, from Woodstock. I wasn't at Woodstock, but from watching the documentary and talking to people who were there, I get the sense that Woodstock was sort of homogenized into a "hippie" event. Monterey was something else. It was the beginning of "the Love Generation." The San Francisco crowd was supporting it, but everybody was into their own thing. There were so many different styles, from Otis Redding and the Mar-Keys, Ravi Shankar to Jimi Hendrix . . . I said to myself, "Now I know what I want to do with my life." At that point, it was crystal clear.

That [decision] meant I had no more interest in formal education. It meant I had to put the band ahead of everything else. We needed to practice; we needed to get gigs; we needed to create our own songs; we needed to design our own visuals. I was heavily inspired by the theatricality of bands like The Jimi Hendrix Experience and The Who. I wanted to blow things up on stage. I would put huge sheets of flash paper between the vox amps and they would ignite at a certain point, and then I had smoke coming out of the sleeves of the outfit I was wearing. I always wanted special effects mixed in with the rock n roll music. That's what my group, TNT, was all about—explosive sounds and explosive visuals.

What kind of music did you play?

In the beginning, we called ourselves The Avengers (after the TV show), and our music was kind of derivative of the California

George Krzyzweski, Steve Goldstein, Tom McLoughlin and Don Silverman are TNT, 1967.

surf music and early rhythm and blues stuff like The Rolling Stones. Then when Chris and I got kicked out of school and we went our separate ways, I started to get involved with other people's bands. I was in a band called The May Wines with guitarist Jeff Briskin and drummer Bob Krasnow. And most of that stuff again was related to what the Stones had taught us. There was a wealth of music in the Southern rhythm and blues tradition, so we were very much into Howlin' Wolf, Bo Diddley, Etta James, John Lee Hooker, Junior Walker, those kinds of artists. We did their music but with more of a rock flavor. And I always sang with a slight Southern twang because it just sounded better. I didn't want to sound like me. I wanted to create a persona. So most of the early stuff was [blues standards], and then I started writing songs that really were more about "got the girl, got rejected." Sometimes it was "girl's not gonna live much longer if she keeps this up."

Like the Beatles song "Run for Your Life."

Yeah. It's funny because if you listen to most of those early Beatles songs, the lyrics are a lot of "he said, she said" stuff. The Stones added a darker twist. So even if you were not really *trying* to piss off your parents . . .

I would think that getting kicked out of school would have done that . . .

My mother would always roll with the punches. And eventually my father just threw up his hands and said, "I don't understand him. I don't know what any of this means." At that point, I think he was just ready to sell me to the highest bidder. That was the period where . . . I wasn't a movie person any longer. I still went to the movies and loved the movies, but I was more interested in being on stage and having girls watching me. Suddenly I felt like I was accepted and doing something that certain people could understand and relate to. The song lyrics all came out of that.

We had a manager—this guy named Jim Demarco, who was sort of tied into what was in those days called the Freak Scene in Los Angeles. That was the Laurel Canyon crowd: Frank Zappa, Mothers of Invention, Fraternity of Man, and the guys from The Factory. It was the beginning of the psychedelic era, and the music that we were creating started to go from rhythm and blues into much more abstract noise. A lot of feedback and a lot of distortion.

Around that time, one of the Mothers of Invention, Elliot Ingber, took a liking to our group. We were young and didn't know what we were doing, so he became a kind of mentor. He was a complete stoner-type mentality, with huge afro hair and beard, and he would sit down and talk to us about how the music had to be. He'd say to our guitarist, "You need to play a . . . orange spider going up a . . . purple cobweb . . . you know what I'm saying?" And we were like, "Yeahhhhh . . . Let's play something like *that*." So the songs suddenly became "Happy Being High," and my lyrics got more and more absurd. I was re-reading *Alice in Wonderland* and anything that I thought I could turn into the kind of abstract lyrics that John Lennon did so well.

Or Jim Morrison.

It's funny that you should mention him, because it was during this period that The Doors became a big hit in Los Angeles, and we were their opening act in a number of the clubs. We got the gigs because we were a very visual act. We weren't the best musicians, but we had a lot of passion and a lot of energy, and the word on the street was "these guys put on a good show." A lot of things would happen onstage. We would try to be outrageous as possible. We blew a lot of things up! I would throw myself into the crowd . . . Whatever came out of my head that day was what we'd do on the stage that night.

We never had a record label. I never had any sense that we were going to be recording artists. It really was about performing onstage. I did five years of heavy duty rock n roll, where we were occasionally the opening act for bands like The Doors, Love, The Seeds, and whoever came to town—The Animals, Chicago (in the days when they were still known as CTA) . . . on and on. We were regulars at Pandora's Box, The Whisky, Gazzari's and The Hullabaloo, which was the old Earl Carroll's Vanities across from the Hollywood Palladium. But we never performed outside of Southern California.

During that period, the Vietnam War was going on. There was an enlistment lottery and, at one point, I was about fifty numbers away from being drafted. I really didn't know what I was going to do if I got called up. I wasn't in school and the idea of running to Canada wasn't very appealing. I was just blindly hoping that I'd figure it out on the day . . . It was so overwhelming at that age to try to have a game plan for something like that. Some did, but most of us were only focused on music. Thankfully, I never got drafted—I didn't have to make that choice to go in or not go into the service. I remained focused on trying to be the next Mick Jagger or Jim Morrison.

Do you have any good Morrison stories?

Yeah. As I said, we used to open for [The Doors] at the Hullabaloo, which is now the Nickelodeon Theater on Sunset, and then at another place called The Cheetah, which was an old dance hall in Venice. The walls of the Cheetah were covered in silver Mylar so all of the surfaces were reflective. There were these huge screens projecting the psychedelic light-show shit. And in the center of this huge ballroom was a stage that was approximately

The May Wines play Pandora's Box on the Sunset Strip—November 12, 1966.

eight to ten feet off the ground. It was this huge box in the middle of the dance floor. People could dance all around it, and the band had to go up the stairs in the back of this thing. And we had to carry all of our gear up there. Drums, amps, everything.

One night, The Doors were setting up their gear right after us. They assembled all their equipment and then the house announcer said: "*Ladies and gentlemen, The Doors!*" The music starts—it was the opening bars of "Break on Through"—but no Jim. The other guys are looking around for him. They know they saw him a few minutes ago somewhere in the house. Finally Jim comes out of some doorway and staggers across the floor, goes up the stairs . . . and you can tell he is just completely out of it. I don't know what he was on—maybe Quaaludes or maybe he's drunk, or some combination of the two. He grabs the microphone, crosses his legs in classic Morrison style and instead of singing he just stands there. Then, for some unknown reason, he decides to do a cartwheel. And he literally cartwheels right off the friggin' platform. Lands flat on his back on the concrete, ten to twelve feet below, legs out, arms out. And the whole place went silent. We figured he had killed himself. He just came down *too hard*. We didn't see him hit his head but we figured he must have, from the way he fell.

Suddenly he pops up. Looks around. Sees where the stage is. Stands. Goes back up the stairs. Grabs the microphone. Crosses his legs. And starts singing: "*Oh the day destroys the night . . .*" He went right into it and did a perfect set, like nothing happened. I don't know if that fall snapped him back to reality or what, but it was a perfect example of how fucked up he could be, on whatever, and still perform.

Whenever I'd talk to Jim backstage, I never really got anything out of him other than "Yeah, how you doing? That's great, man." I never got any real insight from him, or had a real conversation.

I managed to cross paths with a lot of the major musicians during that time. Chris Mancini and I—because his father recorded at RCA—would go into RCA all the time, and run into people. One time the Stones were recording there. I think they were doing *Aftermath*, or the album after *Aftermath*.[5] So here we are and in walk the Stones. We shook hands with each one of them,

---

[5] *Aftermath* was the first Rolling Stones album to be recorded entirely in the United States. The album was released in the summer of 1966. It was followed by *Between the Buttons*, which was released in early 1967.

and I remember it was like shaking hands with a limp fish. Very cold. No hearty handshakes. But they were all very nice and very pleasant.

I also met Jimi Hendrix at the house where Roger Corman shot *The Trip*. He was there getting stoned. I actually shared a joint with Jimi Hendrix, which was pretty intense. Later we were jamming with him and a bunch of other musicians.

Your life is a bit like *Forrest Gump* . . .

Sometimes you find yourself in these situations, and you don't quite understand how or why . . . but you can't argue with it.

What happened with your band?

Over time, I found it harder and harder to get us real club gigs. We were starting to play frat houses, or backing up transsexual strippers at gigs where we had to start at eleven at night and go until seven in the morning. The thing that finally got me out of rock n roll was the fact that the psychedelic stuff took over and the music was just about jamming noise and screaming. And then all these icons were dying: first Janis [Joplin], Hendrix and Keith Moon, and then of course Morrison. People were dying and the music was getting ugly. At nineteen, I just felt like I didn't want to be part of it anymore. It wasn't that I thought I would die. I just didn't see any future in the rock world.

I recently read a book on the Laurel Canyon scene. What struck me were the author's descriptions of the openness and acceptance of the culture. He said that the general feeling in that community in the late 1960s was that people loved everyone around them until someone screwed up. Today, people don't love anyone *unless or until* someone does something cool or helpful.

My first sense of what you're describing was at the Monterey festival. You'd be walking around and you'd run into Brian Jones, and you could interact in a casual way. He wasn't like, "I'm a member of the Rolling Stones." He didn't have bodyguards around him, preventing you from getting close. He was just part of the scene, you know? So many of the great San Francisco musicians were part of the audience that weekend, and there *was* an accessibility to them.

Weed obviously helped to break some of those social boundaries . . . Alcohol wasn't really cool. Some people did drink, but that was more for our parents' generation . . . And that continued to be the case until hard drugs like coke and heroin became readily available. With that came the demons of real addiction, and I started seeing friends overdosing and dying.

Then came the Altamont Festival,[6] where a guy was beaten to death. And of course the Manson murders.[7] Suddenly the word in L.A. was "hippies have gone evil." In places where I had been accepted literally one week before, I was now being asked if I was part of "that Manson group." I remember not getting served in a couple of restaurants. In the beginning, it was just because they didn't like hippies. They'd say, "Get out of here and go get a haircut." Now it was different: "Get out because you could be part of the Manson Family." I remember a bunch of short-haired Valley guys pulling over one day while I was walking on the sidewalk. I turned and they spit at me. It all started to sour in late '69.

The band broke up and then I wasn't part of anything anymore. I didn't know where I belonged. I was living with my girlfriend and suddenly our relationship was falling apart. It was a transitional period. I knew something had to change. Out of that came this bizarre moment when I saw an advertisement about pantomime

---

[6] The Altamont Speedway Free Festival was held on December 6, 1969, in northern California. Promoted as "Woodstock West," the event turned dark when a young man was killed by a member of the Hell's Angels. The Angels had allegedly been hired to provide security for The Rolling Stones.

[7] On August 8, 1969, followers of a cult founded by Charles Manson killed five people at a private residence in the hills above Los Angeles. One night later, cult members killed two more victims at a home in the Los Feliz section of L.A. Manson dubbed the attacks "helter skelter," after a song by The Beatles.

classes in Hollywood. I remembered that somebody had once asked me if I ever studied mime. I didn't even really know what the word meant, but for some arbitrary reason I went to the class, which was taught by a guy named Richmond Shepard. It sparked my interest in learning how to tell stories *physically*.

As a lead singer, I'd already been doing that in my own way. I always wanted to incorporate more and more movement into the songs. So I started writing sketches for the class, and doing my own rebellious, politically-incorrect pieces. From that point on, I started immersing myself in the world of mime.

It wasn't long before Marcel Marceau came along to Los Angeles to perform. I went and met him, showed him some of my mime work at this art gallery where he was promoting his book. And he invited me to come to Paris, and study mime with him there. At that moment, I thought, *Okay—something just fell in my lap. Now I'm going to leave everybody and everything I know, at nineteen years old, and go to Paris.* This made no real sense on a rational level, but it felt like this was the place I needed to go next.

I had no money. I was still living on the last of the money I'd saved from music gigs. So I got the one and only "normal" job I ever had—working at a warehouse, packing up pharmaceuticals and vitamins. In about six or seven months, I had to earn as much money as I could for Paris. While I was there, there was this huge drug bust and a lot of my fellow workers got thrown out. Suddenly I was in line to be foreman. I'm earning three times as much as I was earning initially, and it seemed to everyone else that I was going to become a company man. But all I was doing was quietly saving as much as I could so that, come September, I had money for the plane and hopefully enough money to live on for a year in Paris.

Did you have a specific amount that you wanted to make?

Not exactly. Just as much as I could earn in that time frame. I figured out the budget I had to be on when I got to Paris. The school—by today's standards, it's hard to believe—cost about $75 a month. And I went from nine in the morning until six at night, five days a week. $75 a month isn't much, but when you aren't making any money and you have to pay the rent, plus airfare . . .

I found that the one area I could compromise on was eating. I ate carrots, oatmeal, apples . . . whatever was the simplest, cheapest food I could get away with. I think I dropped down to about 130 pounds, but I was fine, I was healthy, I was doing all this physical stuff every day to stay in shape. It was like a new chapter of my life beginning in 1970-1971.

PART II: COMEDY AND HORROR

Marcel Marceau's School of Mime / Mr. Hulot / Convincing Woody Allen that he's funny / Goofing off with Dick Van Dyke / Studying with the stars at Sherwood Oaks / Meeting Frank Capra / Playing the mutant bear / The second fastest gun in the universe / Psychic vampires / A personal ghost story

Here you are starting your second adult life at the age of nineteen ... Did you go straight to Paris?

First I flew into London and, right away, I felt like I had lived there in another lifetime. I looked out the window and thought, *I'm home. I belong here.* Maybe it was because I had watched so many Universal horror movies and Sherlock Holmes movies that it seemed so familiar. All I know is that it felt incredibly comforting—which was good because, inside, I was freaking out. I had just left everybody and everything I knew, and I was going to a country where I didn't speak a word of the native language. I had spent no time preparing to speak French. I was too stubborn. I thought, *I'll pantomime my way through things.* I had no idea what I was in for.

You went to Paris to study mime under Marcel Marceau. What exactly is the curriculum for mime school?

First of all, Marcel Marceau was not there all the time, because he was touring. He came to do Master Classes, where he would lecture about telling stories visually—creating something that makes the invisible visible. Then there were two or three other mime teachers. One taught Commedia Dell'Arte, which is old Italian comedy. We learned how to perform different types of characters: Pierrot, Columbina, Harlequin, etc.

I also learned what they call the basic grammar of mime, from Etienne Decroux. Etienne Decroux was considered the father of mime. He taught Marcel Marceau and Jean-Louis Barrault. What he did was show us how to break the body down, and to look at the body as separate parts that could all move independently—the head separate from the neck, the neck separate from the chest, the chest separate from the hips. It was like a pianist learning scales. Once you understood the basics of how to move, then you could artistically express yourself. Using those basic techniques, you can make yourself louder. Even though you're working in silence, you can be louder because of the way you use your body.

If you really study Buster Keaton or Harold Lloyd or Charlie Chaplin, you recognize their ability to convey a lot with very small gestures. Keaton, for example, was great at keeping his eyes completely separate from his head. He was expressive in the simplest ways. For example, he would release a huge explosion of energy when he took a fall, and then maximize the silence and stillness when he stopped. He'd just sit there blinking, like, *What just happened?* The extreme contrast is comic. That's what we were learning—how to think of the entire body as an instrument, and figure out what it's capable of.

I got completely immersed in the world of performing arts, studying fencing and acrobatics and mask work and classical dance and modern dance . . . And there was a cinema across the street from my hotel that changed movies three times a day, so I was going to the movies as much as possible. I got to see so many classic foreign films and silent movies that I wouldn't have been able to see in Los Angeles. Then I went to the Louvre and Rodin's Museum to study the sculptures and paintings, and see how all those artists expressed things without words. And because I couldn't speak French, I was completely voyeuristic. I would sit in a café and watch people, and I became a student of human behavior. All of that was part of my education for almost a full year.

When I got back to America, I thought, *Alright, now what do I do with this?* I have all the corporeal training. Now I have to find a way to make a living, using my body as my instrument. That means no more crazy stunts, no more riding motorcycles, no more of anything that could possibly hurt any part of my body. I had no car, no money . . . and my girlfriend, who I'd been holding a candle for during my time in Paris, had moved on. I was starting from ground zero, on a new road to God knows where.

Strange as it sounds, I remember having a dream one night where I was backstage and I heard a voice say, "Ladies and gentlemen . . . Tommy." Maybe it was the influence of The Who's rock opera *Tommy*. Regardless, it was that crazy dream that made me say: "Okay I'm no longer Tom McLoughlin, I'm Tommy." I knew I had to reinvent myself.

Where did you find work in L.A. as a mime?

I started performing anywhere I could—at Joan Rivers's comedy club, The Comedy Store, a blues club called The Ash Grove, which is now The Improv. I did my mime routines as an opening act for Bo Diddley, Big Mama Thornton, Howlin' Wolf, John Lee Hooker. At first, I was a solo performer. Then I put together an act with a girl I met at the Renaissance Faire named Katee McClure, who I eventually married. I founded a comedy troupe called the L.A. Mime Company, with Katee, Mitchel Young-Evans, Tina Lenert and Albert Ash. We performed at theaters, clubs, festivals, and on TV shows. I kept making my canvas—and the mime stories that I was writing and directing—bigger and bigger.

What were the main influences on your mime work?

I created my own comic character. I learned I naturally walk at an angle and have a bit of a lope, and a number of Parisians called me Hulot. I didn't understand what that meant, because I didn't speak French. Later somebody explained to me that Jacques Tati had created a character named Mr. Hulot, and they thought I walked like him. When I finally saw his movies, I realized this guy was doing exactly what I wanted to do. He was doing silent comedy that showed the influences of Chaplin, Keaton and Lloyd in *Mr. Hulot's Holiday* and *Mon Oncle*, but he was also satirizing the modern world in movies like *Playtime* and *Trafic*. So he became my new hero, because he was writing, directing, *and* starring . . . and that's exactly what I wanted to do. I wanted to be a one-man operation like Tati.

So my character—who I called Dufus—was a modern guy who just doesn't belong in the modern world. People on the street would say that he looks like something out of a silent movie. He always had the same kind of stupid look on his face. And I threw him into simple situations that were way over his head.

I started making short films on video because that was the only medium I could afford. Those were the days when video cameras were gigantic. You used reel-to-reel tape, or you could only play back the footage on the same camera you shot on, so it was very limiting. But I was happy to be storytelling in that medium . . . All I wanted to do at that time was make the world laugh. I felt

Tom and Mitchel Young-Evans of the L.A. Mime Company

like, if I could be responsible for making people laugh, I was doing a good thing.

For about the next ten years, I would do anything that came along that had some aspect of mime to it. I did about fifty commercials—for Heinz, Bob's Big Boy, McDonald's, Kodak, Honda, you name it. I put together a circus for the opening of the Bonaventure Hotel, with elephants and giraffes and stunt performers. I was sort of the ringleader of the whole thing, and my father was the fire-eater. I did promotional appearances for department stores. One time, I dressed up as Harold Lloyd and Nancy (my future wife) was Mary Pickford, and our other friends played Chaplin and Keaton. So many weird gigs . . . I poured the wine when Orson Welles spoke for Paul Masson. I was the hand model for Winchell Donuts. It was crazy shit, but it paid the rent.

Tom as Harold Lloyd

Nancy as Mary Pickford

I couldn't bring myself to take a regular job. I only took jobs that had to do with show business. There was too much of a performer's ego in me to do anything else.

It was during that time period that I decided I really wanted to be a film director. Of course this is the great cliché: "What I really want to do is direct." My first big break in film came right after I got back from Paris. I got a call saying, "Woody Allen is looking for mimes for a new comedy that he's doing, and he wants to interview you." I was a huge fan of Woody Allen's early movies—*Take the Money and Run*, *What's Up Tiger Lily?*, and *Bananas*—so I went down to the old Desilu Studios and met Woody Allen.

Woody wouldn't really make eye contact with me. There was a pool table in the room, and he'd glance up from the table for a second and then look back down again, and he was pushing these billiard balls around as he talked. I don't do a very good Woody Allen impression, but he was like, [in frantic but halting speech] "I don't know what I'm thinking, I just . . . I-I-I'm gonna do this physical comedy, but I'm not Chaplin . . . I-I-I can't do this." He was doing his self-deprecating Woody Allen schtick, and he said, "I'm hiring mimes because I'm gonna do robots and I want to imitate one, and . . . it doesn't even *sound* funny does it?" And I found myself going, "No, no, no, it sounds great!" Here I was, this kid in my early twenties trying to encourage one of my idols. Ultimately I showed him what I did, and he said, "Well, if you do that, what if I do this?" And he did his hysterical staccato robot moves, and we talked about that. So, three of my friends and I ended up getting roles in *Sleeper*.

My best memories of the experience are of watching how Woody Allen directed in those days. Of course I wanted to be a director, so I watched him very closely. What he would do is go up to his A.D. [Assistant Director] and give instructions, and then the A.D. would talk to the actors . . . Woody had a real hard time telling an actor what to do. Obviously he's gotten past that, but at that time he seemed intimidated by the process. And then they would roll the camera and he would just riff. He would deliver his scripted lines, and then he would keep adding asides. At a certain point he would stop and say, "Okay that's enough."

Woody Allen's *Sleeper*
(United Artists, 1973)

What was so incredible about that was seeing him give himself all these options for later [in the edit].

Sleeper was what got me my SAG [Screen Actors Guild] card, and got me into the union. After that I was in a documentary called *The Incredible Machine*, made for National Geographic.[8] It was a film about how the body worked. I came in and they painted every single muscle in my body, using different colors for the different types of muscles. It must have been a five-hour paint job. And then I had to move and they shot close-ups to demonstrate how the muscles work. Very tedious. But again, it was a job that used my mime training.

While working on *Sleeper*, I also met Joel Schumacher (who was the production designer). A few years later, he directed me in Lily Tomlin's *The Incredible Shrinking Woman* (1981). He called me up and said, "Would you like to come work with these guys who have to act like toys?" There's a scene in the movie where Lily opens a closet door and there's all these toys in there . . . I don't even remember what toy I played . . . I think I might have been the bear . . . But that was another one of those crazy jobs that

---

[8] *The Incredible Machine* was nominated for "Best Documentary Feature" at the 1975 Academy Awards.

The L.A. Mime Company with Dick Van Dyke

came after I got my SAG card. The funny thing is I'm still getting [residual] checks—usually for about two cents—from all those different jobs.

Your big break was on the variety show *Van Dyke and Company*?

Yes. In 1974 or '75, the L.A. Mime Company was performing at a theater in Hollywood called Las Palmas. Dick Van Dyke came and saw us one night and he said, "I'm going to be doing this variety show, or a pilot for a variety show, and I'd love to have you kids on." We were floored because this was *Dick Van Dyke*! Dick is probably the single greatest actor / performer who I have ever met. He is so accessible, so humble, and so honest.

Andy Kaufman auditioned for the pilot too, so we got to watch Andy perform for the writers and do all the material he had at that point. I was already a fan of Andy because I'd seen him perform at The Comedy Store. For the producers, it came down to featuring Andy or us, and they chose Andy as the more important act. But Dick was more excited to work with us. He wanted us as an extension of *his* performance. He literally said, "I want to be the sixth member of the L.A. Mime Company." And he always added something to every sketch I wrote. He understood the mime world so well that he could come up with things that made it so much better. He loved the sketches, and it was a great experience for us to be able to bond with such a major comedy hero.

It took a while before the pilot was picked up and turned into a series—maybe a year or more. There was a period where we were wondering if it was really going to happen. When it finally happened, the producers said to me, "We want you to write these sketches and, in turn, we'll let the mime company perform on the show." We had our own spot just like Andy Kaufman had his spot. Even though they had top writers on that show—I think Steve Martin wrote on the pilot—I wrote all the physical comedy stuff each week. It was an incredible honor for a twenty-six-year-old mime who hadn't really done much else.

Each week they'd say something like, "Okay, Freddie Prinze is going to be the guest star this week, so we need something for Freddie. And this is our Thanksgiving show, so come up with something that is Thanksgiving themed." That was the challenge. Or "Lucille Ball's gonna be on this episode, so write something great that Lucy and Dick can do together." Or Carol Burnett, Harvey Korman, Tommy Smothers, Sid Caesar . . . Each sketch had to be tailored to the guest star, and then I'd choreograph with them what I had written.

I tried to write around their comedic skills. With Tommy Smothers, I didn't know how good he would be with slapstick comedy, so we did a chiropractor sketch where it looked like he was bending Dick in half and pulling him apart. Then we built a "squash suit," like from a cartoon, so Dick's head and hands extended upward and outward but the bottom half of his body looked like an accordion. Dick would walk with his legs bent, and it looked like he'd been hit with a hammer and squished down. Then it was up to Dick and Tommy and Katee from the Mime Company to react to what they had done to this guy.

Tell me about working with Lucille Ball.

Lucy was amazing. I've never seen a woman—*or a man*—create such fear on the set. She was such a perfectionist and had been doing it for so long that she automatically took over. She wouldn't do anything without knowing everything about it. "*Is that my key light? That's my fill light? How long am I going to be sitting here before something happens?*" If I was pantomiming handing an object to her, she'd say, "Don't just *show* me the size. How heavy is it?" I said, "Well, it's about a half a pound." And she'd say, "Okay and . . . is it plastic?" She focused on details that nobody else would ever think to ask about. That was her process. She would question you to see if you had an answer. And if you didn't, she would let you have it. She'd say, "If you don't know, who's supposed to know?"

One day, there was a very uncomfortable moment where Dick and Lucy were waiting while the crew took care of some technical detail. And Lucy was getting impatient. Finally she turns to Dick and says, "What are they doing?" And he says, "I don't really know." And she just glared at him and said, "You don't know? This is *your* show and *you* don't know what's going on?" It was rude, but that was Lucy—she was a "go for the throat" person.

I learned very quickly that all of these great working professionals—Sid Caesar, Carol Burnett, Harvey Korman—were excited to do a mime sketch. They had a lot of experience and enthusiasm because they were getting to do something they don't get to do as much anymore. That's how I knew that these people truly loved what they were doing.

As great as it was working with people like that, I started to get frustrated with the show because the Mime Company sketches

L.A. Mime Company members Katee McClure, Tom McLoughlin, Tina Lenert, Albert Ash and Mitchel Young-Evans

L.A. Mime Company as "Visitors from Outer Space"

kept getting cut. On the day of taping, the producers would cut it. Or, if it did get taped, Andy's bit would end up being fifteen minutes instead of five minutes, and they'd say there wasn't enough room on the show. So I was writing all these sketches for the celebrity guests, but I wasn't getting paid or credited because I wasn't in the Writer's Guild. My payment was supposed to be the time that the L.A. Mime Company was featured on the show. That was the carrot they dangled in front of me . . . but it kept getting further and further away. When the show was nominated for an Emmy, I finally went to the Writer's Guild and fought to get my name put on the show as a writer. I had two routines in the nominated episode.

What happened to the series?

NBC kept changing the time slot. Usually when that happens you start to lose your audience, because they just don't know where to find the show. One day, Dick was driving up to the NBC lot and the guard at the gate said, "Oh, so sorry about your show, Mr. Van Dyke." He goes, "What?" "Well, about the show being cancelled . . ." "The show was cancelled?" That's how he found out. It's a great example of how callous our industry can be. He was devastated. I felt really bad for him.

Possibly the reason it was cancelled was that the world of comedy was changing. *Saturday Night Live* had just come on, and it was the beginning of a new age. The old variety shows were a dying breed. *Van Dyke and Company* came along during that transition, and the show was not given a fair shake. The network kept moving it around and the public moved on to other things. Its failure had nothing to do with Dick. His talent remains unsurpassed even today.

How did you move from television into film?

I was twenty-six or twenty-seven years old when *Van Dyke and Company* was cancelled. And I remember thinking that Orson Welles had directed *Citizen Kane* at twenty-six and Michelangelo painted the Sistine Chapel at twenty-six. I felt that if I was going to "make it," this was when it was supposed to happen. But I wasn't where I wanted to be. I wanted to be a comedy filmmaker, not just a mime on a TV show. So I felt like I had to turn what I was doing into what I really wanted to do . . . but I didn't know how.

So I started attending filmmaking classes at the Sherwood Oaks Experimental College on Hollywood Boulevard. I took classes in directing, editing, and production. While I was there, I saw *Rocky* for the first time before it was released. Sylvester Stallone came to talk to us about it. Then John Cassavettes came in with *A Woman Under the Influence*—a cut that was maybe an hour longer than the released version. Martin Scorsese came with *Alice Doesn't Live Here Anymore*. He asked us to give him feedback, because he felt that he was working in a genre that he had no business being in. He was so open about it. He kept saying, "Talk to me, tell me what's wrong." Of course, nobody would say anything. We were all too shy, too inhibited. What is a bunch of nobodies supposed to say to Marty Scorsese?

I was blessed to have Rod Serling as a writing teacher for six weeks. I took extensive notes on everything that came out of his mouth. Not only was everything that came out of his mouth fascinating, but what *didn't* come out of his mouth was also fascinating. He smoked these non-filtered cigarettes, and he would take a huge drag and suck the smoke in through his nose and into his mouth. Then he would begin to talk. And I'd watch him, waiting for him to exhale the smoke. Over time, the smoke had to be coming out . . . but you could not *see* it.

Truffaut came and talked to us about *Small Change* . . . John Badham came and talked about *WarGames* . . . I took Syd Field's screenwriting class when Syd Field was still a fledgling screenwriter himself . . . Irving Kirshner taught one of my directing classes . . . Dan O'Bannon was my editing teacher . . . I'd have to look at my notes. There were so many people. I planned every day of my life around going to see films, auditing film classes as USC and UCLA, and attending seminars at Sherwood Oaks Experimental College, where I got the benefit of meeting all these industry insiders.

You're a great walking advertisement for Sherwood Oaks . . .

The guy that put this together is Gary Shusett, and Gary has got the balls of King Kong. He would go up to *anybody* in the industry and ask them to come to his little experimental college and talk. He would literally knock on their front doors . . . And he always got them! I'm enormously indebted to his chutzpah because it benefited me with a film education from industry people.

How did you develop a relationship with Frank Capra?

He came to Sherwood Oaks to screen *It's a Wonderful Life* and to talk about it. This was before *It's a Wonderful Life* was the classic that it is today.⁹ While I was watching the movie, I noticed certain elements that really spoke to me—especially the Jimmy Stewart character and the idea that he was just trying to be a good person even though all these horrible things were happening to him. The thing that really got to me was the ending, with the family, the money and the bell. I had seen that sequence a number of times on TV. Somehow, I had always managed to catch the movie at the end and that scene always got to me emotionally, even though I had never seen what led up to that point. Now that I knew what had come before, I had this wonderful moment of revelation: "Oh, it's *that* movie!" I felt compelled to approach Capra afterwards, and I said, "I need to know you. I need to understand what you do, because I want to do the same thing." And he was kind enough to give me his phone number and address so I could get in touch with him.

After that, I was on a mission to see all of his movies. They weren't available on video yet, so I had to wait until they came to the revival houses. Each one had a strong effect on me, because he consistently embraced that theme about the little guy against big odds.

When he worked for [producer] Mack Sennett, Capra was a silent gag writer for Harry Langdon, who in turn was a huge influence on me. There was a lot of Langdon in the character that

---

[9] The film earned its status among younger generations in the 1970s and 1980s, when it became a staple on network television during the Christmas season.

Tom and Frank Capra

I created in the Mime Company. He had that man-child quality. Langdon's character, particularly in the films that Capra was involved with, had a humanity that made him watchable and likable even though he was a cartoon in the middle of a realistic world. It's the same quality that Jimmy Stewart has in *Mr. Smith Goes to Washington*. Or Gary Cooper in *Meet John Doe*. People treat him like an idiot, but he's not an idiot. He's an innocent with uncompromising morals and an incredibly strong sense of self.

How would you sum up Capra's influence on you?

His attitude was that movies are a people-to-people medium. If you don't care about the people, you don't care about the story. You can have all the fancy camera tricks and special effects in the world, but it means nothing if the audience doesn't care about the characters. And I try to take that idea and put it into everything that I do—whether I'm doing a horror movie or a romance or a drama. If you care about the people, you get taken in. I'm not necessarily using a Capra-esque story structure or a Capra-esque character, but I'm very consciously thinking I've got to get the audience to like the characters and relate to them so that, when things start to happen, you're rooting for them. You want to see them succeed and, on some level, you want to *be* them.

I remember a couple of other things that Capra said that really stuck with me. One was, "If you get a chance to talk to people for two hours in the dark, you must have something to say." That made sense to me because I know the effect that movies have on me. I carry the experience of certain movies around with me for a long time. I know how many times I've been in a really tough situation in my life and the image that comes into my head is George Bailey at the end of *It's a Wonderful Life*, or Rocky Balboa pulling himself up in the fifteenth round to keep fighting. I love those scenes that represent the human desire to keep trying, no matter what.

When you were going to the movies during this time period, did you feel like you were doing research for a future career?

For me, the late '70s was a period of studying to be a filmmaker—taking any job I could that would pay the bills and allow me to be on a set. That was my mandate. When I was working [as a stuntman] on the movie *Prophecy*, I'd check in with the A.D. every morning. Even if they didn't need me that day, I'd hang around. They didn't have video monitors in those days, but you could trail behind the director if you wanted to see what was going on. The crew would set up the shots while the director and the actors went back to their trailers, and during those great spaces, I had the opportunity to talk to all the different crew members and learn about what they did. That was the kind of experience that my dad believed was far better than film school.

Since you brought up *Prophecy* . . . How did you end up getting the role of the mutant bear in that movie?

Because of my mime background, I was called to meet with

[director] John Frankenheimer and [producer] Robert Rosen. They needed someone to get into this monster suit and run on all fours. They showed me some early sketches of the monster, which looked like a weird mix of Godzilla, Mothra, Rodan—all the monsters from the Japanese horror films. The movie was about a mythological creature called Katahdin, and Katahdin is supposed to be this combination of all of God's creatures. So their early sketch of the monster was accurate in that this thing was a combination of bird and mammal and all these other creatures combined . . . It had a beak and a wing and a claw and sort of a bear-shaped body. I looked at it and they said, "What do you think?" I was trying not to laugh; trying not to lose the job. So I said, "Well, I sure wouldn't want to be in the same room with that thing." That was the kindest thing I could think of. Eventually Tom Burman stepped in to redesign the monster, and he came up with the notion of the mutated bear.

What was it like inside that costume?

It was me and another guy, a dancer named Charles Flemmer, who wore the bear suit—the idea being that if one of us got worn out, the other would take over for a while. And we did get worn out because this bear suit weighed about 150 pounds, most of which rested on our heads. We were eye-level with the neck. The bear head, with all the hydraulics in it, was perched on top. We had to do a lot of conditioning to make sure our necks were strong enough to handle that. Then we had to run on all fours, with extenders on our arms and legs. It was a real endurance test.

At one point I had to get into scuba gear for a scene where the bear emerges from underwater. I realized very quickly that this suit—which was rubber—absorbs water. The first time it happened, I couldn't stand up because the thing was so heavily weighted. I think they finally just cheated the shot. A stuntman put on the head, got into the water, and then they blasted water up around him as he stood up.

There were so many crazy shots where we were fighting to make this thing look as big as it was supposed to be. I remember

Famous Monsters of Filmland, July 1980

the scene where I'm chasing the Native American character, played by Victoria Racimo . . . They put her on a dolly, on her knees. Then they pulled the dolly while I was running behind her. It was the most absurd-looking thing as we were doing it. As I was in there, I was just thinking: *I'm paying my dues. My goal is I'm going to direct one day.* That's what got me through.

Famous Monsters of Filmland, July 1980

Prophecy was a grueling job . . . I even had to run through fire! I caught on fire twice while wearing monster suits—once on *Prophecy* and once on *Alice in Wonderland* [1985], when I played the Jabberwocky. The wing caught on fire because they had real torches on the set. I remember hearing somebody say, "The

Tom and Natalie Gregory on the set of *Alice in Wonderland*

Jabberwocky's on fire. Can we put him out?" I'm inside the suit, looking back and forth, going . . . *huh? Put him out??*

Tell me about being directed by John Frankenheimer.

For me, it was a chance to work for nine months with a living legend. John Frankenheimer represented to me what the great classic directors, like Ford and Hawks, would have been like. He wore the boots; he had the power. When he went on location, forty people followed him wherever he went. If he walked into the river—which he did one day to look for a shot—everybody walked right into the river with him. He was in charge and you did whatever he said.

At that time, I was a frustrated wannabe filmmaker and I actually had the stupidity to make some suggestions to the director. As much as I respected Frankenheimer, there was a part of me that regarded the filmmaking process as communal—because when you make little films, everybody throws something into the pot and it's up to the director to sort everything. I had the idea that's how all films were made. So when there was a scene that involved me, I would say, "Mr. Frankenheimer, what if the camera was down here and then we could get the monster's point of view from over here and then . . ."

The crew must have been thinking, *Why is this mime in a bear suit telling John Frankenheimer how to direct his movie?* The first time, John was like, "Yeah, well, thank you Tom, I appreciate that." He blew it off. The second time, he said, "Can I talk to you for a second?" He pulled me aside and he said, "I know you haven't done this a lot, but you don't tell the director where to place the camera. That's my job. It's not that your ideas aren't good—in fact, I'm going to use that idea—but in the future if you have an idea, come to me privately. Don't do it in front of the whole crew. You're just embarrassing yourself." I thought that was very nice of him to address my stupidity that way.

As years have gone on, the more I think about it, the more I cringe. I can't believe I had the nerve to do that. But it was an innocent, well-meaning gesture. I was just thinking, *Gee, we're all making a movie together, and I've got an idea to contribute.* I still genuinely love that sense that movies are a group effort. I think people are always more committed when they feel like it's not just one person's movie. Film is a communal art form, and you want everyone in the group to be excited and share their best work.

Was everyone else as excited about making a monster movie as you were?

John did *not* want to do a monster movie. In fact, if you

referred to *Prophecy* as a monster movie at any given time, you were fined or yelled at by John—and you didn't want to be yelled at by John. I think he had convinced himself that he could call this a political movie about environmental problems, because they developed the monster around this Indian mythology about the destruction of nature by the white man. And he probably thought it would be a big money-maker.

No such luck.

When I went to the preview screening of *Prophecy* at Grauman's Chinese Theater, people were laughing at it. It was really hard on some of the people who worked on the movie. And hard for the studio, which had put a ton of money into it. I remember somebody told me that the production costs were $40,000 a day . . . And on some days we only got one shot. That's $40,000 for one shot! Plus we started shooting day for night, and when the studio execs saw the footage they scrapped all that material and started over. They built a forest on the sound stage sixteen at Paramount and started all over again. That's when the realities of excessive studio spending became very clear to me.

And all for a movie that then gets laughed off the screen.

Well, at the first preview anyway. But I think there might have been some people in the audience who wanted to sabotage it. The movie really did work on one level. It was very intense. The problem was that the monster just . . . wasn't . . . scary. And because the actors were taking things so seriously and the monster was so ludicrous, it seemed like a joke. And all it takes is one person to start laughing. Suddenly everybody in the theater is going, "Is this supposed to be funny?" It's like a fart that starts to permeate the room, and it wasn't long before the mood in the theater changed. It just became a farce, and I was started slowly sinking down in my seat too.

The best thing that came out of *Prophecy* was I met my wife Nancy on the set. The head of security had a daughter who was best friends with Nancy. I met her on stage sixteen as I was

Nancy McLoughlin

crawling out of the ass-end of this monster. Picture this: I'm wearing an electric blue leotard and tights. As soon as I get out of the costume, I immediately start to exercise—because my muscles would get so hot in that suit and I couldn't let them get cold or everything would tighten up. I had a routine that I had to do—because I knew that, when I got back into that suit, my muscles couldn't be cold or I would really hurt myself. So I was doing my routine and she made eye contact with me and I with her. Her immediate reaction was, "He's gay. Has to be. In leotard and tights, looking like a ballet dancer . . ."

I managed to find out that she worked as a waitress in a restaurant on Sunset Boulevard, so after we wrapped that night I went home, cleaned up and went to the restaurant. I walked up to her and she was shocked to see me. I think I said something corny, like "I was afraid I was never going to see you again." Which was terribly romantic to her. And then, "What time do you get off? Let's meet for coffee." That was the beginning of our relationship. Thirty-four years later, we're still together.

In your next film, *The Black Hole*, you played the second-fastest robot gunslinger in the universe...

I was originally hired as a sort of sentry robot / humanoid stunt choreographer, which was the case on many projects in those days. The film featured two different kinds of robot characters, and the director, Gary Nelson, wanted somebody to train those guys to move in a consistent way. With the humanoids, I went for a slow-motion floating walk. With the sentries, I decided to use Nazi goose steps. We kept their movements very staccato, so that they would still look like machines.

I wasn't hired to act in the movie, but one day Gary came to me and said he was thinking about creating a new character called Captain S.T.A.R. He was the original prototype before they turned to clone robots, and he's incredible at these laser video games. They basically wrote that part for me, and then they created a suit where the arms were rubberized instead of plastic, so I could spin the guns and do that kind of stuff. So that became my little cameo in the movie. I was surprised to see myself listed on the credits with all the top-name stars.

When did you get interested in horror again?

The "dark side" never stopped fascinating me. While I was auditing classes at USC and UCLA and going to seminars at Sherwood Oaks, I decided to write a horror movie. I really wanted to make a comedy, but comedies really weren't selling. Horror *was* selling, and I loved those too. When I saw *The Exorcist*, I decided that if I was going to do a horror movie, I wanted it to be something like that.

Tom as Captain S.T.A.R. in *The Black Hole* (Disney, 1979)

What was so compelling to you about *The Exorcist*?

People who saw that movie couldn't sleep. For so many people . . . it really affected their lives. *The Exorcist* changed my life too, but in a different way. It made me realize the potential of a movie like that. One of the big reasons I wanted to be a filmmaker was because you really can affect people on a level beyond entertainment. A good movie goes much deeper.

I was fortunate to see *The Exorcist* in the optimum conditions at the National Theater here in Los Angeles. I saw it on the third day of its release, and the lines were enormous. Word had spread through the city that you *had* to see this film. [Director William] Friedkin and [writer William Peter] Blatty were out on the sidewalks in front of the theater, passing out coffee and hot cocoa to people waiting in line. So we went into the theater with this sense that we're going to see something *evil*. I mean, this was going to be really *an experience*. People came in with that anticipation. They expected to be traumatized. And sure as hell they were.

People ran up the aisles with their hands over their mouths, about to throw up. Many did. One guy stood up and just passed out. Sometimes it was the needle into the arm scene that did it, when she [Regan] was getting the spinal . . . or the scene when her throat bubbled up. There was so much tension in the theater, and visuals like that would just push people over the edge. My favorite memory of that screening is when the movie was over and the credits were rolling, and I saw that some people *couldn't move*. I saw them standing to leave—people with a coat half on—and they were not able to move any further.

Needless to say I went back the next night and the night after that. It became an obsession—trying to understand every aspect of how they put this thing together and trying to separate the myth from the truth. *Did bad things really happen on the set? Were there really things on the screen that were subliminally affecting viewers in the audience?* I eventually came to realize it was just one hell of a dog-and-pony show. But that movie sent hordes of people back to church . . . because they didn't want whatever got that little girl to get them. It created a phenomenon like we've never had since. It actually changed people's lives.

Entrance to the Catacombs of Paris

Was that the inspiration for *One Dark Night*?

I went to the catacombs when I was in Paris studying with Marceau. Went down six stories of stairs and found myself wall to wall with skulls and bones from hundreds of cemeteries. It's different now but, in those days, everybody in the tour group was given a candle and you walked through the catacombs with it. There was no artificial lighting . . . Talk about gothic.

I let the tour group go ahead of me and I stayed back alone, to kind of experience this on my own. And it was the first and only time I ever experienced supernatural fear. By that I mean, I know there's nothing in there that's going to get me, but I felt that sensation that starts at the bottom of your spine and rises. I knew I shouldn't be there all alone. It was part claustrophobia; part awareness of the dead all around me. I found myself hurrying to catch up with the group. And that impression was the thing that created *One Dark Night*.

How did you and Michael Hawes work together to write the script?

Hawes and I always went to horror movies together, so we were both anxious to try writing a horror script. I would have not written that piece if he had not kept on me. I wrote things out by hand, then bounced ideas off of him and he would say, "Yeah that works" Or "How about this instead?" The objective was that we wanted to create a claustrophobic Edgar Allan Poe kind of horror movie, but it had to be teen-oriented because that was the target demographic that made money. Once we had a script, we started to shop it around . . . but nobody wanted it because it wasn't a slasher movie. Hollywood only wants to copy what is successful *right now*. So we kept shopping it around for years. Lots of attempts; lots of closed doors.

We used to joke about how scripts would always come back with coffee cup stains on them. You couldn't help but wonder: *Did it end up just being a temporary coaster?* Or, if it was all rolled up: *Was it a door stopper?* You have to make jokes about the rejection. It's either laugh or cry.

At writing seminars, the top screenwriters say, "Get ready to eat a lot of cheese—because your first six scripts are never going to sell." I heard Lawrence Kasdan speak right after *Raiders of the Lost Ark*, and he said the same thing: "Do you know how many scripts I've got sitting in my drawer at home? What I'm going to do next is revise all these things that I wrote years ago . . ." Because once you get the door open, people will start paying attention. So I'm thinking: *Does this mean I've got to write another script? That I'm never going to get anywhere with this one? Or do we just need to find a better way to make people to see this movie idea the way we see it? Maybe they're just not getting it . . .*

I realized that I had no credibility as a filmmaker, so I decided to surround myself with people who did have credibility. I went after people who were involved with movies that I really admired . . . like *Halloween*. I got a hold of Craig Stearns, who was the set decorator on *Halloween* and the production designer on *The Fog*. He's a really nice guy and I went to his house and we instantly bonded, and I said, "Would you give me a letter of intent, saying that you would be willing to do this movie?" He said, "Yeah, sure." So I made up some letterhead and he wrote: *I believe in Tom McLoughlin and in this movie. And would love to be a part of this.* And then I tacked his credits to that letter.

[Makeup designer] Tom Burman, who had worked on *Prophecy* with me, also gave me a letter of intent. I had an art director, director of photography, production designer . . . and I got a letter of reference from The Academy of Science Fiction and Horror, which is where I went every Sunday morning to watch horror movies. They wrote a letter saying that they read my script *Mausoleum*, which was the title of *One Dark Night* at that time, and they saw it as something in the classic tradition of horror movies, and something that could probably compete for a Saturn Award. So I put that whole package together, attached my own stinky credits and added a letter about the style and look of the movie I wanted to make.

You really shifted into the role of businessman, which is a jump that a lot of writers never make.

You do what you've got to do . . . but a few more months went by and still nothing was happening. So I'm thinking, *Shit, what do I have to do now?* I went to a seminar on how to get your script made and the speaker presented the idea of hiring an actor who had [lowering voice to sound like a radio announcer] *one of those voices*, to do a radio spot saying, "It's the most horrifying thing you've seen since . . ." Then add sound effects to jazz it up. I figured, *Okay, it's cheap. We'll just record an audio tape and then go into somebody's office and say, "Here's what the radio spot would sound like."*

Then Hawes and I thought: *We're going to go one step better. We're going to do a* slideshow *presentation!* Hawes was a photographer and I knew an actress who looked like the fresh-faced girl next door, so we went to the Hollywood Mausoleum and shot her walking through. We got long shots of the hall, close-ups of her

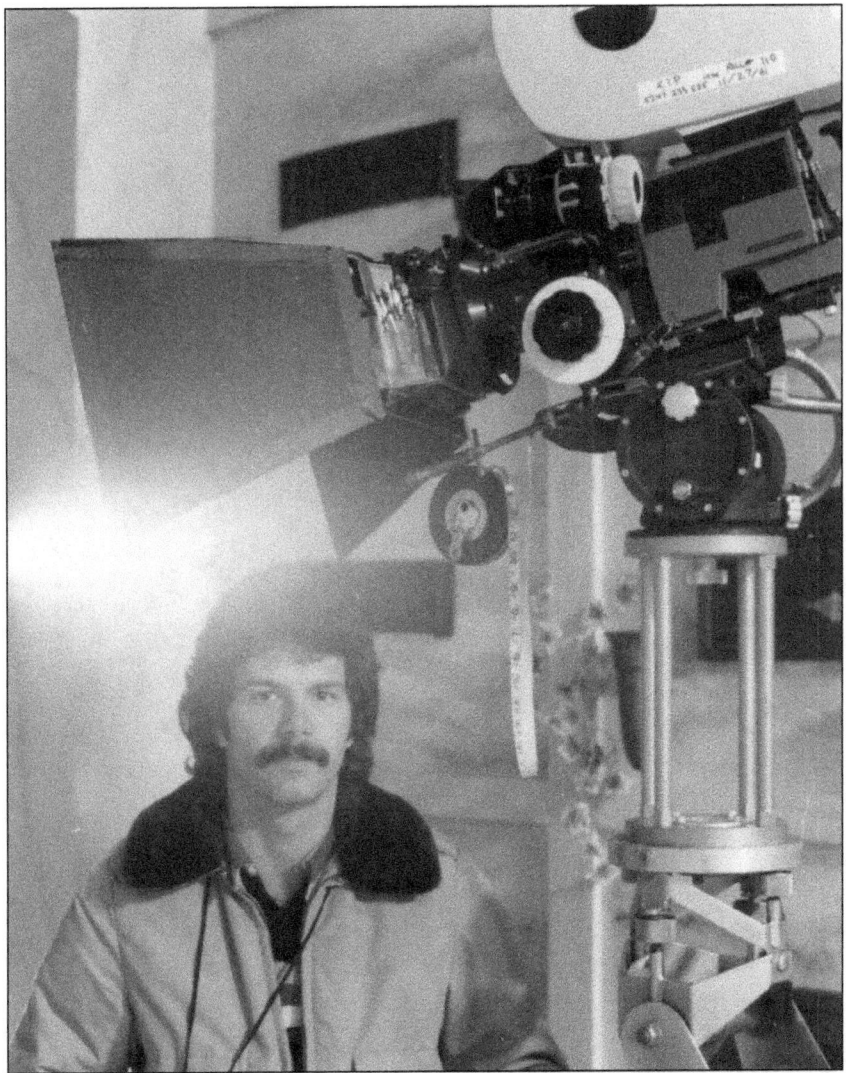

Mike Hawes on the set of *One Dark Night*.

face, point of view shots . . . Then we took the music from *The Amityville Horror* because it had a great build. The music went up and up and up, and then . . . *"Mausoleum!"*

Of course, that turned out to be ridiculous. We had to continually drag the slide-show projector around with us and project the images on the walls of darkened rooms. But it was better than nothing because I was showing people my vision for the movie. Ultimately, believe it or not, we brought that slide projector and

Early concept art for *One Dark Night*

our little tape recorder to Provo, Utah, to meet with the head of a company called ComWorld. We went into this guy's bedroom, because it was the only place with open wall space—right above the baby's crib—and we projected this thing and turned the sound way up. Afterwards, the guy said, "I don't know anything about horror movies, but this looks scary to me." He represented a group of Mormon investors in Salt Lake City that needed a tax shelter, and they said, "If you can start in three weeks and we can show a cut in the Bahamas a week after wrap (to qualify as a tax shelter), we will give you one million dollars to make this movie." In the end, they ponied up $850,000. That's how it happened.

I understand you did a lot of research on psychic phenomena for *One Dark Night*.

Mike and I, and a number of people that were involved in my life at that time, were really interested in the idea of mind control.

After Ron Hubbard created Scientology,[10] there were a number of offshoots of that. One of the offshoots was a thing called *est*.[11] Est took some of the ideas from Scientology and combined them with ideas from Eastern philosophies. And then there were a lot of little variations on est, like Silva Mind Control. Silva Mind Control was a method of learning how to lower your brain frequency so that you could perceive things beyond the five senses and actually reach out with your mind and cause things to happen just by thinking about it.

A woman named Helen Virginia Bangs had created her own program called Mind Psi Biotics, and she held workshops in Orange County. I can't remember exactly how we heard about her, but we went to a seminar and she talked about how you can stop bleeding and stop pain through the power of your will. What you do is bring your brainwaves down to a level called theta.[12] In that state there's an energy that somehow stretches beyond the human body as we know it. That led to our studying Kirlian photography.[13] You really can photograph a person's energy [moving beyond the surface of their body].

But we weren't 100% buying the idea that we have psychic powers. We weren't ready to be converted or anything, but we figured, *Why not? Let's see what happens.* She talked us through this process—it was almost like self-hypnosis—and we found that we could do things that were pretty cool. One time while I was in a meditative theta state, someone handed me a wedding ring

---

[10] The "Church" of Scientology was established in 1954 in Los Angeles by science-fiction writer L. Ron Hubbard.

[11] Erhard Seminars Training offered intense two-weekend seminars utilizing "the technology of transformation," from 1971 to 1984.

[12] In the state called theta, brain waves have a frequency rate between 5 and 8 cycles per second. This state is commonly associated with daydreaming and repetitive tasks such as long-distance running and freeway driving.

[13] The Kirlian technique is a form of contact photography in which the subject of the photograph is placed in direct contact with a film on a metal plate that is charged with high voltage, high frequency electricity. Resulting images show electrical discharges emanating from the subject of the photograph.

and I started describing what came into my mind as I was holding it. When I opened my eyes, the other person said: *You just described my grandmother.* Another time, I was given a name and a city. My imagination seemed to make up what this person looked like. I saw heat coming off of his chest and then I found out that he had lung cancer. It was unbelievable. Everyone in these classes was able to accomplish these seemingly supernatural deeds. Businessmen, housewives, students, truck drivers, anyone. We came expecting to find that this was a fraud, and we became total believers.

Afterwards, I thought: *Well what if somebody could do these things, but they used the power for dark purposes? What if they could actually drain the energy off of people? And what if, when they die, that energy still resides in their body?* I did some research and found out that, when you die, your hair and fingernails continue to grow. There is still a life energy in dead bodies. When I learned that, I began to think maybe that's what ghosts are. People say that if you go into the house where the Manson Family murdered Sharon Tate, and you are at all "sensitive," you will feel this negative energy—because what happened there was so horrific and that dark energy remains. They eventually torn that house down.

I took what I'd learned and put it into our script. In *One Dark Night*, a young girl (played by Meg Tilly) has to spend the night in a mausoleum to pledge into a high school club. The other members sneak in that night to scare her. On that same day, a Russian psychic named Raymar is entombed there. His body is deceased, but his bio-energy is very much alive, and he scares the girls to the point that their energy helps bring him back to life.

I didn't want the audience to get too hung up on trying to understand all that, but we needed to explain things somewhat at the beginning of the movie. I thought of it like the Ark of the Covenant speech in *Raiders of the Lost Ark*. Lawrence Kasdan said that it killed him to interrupt the momentum of the movie with that speech, but it was necessary to explain why the Nazis wanted the Ark. So I hired my acting coach, Don Hotton, to play Raymar's former associate and explain Raymar's power. He used these Kirlian photographs that we got from a well-known parapsychologist

Raymar concept art by Tom Burman

named Thelma Moss. And basically it was our Ark of the Covenant speech. It allowed the audience to say, "Okay he's got these superpowers... Now let's get on with the scares."

It's interesting to me that you weren't just looking at the idea of the "psychic vampire" as a high-concept gimmick or a plot device for a horror movie, but as part of a worldview that acknowledges but can't entirely explain the unknown. Ultimately, the movie was more about that *feeling* you had in the catacombs than about the psychic vampire plot device... and that feeling came from questioning what's real. There is very real power in imagination. When you *believe* that something is real, it is—for you, in that moment—as real as anything...

Exactly, and that's something that was important to get across the audience. To make Meg's character even more susceptible, the girls gave her a sleeping pill—something to make her disoriented so that she'd wake up and not really know what was going on, and then feel really vulnerable. They know she's a girl who doesn't take drugs.

Or hang out in cemeteries . . .

Right. In classic horror movie fashion, they all happen to be in the wrong place at the wrong time, because Raymar was just entombed there. And we've already set up the idea of psychic vampirism . . . which is something we have all experienced in our lives, even if we've never heard the term "psychic vampirism."

Everybody has to agree that there are certain people that can drain the energy out of you in a casual conversation. Most have no idea they're doing it, but they somehow use other people's energy to keep themselves going. And then there are people who do the exact opposite. When I worked with Bette Midler, she had such energy that, after I talked to her, I was buzzing. Quentin Tarantino is the same way. I remember a few years back, he told me about *Grindhouse*. I saw the entire movie as he was explaining it, and when he left I was on a high. That's a gift. This phenomenon exists in life.

Now let's take it to the next step, which is that Raymar is using the girls' energy to open up crypts. Now we're into pure horror movie visuals—coffins coming out of the wall and opening up. That's many people's greatest fear at funerals. Thinking: *I don't want to see what's in that casket. I don't want to look at death.*

I've heard that Meg Tilly was genuinely frightened when you were filming in the mausoleum.

Oh yeah. And it shows. A lot of times when I'm directing actors in scare scenes, I tell them *not* to go for the fear—because it usually becomes too big, too much, and then it becomes funny. I tell actors to try *not* to be afraid. Try *not* to freak out. You know that you're seeing someone walking toward you with a knife in their hand, but try to be cool. Seeing inner-conflict makes me, as a viewer, more uncomfortable than seeing someone express fear. But then if you have somebody like Meg who is so committed

Part II: Comedy and Horror

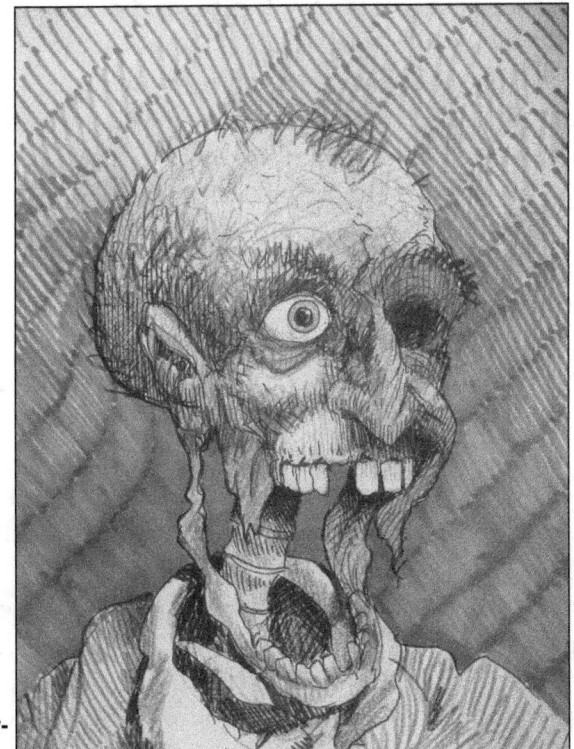

One Dark Night storyboard art

that she really seems like her mind is going to snap . . . It isn't funny. It was as intense as I wanted it to be. When see that an actor has that ability to really go there, you let them.

Because if it seems like they truly believe that they're being attacked by zombies, then the audience will believe it too . . .

Hopefully. The other thing I wanted to do was to change the accepted theory that when the dead come back to life, they walk. [In *One Dark Night*], the zombies were hunks of decomposing or mummified flesh that are being manipulated and moved through the air by a type of magician.

There's an old Army vet, a heavy-set woman, an old man, a little girl buried with her doll . . . I looked for personalizing touches because that's what I would notice when Mike [Hawes] and I visited real mausoleums. The crypt-keepers would take down the dead flowers, but they left behind photographs and notes, Christmas cards, birthday cards . . . and some of them were really personal. The things people said in those cards were things they couldn't say in life. They know that they're never going to get a response, but they have to say it anyway . . . I really wanted to get those details into the movie, so that when Meg walks into the mausoleum, we understand that she's afraid of being in there with people's *memories*. The longer it took to get the movie made, the more of these things I kept putting in the script and the more personal it became.

Just before the movie came out, some reviewer saw it and they asked to do an interview with me. I was able to do what I'm doing now and talk about all the reasons why it was important for me to make this movie, and to express my feelings about death and about having respect for the dead. And the article that came out of that was wonderful. You could tell that the critic didn't really buy everything in the movie. He was like, "Well yeah, it was fun, but . . . the most interesting thing is the way that Tom McLoughlin wants to honor the dead." He wrote, "Maybe one day the dead will come back and make him an honorary member." I loved that.

One Dark Night storyboard art

Do you believe in ghosts?

I've had a number of—for lack of a better description—"encounters" with things that are beyond reality as I know it. And I wasn't in any sort of hyper-state or drunk or stoned or anything else. The first one happened when I was sixteen. My girlfriend Amy's parents were part of a unique group . . . Believers in the paranormal. They met every Thursday night to meditate and discuss, and they were open to *all* the other possibilities outside of "normal" religion. I was a sixteen-year-old kid and my world was all about sex, drugs and rock n roll, so that stuff really didn't mean a lot to me, but my girlfriend grew up in a house where they believed in all these other things. So she always spoke about ghosts.

At that time, Amy was seeing apparitions in the house and was quite frightened. She said things were moving around her all the time. Now, again, I didn't believe any of this. I'm sixteen. She's sixteen. She would tell me these things very sincerely and I sort of wanted to believe her, but I never saw any proof. So I dismissed it, figuring, *I have an attractive, artistic girlfriend with a very vivid imagination.*

Anyway, a Ouija board was discovered in her family's attic. Nobody could explain how it got there. When this group learned about the Ouija board, they asked my girlfriend and I to sit in on their meeting so they could figure out what was going on with her. They made a fire in the fireplace and took out the Ouija board and the planchette, and once the fire was big enough, they put the whole thing into the fireplace. We're all just sitting there, waiting for it to burn . . . and it didn't burn. You could probably come up with a logical explanation—the lacquer on the bottom of it wasn't flammable . . . or whatever.

But then—I kid you not—different sections of the Ouija board lit up in different colors. A blue flame, about an inch and a half around, came up from one section. Then a red flame, same size, from another section. Then an orange flame, a purple flame, a green flame . . . all in different sections of the Ouija board. And each time one of those flames came up, they gave off a screeching sound. It sounded like these old fireworks that were called Piccolo

Petes. So there are six or seven of those things going off at the same time, and everybody in the room was in a state of shock. Suddenly the whole thing just went poof and disintegrated. The flames engulfed the board and it was gone. We must have sat in silence for five minutes after that. Nobody knew what to say or what to do. No words of wisdom. Just . . . wow. It was like we'd just witnessed a horrible accident and everybody was frozen and speechless. And that was it.

The next night, I went back over to Amy's house. At the end of the night, I was standing out on the front porch, saying goodnight, and I remember feeling like there was someone else there. I didn't think too much about it at the time—it was only as the night went on that I really had to secretly acknowledge feeling like there was something *with me*. I went home and went to bed, still feeling a little weirded out.

Around three in the morning, I woke up . . . just woke up abruptly . . . and I could see a shape in the corner of my bedroom in front of the closed door. I saw the outline of a head, shoulders, and then a line straight down, like a long cape or something. Couldn't see arms or anything, just this form. And it was like . . . television static, except it was sort of a violet color. And just like the cliché, the room was freezing.

Truthfully, I really was not sure if I was dreaming or if this was real, but after a while I knew I was awake and that this was real somehow. And I was *scared*. So I called Amy in the middle of the night. Her mother answered, and I said [timidly], "Hi, this is Tom." And she goes, "There's something there, isn't there?" I said, "Yeah." She goes, "Okay here's what you need to do. Close your eyes . . ." And I said, "I don't want to close my eyes." It was like this thing was staring at me, as I was talking. I was transfixed. She said, "Just close your eyes. You *have to* close your eyes." So I closed my eyes and then she said, "In your mind, imagine the room is filling with white light. Just picture the room getting brighter and brighter." It took me a while, but I tried doing that. I just tried to imagine I could feel it getting brighter, brighter, brighter. She said, "Don't open your eyes." Of course I was terrified that I was going to open my eyes and this thing was going to be right in my face. Like in a horror movie. After a while, she said, "Now open your eyes." I did and it was gone. The coldness was gone.

I said, "What was that?" She said, "I'll tell you tomorrow." "Well, what if it comes back?" "It won't." Eventually I went back to sleep, still confused by what I just saw. I was still scared. But then another part of me was thinking, now that the thing is gone, *Boy was that pretty cool.* [smiling]

When I spoke to her mom the next day, she said, "I don't know exactly what it was, but obviously it was something related to what happened with the Ouija board. This energy or ghost or specter, whatever you want to call it, somehow attached itself to your energy and left with you. For whatever reason, it had a need to connect." She said, "There's so many different theories . . ." She continued trying to explain paranormal phenomena to a sixteen-year-old kid.

At the time I did not put a whole lot of stock in what she said . . . but I certainly didn't forget what happened to me. It's a story that I have related to people for years, because it was the first time that something like that happened to me. I wasn't necessarily a believer, but it created in me a desire to believe in something more—something beyond the news, weather and sports of the everyday world. That's what it took. My own true, surreal, paranormal experience.

PART III: MYTHS & MONSTERS

The first director's cut / Resurrecting Jason Voorhees / The dying man and his angel / Mysteries from a magic pawn shop / Frank Capra meets Freddy Krueger / Stephen King's greatest hits / Life, death and Indian burial grounds

FILMOGRAPHY

ONE DARK NIGHT (COMWORLD, 1983)
DIRECTED BY TOM MCLOUGHLIN
ORIGINAL SCREENPLAY BY TOM MCLOUGHLIN & MICHAEL HAWES
STARRING MEG TILLY, ROBIN EVANS, ELIZABETH DAILY, LESLIE SPEIGHTS
   Julie spends the night alone in a mausoleum haunted by a psychic vampire.

FRIDAY THE 13TH PART VI: JASON LIVES! (PARAMOUNT, 1986)
DIRECTED BY TOM MCLOUGHLIN
ORIGINAL SCREENPLAY BY TOM MCLOUGHLIN.
STARRING THOM MATTHEWS, JENNIFER COOKE, C.J. GRAHAM
   Tommy accidentally resurrects his old nemesis, serial killer Jason Voorhees, and the maggot-eaten madman continues his killing spree at Camp Crystal Lake.

"AMAZING STORIES"—"GO TO THE HEAD OF THE CLASS" (NBC, 1986)
DIRECTED BY ROBERT ZEMECKIS
TELEPLAY BY MICK GARRIS, TOM MCLOUGHLIN & BOB GALE
   A teenager uses black magic on his English teacher, only to be terrorized by the results.

"Amazing Stories"—"Such Interesting Neighbors"
(NBC, 1987)
Directed by Graham Baker
Teleplay by Mick Garris & Tom McLoughlin. Based on a short story by Jack Finney

A family is tormented by their new neighbors, who seem to have supernatural powers.

Date with an Angel (DeLaurentiis Entertainment Group, 1987)
Directed by Tom McLoughlin
Original screenplay by Tom McLoughlin
Starring Michael E. Knight, Emmanuelle Beart, Phoebe Cates

A week before his wedding, Jim falls in love with a wounded angel.

"Freddy's Nightmares"—"It's a Miserable Life"
(New Line, 1988)
Directed by Tom McLoughlin
Teleplay by Michael DeLuca & Paul Rosselli
Starring Robert Englund, John Cameron Mitchell, Lar Park Lincoln

Bryan is feeling suffocated by his dead-end job in a dead-end town. Things get even worse when a drive-by shooting plunges him into the dreamworld of Freddy Krueger.

"Friday the 13th: The Series"—"Master of Disguise"
(Paramount, 1988)
Directed by Tom McLoughlin
Teleplay by Bruce Martin

Starring John D. LeMay, Louise Robey, Chris Wiggins, John Bolger

Micki falls for a coldhearted actor who owes his success to a cursed antique makeup case.

"Friday the 13th: The Series"—"The Playhouse"
(Paramount, 1988)
Directed by Tom McLoughlin
Teleplay by Tom McLoughlin
Starring John D. LeMay, Louise Robey, Chris Wiggins, Robert Oliveri, Lisa Jakub

A toy playhouse from a cursed pawnshop offers sanctuary and revenge to a pair of children from an abusive home.

"Friday the 13th: The Series"—"The Prophecy"
(Paramount, 1989)
Directed by Tom McLoughlin
Teleplay by Tom McLoughlin
Starring John D. LeMay, Louise Robey, Chris Wiggins, Marie-France Lambert, Fritz Weaver

Micki and Ryan travel to rural France to investigate a nun's prophecy about the second coming.

Steven Banks: Home Entertainment Center (HBO, 1989)
Directed by Tom McLoughlin
Teleplay by Steven Banks
Starring Steven Banks

One-man comedy show about a twenty-something musician in arrested development.

"They Came from Outer Space"—pilot (MCA Television, 1990)
Directed by Sidney Hayers
Teleplay by Tom McLoughlin, Peter Baloff & Dave Wollert
Starring Dean Cameron, Stuart Fratkin

Two horny teenage aliens travel to Malibu, California, to pick up earth girls.

"She-Wolf of London"—pilot (MCA Television, 1990)
Directed by Dennis Abey
Teleplay by Tom McLoughlin & Mick Garris
Starring Neil Dickson, Kate Hodge, Scott Fults

American college student Randi gets bitten by a British werewolf. Her anthropology professor comes to her aid.

STEPHEN KING'S SOMETIMES THEY COME BACK (DINO DELAURENTIIS COMMUNICATIONS, 1991)
DIRECTED BY TOM MCLOUGHLIN
ADAPTED SCREENPLAY BY LAWRENCE KONNER, MARK ROSENTHAL AND TIM KRING (UNCREDITED)
STARRING TIM MATHESON, BROOKE ADAMS, ROBERT RUSLER

Jim returns to his hometown, where he must confront memories of his brother's murder, and save his family from his brother's undead killers.

Tom and Raymar on the set of *One Dark Night*

Were your investors creatively involved in the making of *One Dark Night*? I understand they had final cut . . .

One Dark Night was a wonderful yet incredibly painful experience at the end. It was my first time in the director's chair. I was finally getting a chance to do what I wanted to do, after all these years. There were some rules. ComWorld didn't want any profanity or any sex in the film. But that was the only creative interference, in the beginning. Then they added an executive producer who was a child psychologist. That became a running joke with us, because he would intellectualize every scene. He would say [in a deep, ultra-serious voice], "Okay, this is good because the kids are going to see that Julie really represents . . ." And we'd say, "Yeah yeah yeah." Just to keep him happy . . . And he was a doctor, so he had to be addressed as such. [laughs]

But basically we had a set amount of money, a set amount of time, and we had to make it work. While we were shooting the movie, the editor Charlie Tetoni was putting together master shots and a very rough assembly as fast as he could, because as soon as we wrapped the film had to be screened in the Bahamas to qualify as a tax shelter for the investors. There was no time to do additional sound recording or mixing, so about half of the movie didn't have sound. They screened the edited master . . . That's been called my "director's cut." Of course, it *wasn't* my director's cut; it was the editor's cut. When they screened that version, they added text to the bottom of the screen that said: *Due to technical difficulties, the audio in this portion of the film is missing.* That was how they covered for showing an unfinished film.

After that, they handed the film back to me and I had two or three weeks to cut it. During that period, a guy named Charles Sellier, who we'd heard was a low-budget filmmaking icon in Utah, took over the company. It sounded like a really good thing, because he had done a few movies and he knew something about the industry. He had produced a low-budget horror movie called *The Boogens*. Later he directed *Silent Night, Deadly Night*, which was about a killer Santa Claus. He came down from Utah to meet us, and he was like [very understated], "So this is your first film? Hmmmm . . ." He sat down and watched the entire film. At the end, he said, "Nice job." That was on a Friday and he said, "Let me think about it over the weekend and then we'll talk . . ."

On Monday morning, I went to the editing room and it was gutted. The film was gone, the equipment was gone, everything . . . Holy shit! I started calling people, and couldn't get hold of anybody. I finally got hold of Sellier and he said, "We just felt that it was in our best interest to bring the film up here. We're going to take care of it. We appreciate your director's cut. Thank you so much." I said, "Wait a minute, you can't do this." And he said, "Yes we can." I was devastated. I didn't know what was going

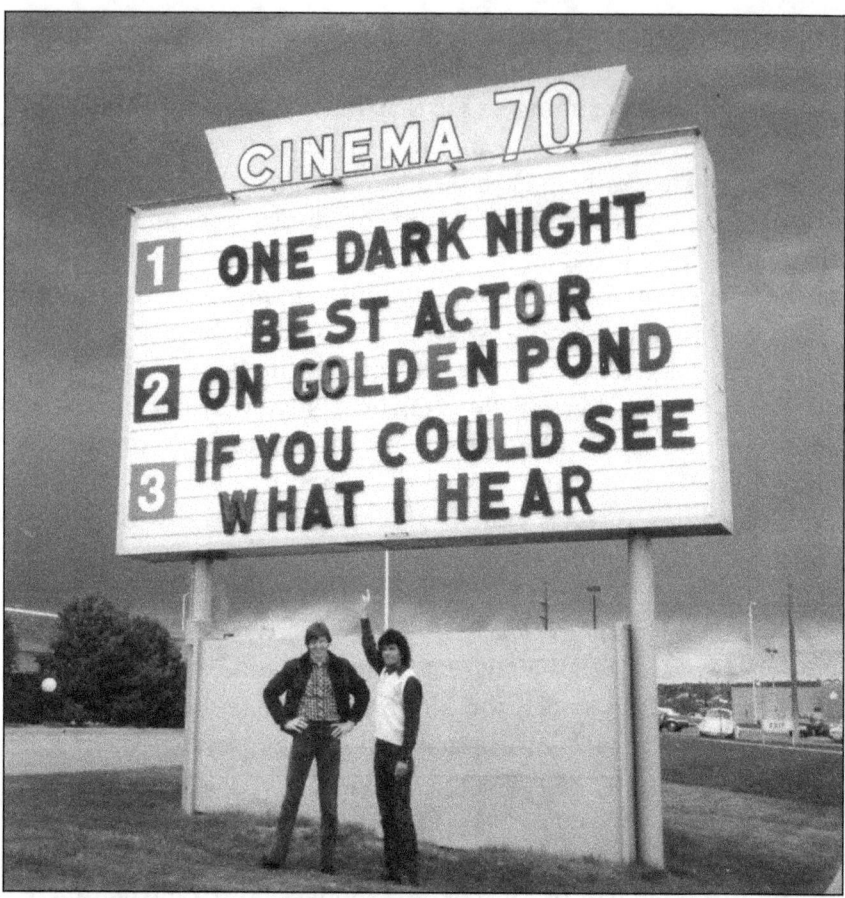

Tom and Mike Hawes on May 22, 1982

to happen. Eventually somebody called and said they were going to preview the movie in Colorado Springs to see how it played. So Mike Hawes and I bought cheap plane tickets and went to see it.

We were shocked to see that the beginning was totally different. They took the title sequence and made it into one long Steadicam scene for no good reason. They got actress Melissa Newman to do an additional scene where she wakes up out of a dream. There were all these things in the film that we had not planned. Then there were other sections that were left completely intact. The opening of the crypts sequence was exactly the way we wanted it to be . . . Then we got to the ending. The Meg Tilly character just walks away and they roll credits. And you could hear the audience going, "Huh? What? That's it?"

During production we used the contact lenses that Tom Burman designed for Nastassja Kinski to wear in *Cat People*. We put them into Meg Tilly's eyes so that when she turns and looks at the camera, you see these dark eyes—suggesting that Raymar had possessed her. It was corny and might not have been exactly right for the movie, but at least it was *something*. At the screening, we realized that it just wasn't enough. So we opted instead for the old *Carrie* ending that so many people were doing. And that only happened because I got on the phone with somebody at ComWorld and convinced them I could give them a new ending that wouldn't cost a thing.

I had two set pieces left over from the crypts that Craig Stearns had built for the photo sessions to help sell the movie. Somehow we convinced Panavision to loan us a camera for free. We only paid for the film stock, which wasn't much because it was such a short sequence. We got the actresses back and did this silly jump scene ending. You're supposed to think it's all over, and then we hit you one more time. I'm sick of this technique—it's such a cliché. Everybody sees it coming, but it really did work. It wasn't great, but it was better than what was there before.

Let's talk about casting the picture, since you've said that the first secret of good directing is good casting.

I have always believed very strongly in what Capra said—that this is a people-to-people medium. If you get the audience to love the characters, you can tell any story any way you want and they'll be right there with you. If they're invested in the characters and you do something surprising, they'll go with it. If they're not invested in the characters and you throw a curve ball, they'll just say, "That's stupid. That would never happen." It's the character that makes you believe something is really happening or not happening.

Meg Tilly was the polar opposite of what I was looking for. I was looking for a blonde, blue-eyed, sweet California girl—but Meg was the one who blew me away as an actress. Thank God for Elza Bergeron, my casting director, who convinced me to be open-minded about this young girl from Canada. The casting of that film really was a combination of discovery and bullheadedness. And using friends. My ex-wife is in there—she's one of the reporters. My brother is in there. My best friend Steven Banks is in there . . . And my soon-to-be wife Nancy has a great scene.

The most unusual casting decision was Adam West.[14] My casting director said to me, "I don't know if you should cast him, because people perceive him as Batman." I immediately thought: *Just because an actor does something that everybody loves him for now, it's hard for him to get other jobs?* I cast him purely for that reason. Then, when we were shooting, I realized that Adam had done the Batman voice for so long that it had become part of his acting persona. I worked so hard to get that out of him. Of course, when the film was taken away from me and the producers looped him, I wasn't in the looping session and the Batman-style readings came back in.

How was the film received by critics and audiences at the time?

I remember Allen Daviau, who was friends with our cinematographer Hal Trussel, came in one day while we were editing. Allen had just finished shooting *E.T.* He saw some of our corpse footage and he asked us when the film was coming out. We said January and he said, "Good . . . because I just saw some footage from Steven [Spielberg]'s movie *Poltergeist* and there are a lot of similarities here." Well, as it turned out, our release was delayed. There was a change of leadership at the distribution company and we came out after *Poltergeist*. Thus all of the reviews said, "Obviously the filmmakers saw *Poltergeist*." I was very impressed with *Poltergeist*—I thought it did all the things that a modern-day gothic horror movie should do—but it wasn't an influence on *One Dark Night* at all.

That's the risk you run when you do these things. It's all about who gets there first. You can look back through movie history and see that filmmakers in France, in Germany, in America . . . All seemed to be doing the same things around the same time. I've

---

[14] Adam West played the dual role of Bruce Wayne / Batman in the TV series *Batman* (1966-1968).

always wondered if that is a coincidence, or if there some giant radio signal that beams ideas out for creative people to pick up on. I don't know. Maybe it is just somebody seeing something in France or wherever, and coming back to the U.S. and saying, "What would be good is to do something we just saw in France. Nobody knows about it yet."

One Dark Night is a very traditional horror movie, which made it stand out during a time when most horror movies were slasher movies. How did you go from One Dark Night to one of the biggest slasher franchises of all time?

Frank Mancuso Jr. offered me a *Friday the 13th* sequel based on *One Dark Night*, and I said, "I'm not really interested in doing that because I don't know what I could do that would make it any different from the previous films in the series." But he was determined to get me to do the job—for some reason. I came up with this notion that if I could put humor in it, and I could make the characters likeable enough that the audience wouldn't want to see them get killed, it would be worth doing. So I eventually said, "Okay I'll write and direct this."

Then I had to sit down and watch all the *Friday the 13th* movies in a row, in a screening room at Paramount. I had seen the original Friday the 13th but I hadn't seen any of the sequels . . . Talk about déjà vu. Each movie was a variation on the exact same thing. After that I had a sense of what the mythology needed to be, so I decided to craft a scene where one of the characters presented the legend so far. Then I set up my own rules. There were going to be thirteen kills in my movie and it was actually going to take place on Friday the 13th. And Jason was going to come back to life in a completely Gothic way—like Frankenstein's Monster when he's struck by lightning. Then, on a three million dollar budget, I tried to put as much action into the story as I could. There's a car chase, there's an underwater fight sequence . . . It was all incredibly ambitious, but that was the challenge and the fun of it.

Storyboard art from *Jason Lives!* (Paramount, 1986)

You also had some new ideas for the Jason character . . . how he should move . . .

I was recently interviewed about it, and someone said, "Your Jason seemed to be much more communicative." I said, "That's because I was dealing with a mime character." When he sees the motor home bouncing up and down because a couple are having sex in there, Jason just stands there and stares, with his head tilting back and forth—like a dog trying to figure out what's going on. It got a big laugh. I wasn't making fun of Jason . . . I just figured he would be processing what was going on in that motor home. Whenever I find a way to put my mime training to use in storytelling, I do it.

You've talked about this being one of the better moviemaking experiences you've had . . .

To this day, whenever somebody asks what film I had the most fun making, I say *Friday the 13th*. It was six weeks of night shooting.

Jason Voorhees (C.J. Graham) and Nancy McLoughlin

We shot six days a week, and then on Sunday night we'd go to a club in Atlanta and dance all night. Then get up on Monday morning and continue with the show. It was so much fun. I was amazed that the finished film was actually perceived the way I wanted it to be perceived—as a satire on a slasher movie that also worked as a slasher movie. Frank told me, "Just don't make fun of Jason. We need to keep Jason scary." So we did that, but I also got the laughs I wanted in there.

Tom and Nancy McLoughlin on the set of *Jason Lives!*

I set up a lot of visual gags—like when my wife Nancy is killed by Jason. She tries to bribe him, offering him her wallet to keep him from killing her. She's got money and a credit card in her wallet, and when Jason kills her in this giant mud puddle, the money sinks and the American Express card floats. I held on that shot for a few extra beats because I knew there would always be some joker in the theater that would yell, "Don't leave home without it!" And someone always did. I've done that sort of thing a few different times before. In *One Dark Night*, I named a character Kitty so that when her friend Carol loses her in the mausoleum, she calls out "Kitty?" Some joker in the audience would always meow. Everybody else would laugh, and then a jump scare that came right after that—just as soon as they let down their defenses. I tried to design these movies for the theater audience involvement.

Why was it so important to you to add humor to the slasher movie formula?

I didn't want the film to feel like I was being passionate about the senseless butchering of human beings, and particularly girls. I was just interested in scaring people. I have never believed that gore is a true scare. I wanted to do what Hitchcock did in *Dial M for Murder*. Before the woman gets choked, the audience sees that it's about to happen and thinks, *Oh shit, I don't want to see this happen to her.* I tried to build up the characters so that hopefully the audience is rooting for them . . . because they had a sense of humor about life and were not worried about death.

There's a scene where the character Paula tucks a little girl into bed and, as she's walking away, we see Jason through the window and he's following her, almost like her shadow. So as soon as she steps outside, you're expecting her to get killed. She hears something, goes around the corner, and you're expecting it to happen . . . but it doesn't happen. I just kept milking that, because to me that's where the emotion was. Eventually she goes back inside her cabin. Then the wind blows the door open, she goes and sees Jason standing there. The door blows shut again and that's the end of the sequence. You don't see the kill because by that point there's nothing I can do that's going to be better than the buildup. I just figured I'd take away the kill and let the audience imagine how horrible it will be. That was absolutely a conscious choice. Did it work for the fans? Some yes, some no. I think if you wanted to see her sliced and diced . . . Well, that's someone else's *Friday*.

I heard that you paced the entire movie for that kind of slow build and then had to add some kills at the producer's request.

Because I'd seen audiences get restless in the first half of *One Dark Night*, I wanted to hit the ground running with *Friday the 13th*. The movie opens on a foggy night with a truck roaring around the corner. The first thing you see is this dog eating road kill, with that [lip smacking] sound—so that the audience goes *uggh*. Then here comes Tommy with his agenda: *I'm going to make sure Jason is truly dead.* And then thunder, lightning, maggots on Jason's face. He climbs out of the grave and now he is unstoppable. The scene where he punches out Ron Palillo's heart was my way of giving the fans something they came to see right at the top. That also made it clear that Jason is now a supercharged monster, and there's stuff he can do that a human couldn't do.

That was a new idea in the *Friday the 13th* series. You transformed Jason from a serial killer into a zombie. I suppose that's why you ended the film the way you did, with Jason chained to a rock at the bottom of the lake . . . Because he isn't killable. When the hero puts Jason back at the bottom of the lake, that's the best he can do.

Having watched all the previous movies, I knew I had to do something different. Of course I'm also dealing with a franchise, so there are set expectations. Few rules, but a lot of expectations. The basic idea was to first create an environment that is somewhat removed from the rest of the world—a place where no one can hear you scream. You're out in the middle of nowhere and you're facing an unstoppable killer who, no matter what you do, keeps coming after you. That's what Michael Myers was, and

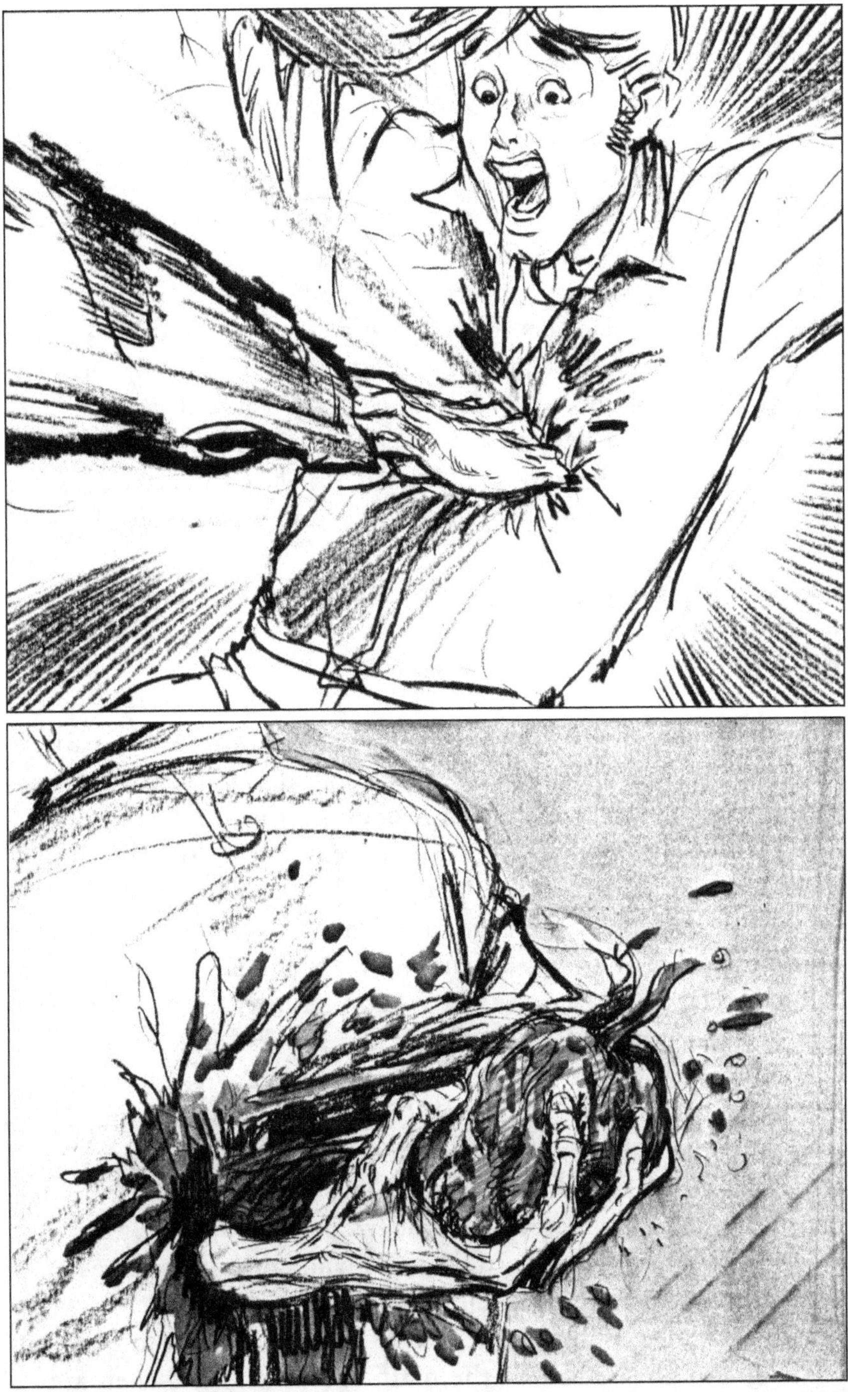

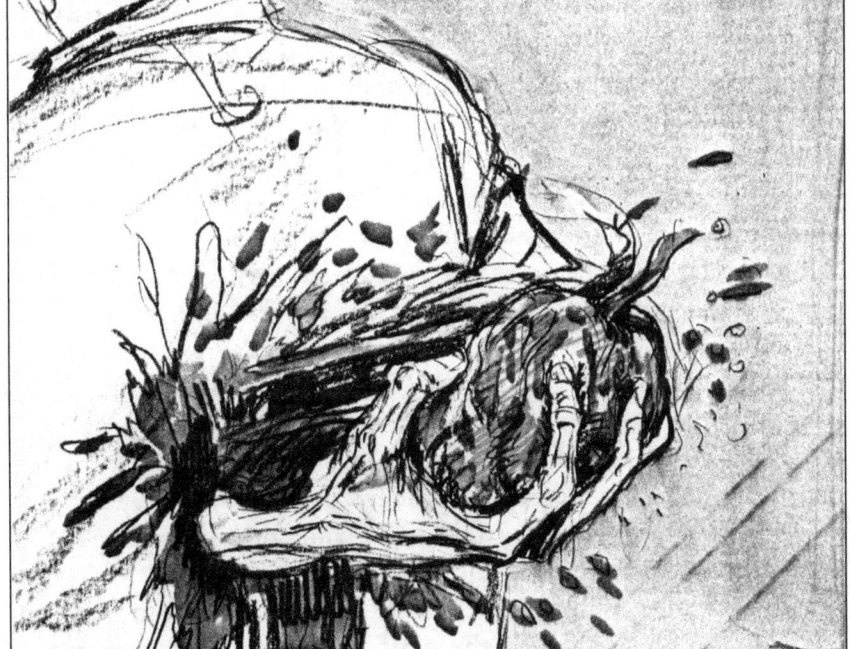

Storyboards for the "heart attack" scene in *Jason Lives!* (Paramount, 1986)

that's what Jason became after a few films. Frank Mancuso wanted to do another one of these.

So I needed to figure out a way to bring Jason back. I did not want to say that it was somebody else dressed up like Jason, which is what the previous film did. In the earlier films, it *seemed* like Jason was unstoppable—because he was so angry. Then [in Part 5] we've got some guy who's pissed off because his kid got killed . . . and he didn't last very long, because it didn't make sense to give him super-human powers. I knew that we had to somehow go back to the real Jason, and we needed to keep the hockey mask because that was iconic. I didn't think Jason would have been buried with the hockey mask, so I came up with this ritualistic scenario in which Tommy brings the mask with him so that he can burn the mask and the body and be done with Jason.

You made the decision to stick with Tommy—the only character who appears as the lead in more than one *Friday the 13th* movie . . .

And we tried to get John Shepherd, who had played the part in the previous film. I thought he did a good job, but he turned it down. So first we had to find somebody for the role of Tommy, and Thom Matthews was the best choice. He had done another horror movie [*Return of the Living Dead*], so I knew he would bring a bit of genre knowledge to it. Then we needed a beautiful blonde because that was a mandate from Frank Mancuso. I wanted to find one who could act—and Jennifer Cooke was great. She had just done the miniseries *V* and she had quite a bit of experience. I thought she was terrific in the movie—she had the spunky 1940s Barbara Stanwyck / Jean Arthur quality that I wanted in there. (Even in a horror movie, my Capra influences were a big part of the foundation.)

Tom Fridley played one of the sidekicks. I thought he was great. Renee Jones—a beautiful actress who's now doing *Days of Our Lives*. I wrote a part specifically for my wife Nancy, who plays one of the camp counselors. I tried to set up the scene so that you think she might be one of the main characters, and then are surprised when she's snuffed out. Like Janet Leigh in *Psycho*. I was

Tony Goldwin and Nancy McLoughlin in *Jason Lives!* (Paramount, 1986)

also fortunate to get Tony Goldwyn at the beginning of his career, before he did *Ghost*. David Kagen, who plays Sheriff Gariss, was another great find. And Vinnie Guastaferro, who plays the sidekick Rick. He was an actor that I'd worked with in a play called "Bullpen." I've done three or four things with Vinnie, and he is a pure Chicago character actor. You put Vinnie in something and he just brings *himself* to the role. Basically I hired people that I knew, people who auditioned incredibly well and who understood my sensibility with the comedy—the dryness and the sarcastic edge of the humor.

Horror fans acknowledge you as the filmmaker who resurrected Jason, literally and figuratively. Your film was successful enough to allow the series to continue . . . Are you proud of that?

On Wikipedia, I'm listed as "an American writer/director most known for my *Friday the 13th* film, because of its infusion of humor into the series." That's my whole identity in the wonderful world of Wikipedia: I made a humorous *Friday the 13th* movie. That's hard for me, because I've had an eclectic career . . . I was really confident about my next movie, *Date with an Angel*, because of my dedication to Capra. And then when that movie got crucified by the critics, I thought, Am I that far off base? It was crushing, because at the time I didn't want to be known only as a horror director. I wanted to make movies that were more uplifting.

Eventually I started to do a lot of dark material again on television, but with a sense of humanism and hope that helps the characters to survive the conflict and go on. My own sense of the balance became a little clearer. I didn't want to do nihilistic horror. I wanted to create modern fairy tales that were grounded in reality.

How did you end up making *Date with an Angel*?

It was my main passion project for many years, but no one wanted to put a fantasy creature in a real life movie. That was before *E.T.* Then once *E.T.* broke out, all anyone wanted was cute alien fantasies.

There was a period where Anson Williams really wanted to produce it. I was going to pitch meetings with Potsie from *Happy Days*! I'd just stand there while he'd say, "This guy wrote the best script." As an actor, he'd pitch the thing for me. Then one day, he said, "I was talking to Ron Howard and he just acquired this thing called *Splash*. It's a mermaid story . . . It's got some similar elements . . . But we're going to get there first." I was already nervous because Warren Beatty was doing a remake of a mermaid movie [*Mr. Peabody and the Mermaid*]. I knew we had to get there fast. And obviously we didn't. Anson eventually went on to some other project; Ron made *Splash*; the Beatty movie got cancelled—I think, because of *Splash*. Then *Mannequin* and a bunch of similar films with female fantasy characters came along.

After my *Friday the 13th* was well-received, Dino DeLaurentiis came into my life and said, "Tom, what do you want to do?" And I said *Date with an Angel*. He said, "Fine, you do angel movie." And just like that, I got to do the angel movie. But by that point *Splash* had come and gone; *Mannequin* had come and gone; *Weird Science* had come and gone; and the critics were like, "Here comes another one. Oh my god, there's so much fucking sugar in this thing, one of my teeth is starting to ache." It was even called "Capra-corn." But I took no offense at that.

Emmanuelle Béart in *Date with an Angel* (DeLaurentiis, 1987)

And yet . . . just yesterday, I met this agent. She's maybe thirty. The first thing she said to me was, "You have no idea how much I love *Date with an Angel*." And I laughed and said, "Thank you, that's very sweet." And she said, "No, I'm serious. I watched that movie so many times I wore the tape out. I was so happy when it came out on DVD." And she was genuine. A similar thing happened about a month ago. I went to the Magic Castle and when one of the magicians there was introduced to me, he said, "Are you the guy who did *Date with an Angel*?" I said yeah and he goes, "Can you talk to my mother? I know this sounds really weird, but after my father passed away, she made us watch *Date with an Angel* every holiday. This was *her* movie." So I got on his phone at the Magic Castle with his mom in Florida. She was incredible, going on and on and on about the movie. I thought to myself: *Maybe this is why I made this movie—for these wonderful people that it deeply touched.*

I always wonder why some people were so affected by that movie, and the others were just like "Oh please . . ." It was so painful to read the initial reviews. You'd think I was doing something sick and twisted, rather than just trying to tell a story that I thought would be heartfelt and sweet. I can understand how critics watch violent movies and say, "Why do we need this on this planet? Don't we have enough violence?" But when you're just trying to make a valentine . . . I just wanted to create something gentle, fun and romantic. I was shocked by the fact that certain reviewers were so cynical about it.

Maybe cynics feel just as insulted by the sugar-coated valentine as the moralists do by excessive violence . . .

I guess. Or maybe *Date with an Angel* just wasn't smart enough or slick enough. Or it simply arrived too late to be considered original.

You've said that the finished film isn't quite what you intended. What went wrong?

When I finished *Date with an Angel*, we did nine test screenings. *Nine!* Every time, it was tested for a different demographic. Joe Farrell was the guy who used to run those things. I don't know if people understood how much he controlled this industry at the time. The average person doesn't know his name, but he and his organization NRG [National Research Group] became incredibly powerful in terms of shaping movies before their release. He would hold these screenings and generate printouts for test audiences to write their comments on. Then he would sit in a room with the producers and say, "Here's what you need to do with your movie." And all of us insecure bastards would say, "Okay."

Do people hold test screenings a lot of times just to avoid responsibility for a film's success or failure?

That's a smart observation. Yes. Anything to avoid responsibility. Find a way to have somebody else make the statement about what works or doesn't work . . . Because most things do fail and you don't want to be the guy that was behind the failure. It takes a lot of guts to put yourself out there and say, "If it goes down, it's my ass." You've got to have a maverick sensibility and not worry about what your next job is going to be.

Do you think *Date with an Angel* suffers in tone as a result of all the screenings?

Definitely.

Do you still feel like it's *your* movie?

Yes. Absolutely. For better or worse, it's my cinematic baby. It was such a labor of love for me, because it's so autobiographical. I wrote the story around the three guys I had a band with—George, Don and Rex. The Jim character was basically me. He's a guy wants to do something creative with his life instead of something practical. What he really wants is to make music, but he's on the wrong track. He's getting ready to marry the wrong woman and go to work for her father, and he's rationalizing about the life that he's creating for himself. I felt very strongly about those conflicts.

What really drove me on was the basic idea of searching for some kind of meaning in life. The main character had a terminal disease that he was totally oblivious to. All he knew was that he was having headaches. I used to get constant headaches when I was a kid. When I started getting them again as an adult, I began paying attention to stories about people who have brain tumors and don't know it and suddenly one day they pass out and go to the hospital and the doctor says, "You have a tumor the size of a softball. There's no way to operate on it. It's over." In a situation like that, you have to hope there's a master plan, and that your death is part of some bigger scheme. You have to believe that. That's what the movie was about.

When I started making the movie, Dino was really eager because he saw *Date with an Angel* as another *Splash*, another *Mannequin*, another *Weird Science*. He liked the idea because commercially it had already worked, so "let's do our version of that." He had a strong desire to play up the comedy as much as possible, which wasn't my intention. My first cut of *Date with an Angel* was two and a half hours. It was cut down to ninety minutes, so you can see how much material was lost.

I fought desperately to hold onto the original romantic theme song. Randy Kerber, who was one of the pianists for the L.A.

Mime Company, composed this wonderful theme for when the angel first appears and Jim finds her in the pool. We reprised it when she takes him to heaven. When I was flying around the world, looking for an actress to play the angel, I listened to that theme over and over and my heart soared every time I listened to it. I did not want contemporary rock music in the film. But that happened because Dino's wife Martha was friends with Frank Mancuso's wife Becky. Becky was the person that you went to if you wanted to spot your movie with hit pop songs. I had planned to rely exclusively on the Randy Kerber score, but suddenly we were using Steve Winwood and The Cars. Not that I don't love their music . . . but it changed the tone of the movie.

In the end, *Date with an Angel* suffered as a result of too many previews and too many chefs in the kitchen. We lost more and more of the romantic moments that were my reason for making the movie. The cutdowns were scenes like when Jim can't find the angel and he wanders into the forest and sees her communicating. From a Biblical standpoint, it looked like she was communicating with God. From a sci-fi standpoint, it could be anything. I wanted it to convey that sense of awe, that she is a creature that belongs somewhere else. I also thought it was highly romantic that they had run away to live in a tree house in the forest. All those romantic fantasy elements were the things that drove me to make the movie.

You were mentored by Capra, who was one of the leading proponents of the auteur theory—"one man, one film"—so I assume you must have fought pretty hard for your personal vision . . .

I remember one specific instance . . . I was working with an incredible visual effects team led by Richard Edlund. He'd done *Star Wars* and so many other incredible films. He did the angel concept. Whenever I'd see the flying sequence, I'd say, "You've got to do it again." He'd say, "Dino's not gonna pay for it." "Well then I'll talk to Dino. But it doesn't look right yet." You have to remember that I was a guy whose last credit was a *Friday the 13th* movie, so they had to be asking themselves, "Do we listen to this

Communicating with God in *Date with an Angel* (DeLaurentiis, 1987)

guy or do we listen to Dino, who might hire us again?" But they were very good at giving me what I wanted, and I was really determined not to cave in. I kept pushing until finally someone broke the door down and said, "That's it." But at least I got closer to what I really wanted.

Let's talk about casting. How did you cast Emmanuelle Béart as the angel?

This was the biggest casting call of my career—probably bigger than a lot of people's careers. Without exaggerating, I saw probably 6,000 candidates—not all in person, but in photos, tapes, etc. We held open casting calls where the lines stretched all the way down Wilshire Boulevard in Beverly Hills. Dino DeLaurentiis got the media on it, so every aspiring, attractive actress wanted to be the angel in this movie. It was massive. I went to so many countries for auditions. Visited all the top modeling agencies. Because I was a fan of silent movies, I wanted to be find an actress who could convey her thoughts without saying a word. I wanted to be able to look in her eyes and understand her.

After months, we just ran out of candidates. We did screen tests with the three actresses I had—one was from New Zealand, one

Emmanuelle Béart in *Date with an Angel* [DeLaurentiis, 1987]

was from Sweden and one was from America. We had Michael Knight audition with them. When we were done, I knew we didn't have her yet. I was praying that when Dino saw the screen tests, he would feel the same way I did. Thank God he did. That started the process all over again, and I ended up taking a trip to Paris to see some French model. I was walking down the Champs d'Elysees one day I saw a poster of Emmanuelle Béart, who was the biggest star in France at that time. And immediately my quest became a quest to get *her* in the movie . . . But the other posters around town were *Jason le Mort-Vivant*, which was my *Friday the 13th* . . . And how's a guy who made a *Friday the 13th* going to get France's latest star in his next movie? I managed to do it by going to Montreal, where she was doing a press junket for her film *Manon des sources*. I pitched the story to her. She cried at the end and agreed to do the movie. I had my angel.

Michael Knight was already cast only. I'd gone through a lot of casting calls for his part as well, and seen every twenty-something male with comedy chops, from David Duchovny to Tim Daly to Judd Nelson . . . . When I go back and look at the casting tapes from this movie, I'm amazed. Jennifer Connelly read for Phoebe's

Tom and Phoebe Cates on the set of *Date with an Angel* (DeLaurentiis, 1987)

part. So did Uma Thurman. So many now-famous people in the early part of their career. I initially wanted Jim Carrey for the lead. At that point he had only done a couple of small films and a TV series. I thought he was perfect, but Dino didn't agree. For the supporting characters John, George and Rex, I tried to cast as close to the real guys that I'd hung out with. David Dukes played the father. I had done a stage play with David at the Music Center, called "Light Comedies," and I thought he was brilliant.

How did you end up casting Phoebe Cates?

She's just one of those people that everybody likes instantly. There's just something about her that is very open. She's also very mischievous. Sometimes I'd look over and see Phoebe, and I could tell that her wheels were turning. She was always scheming something funny. Michael Knight also had a great sense of humor, but because he was the male lead, there were moments when he would get ultra-serious. And Phoebe went after that. She looked for those vulnerable moments, and she make him feel insecure about his hair or whatever. Just to play with him. Through it all, she was a consummate pro.

Oh and Charles Lane—who played the priest! Charles Lane was in almost every Frank Capra movie. I don't know how old he was at that point. He was one of those guys that used to go to work at Columbia every day and wait in Gower Gulch. He was under contract as a character actor. He told me, "I never had any idea what I would be doing at the beginning of the day. One A.D. would put me into a Western and I'd be done by lunch, and then somebody else would say we need a guy to play one of the gangsters on this other picture." Sometimes he'd do three movies in one day. His resume was unbelievable—and for me to have a long time Frank Capra actor, part of his stable of actors, was like a dream come true.

I also did a little cameo in the church scene. I wanted a guy to come out of the confessional and be so enraptured by the sight of the angel that he would back himself into the candles and set himself on fire. Believe it or not, Kevin Kline was on set to see Phoebe—because they were just starting to date—and somehow he'd heard about it and he said, "Hey, I'll to do it as a cameo, but I don't want a credit or anything." I said, "That'd be great." He said, "I'm going over to England—I'm doing this little movie with some of the Monty Python people and maybe when I get back, if you still haven't shot the scene . . ." It's that kind of humility, that kind of team-player attitude, that makes him such a great guy. He can do anything and there's no big ego about it. So I told him I'd try to put it off until he got back.

He went and did *A Fish Called Wanda* and when he came back, I was still shooting . . . which is pretty amazing, considering that most of the movies I do now have seventeen or eighteen day shoots . . . But by that point I'd already had to shoot the scene. Hiring a stuntman was expensive, so I ended up doing the gag myself. It wasn't the greatest moment in the film.

I can't believe they let the director set himself on fire. If something goes wrong, the movie doesn't have a director . . .

I've certainly been on a lot of other shows where I haven't been allowed to get away with things like that. Why they allowed me to do it, I don't know . . . Maybe by that point they were like, "Fine.

Set him on fire. Screw him. If he dies, we'll collect the insurance." That was a George Bailey "worth-more-dead-than-alive" moment.

Save that shot until the end of the shoot and they'll be glad to set the director on fire . . .

It would have scared me if it was that well-plotted. [laughs] No, we shot it way before the end.

Did Capra see the finished film?

Yes he did. I sent him the movie and he said he really loved it. I said, "Would you mind giving me a quote because a quote from Frank Capra on this movie . . . that's like doing a western and getting a quote from John Ford." So he actually gave us a quote. He said, "A wonderful movie. I loved it." Dino wouldn't put it on the poster though. He said, "Who'sa Frank Capra? These kids today don'ta know froma Frank Capra . . ."

My God, Capra was so kind. I have a picture of me and Nancy with him, and another photo of him holding my script when I gave it to him in Palm Springs. He was just so open. It was great. When I would contact him and say that I couldn't get anybody to read my script, much less want to make it, he would just say, "Nobody wanted to make most of my pictures either. You've got to fight." He said, "Just do it." The fact that it was coming from Frank Capra was really inspirational.

After *Date with an Angel*, you had a long period of working as a writer/director on several TV series, starting with *Amazing Stories*.

That was really a blessing from my friend Mick Garris. He had gotten into that world because of his connection to Spielberg and he pulled me in to co-write an episode that Rob Zemeckis directed. Later I wrote an episode on my own called "Such Interesting Neighbors." I got to go on set and watch some of these people direct: Spielberg, Martin Scorsese, Clint Eastwood, Joe Dante . . . They had such an array of huge talent on that series. I knew I could not aspire to direct one of those. It was just a compliment that I could write a script that Steven Spielberg would actually read and make notes on. It was chance to do something for people I admired, so I looked at that as a wonderful step in my career. Thank you, Mick.

I tried not to take too many jobs in episodic television. I was worried that I would lose control of my personal storytelling goals if I became a director-for-hire. There's nothing wrong with series work and I would never say that anybody should turn down work. But for me the goal had always been to do projects where I could either create from the beginning or add my own storytelling ideas. On a lot of TV shows, the scripts aren't ready until the day before you shoot, so you only have a bare bones idea of what you're going to do. In a situation like that, I felt I couldn't do much beyond shooting standard coverage. I can do it, but I don't really enjoy it. To me, a "vision" is everything. A part of who you are should be in the work.

Film is an expressive medium that requires the storyteller to give a point of view in the process. The viewer has to have a sense that someone is guiding the story. If I can add some of my own personality or something that means something to me, I'm far more inspired and invested. That elevates the work.

You wrote several episodes of the TV series *Friday the 13th*. How did you get involved with that show?

Frank Mancuso was going to do a series based on a pawn shop full of cursed objects. The former owner of the pawn shop cursed all of the objects so that they would empower their owners in different ways—making them a better singer, a better dancer, richer, younger, whatever it is. The series was about the new owners of the pawn shop, who have to reclaim these objects, to keep them from hurting or killing people. It made no sense to me that he could make a series off of that, so I was amazed when he managed to make that work—especially for three seasons. The show was given a terrible time slot (it was on at midnight) and it never got any decent publicity. Each episode was as good as its villain, who came into the show along with whatever the cursed object-of-the-week was.

I was in between feature jobs when Frank came to me and said, "Would you like to direct one of these things?" I thought, *Why not?* So I did an episode called "Master of Disguise." I liked the story [by Bruce Martin] because it was about the film industry, and I knew that I could have fun with the kills . . . like using an Oscar statue to beat someone's head in, or electrocuting a nasty film critic while he watches his own TV show. I purposely cast that actor to look like a local critic who had given me a bad review on *Date with an Angel*. But the coolest thing was the fact that John Bolger, the actor who played the killer, had a Timothy Dalton / James Bond quality to him. When I met him for the part, I thought it was great that this horrible killer looked like James Bond. Through the power of his cursed makeup case, he was movie-star handsome and had every woman going crazy over him. But, in truth, his face was deformed.

I also wrote and directed an episode called "The Playhouse." That one was very personal, because it dealt with children and now had a young son. In this story, I wanted to empower these kids through the supernatural. The horror in the episode comes from their everyday home life. I thought, *What if they could take their pain and rage and use that to build a fantasy land that they had all to themselves?* Unfortunately, because of the budget, we couldn't execute it as well as we could have in a feature film. To me the idea was far more complex and interesting than what I was able to execute. But both of the child actors, Lisa Jakub and Robert Oliveri, were sensational.

In the third season, I become a story editor on the series, so then I had a chance to pick many of the stories. Despite the budget restrictions, I'd go after anybody and everybody who might want to be involved. Directors on the series had a lot of creative freedom, so that helped—but we had no time, no money, and every day was an eighteen-hour day. Thankfully, the Director of Photography, Rodney Charters, was able to roll with whatever was thrown at him.

You wrote an extremely ambitious two-part episode called "The Prophecies," which seems to be heavily influenced by *The Exorcist* . . .

Tom with Lisa Jakub and Robert Oliveri on the set of "The Playhouse"

Tom inside "The Playhouse"

That was part of the marching orders for the beginning of the third season. Frank Mancuso wanted to do an exorcist story and John D. LeMay wanted to leave the series. He was getting movie offers and he wanted out, so Frank said, "Okay, kill him off . . . But kill him off in such a way that he could potentially come back later. And make the episode somehow like *The Exorcist*." "Sure," I said. "No problem." *Yeah right.*

So I dove back to my Catholic background to see what I could find there. I was intrigued by the idea that the best way to destroy the faith of the faithful is by destroying their heroes. As a kid, I saw how the assassination of John Kennedy affected the entire country. That was a turning point, because they killed *the* symbol of hope in America's future. And then Martin Luther King and Robert Kennedy. It seemed like there was this vast conspiracy to take away our faith. So, in the episode, I wrote about a nun who had a vision of the Blessed Virgin saying that there will be this little girl who will be the hope for the future. That child became the target of the archangel Astaroth, who was leading this anti-Catholic conspiracy. John LeMay's character ended up getting possessed by Astaroth and killing the nun, who was leading this big supernatural conspiracy. I don't know how well it all worked, but it certainly tapped into my Catholic background. For a TV series, there was a lot of religion woven through the storyline.

Tell me about your episode of *Freddy's Nightmares*, "It's a Miserable Life."

That was a very different type of horror series because they really didn't know what they wanted to do with the show. They just knew that Freddy was going to be in the middle of it. Everybody got to do what they wanted as long as you didn't go over budget, which meant you didn't shoot more than twelve hours a day. And I was always pushing the envelope . . . every day.

The script by Michael DeLuca, who is now a major producer, was not completed when I came on. I was working with a series of loose ideas that hadn't really been fleshed out, so there was a lot of improvisation. But DeLuca had a great energy and he loved all this crazy shit that I was doing with it. There really were no rules on that series. We could make the comedy as absurd as possible. We could do surreal images just for the sake of surreal images. Whether or not it all tied together and made any sense to anybody whatsoever, I don't know. I've always had this dream of being able to do a movie that is just pure surrealism, where I just track from person to person, listening to each person's thoughts for a few moments and then moving on to the next person. It's a very uncommercial idea but I personally think it would be a very interesting indie film. I'm a major Luis Buñuel fan. He and Fellini have had a great impact on me—the way they blend dreams and reality.

Anyway, when we finally had the premiere of the show, I remember Bob Shaye [then-head of New Line Cinema and executive producer on the *Freddy's Nightmares* series] came up to me. He'd been really angry at me because I had gone over budget, but he came over and said, "I really thought yours was one of the better shows. It was really scary." That meant a lot to me, because I've always said I'd rather get fired for trying to do what I thought worked, than get fired because I was just phoning it in.

In 1990, you adapted Stephen King's short story "Sometimes They Come Back" to the screen. Are you a Stephen King fan?

I'm a huge Stephen King fan. Obviously King saw the same *Twilight Zones* we all saw, the same *Outer Limits*, the same Corman movies—he loved that stuff—and because of his amazing writing talent he was able to take those basic ideas and stories and fill them with the thoughts of his characters. That's his brilliance. He shows us our dreams and our nightmares in [his characters'] thoughts, which allows his readers to have a personal relationship with the stories.

In my opinion, most of the Stephen King movies don't work. You can't get that same experience [of the characters' thoughts], so the filmmakers usually substitute something else. The movies that really succeeded were the ones that had stronger characters—*Stand by Me, Carrie, The Dead Zone, The Stand*. But a lot of the other ones didn't quite get there for me, because you're trying to condense something that's so rich in the books into ninety minutes of screen time. You can sell it by its title and you can sell the idea, but ultimately it's got to be fleshed out differently.

I think that's what *Sometimes They Come Back* suffered from—it wasn't fleshed out properly. The writers had to expand a short story, so they put a lot of "Stephen King's greatest hits" moments into it. Like an evil car [*Christine*], a train [*Stand By Me*] . . . a lot of things like that were borrowed from his other works to flesh out the story.

I have to admit that when I watched Sometimes *They Come Back*, I was confused about the nature of the monsters. Are they ghosts or are they the living dead? Do they exist in the flesh or only in the main character's imagination? What are the rules?

When Dino DeLaurentiis offered the project to me, I remember saying to him, "This really doesn't work." The writers had moved on because they were not going to do another rewrite without being paid a fortune, so Dino brought in Tim Kring, the future creator of *Heroes*. Tim is a great guy and very smart, and we saw eye to eye right away. But whenever you deal with Dino, there are a lot of stipulations—"don't lose this, don't lose that, because I like that . . ." So we were trying to Frankenstein things together.

Eventually the main question was whether or not the audience would accept that we're in this realm where anything can happen. I think if you're a horror aficionado, you know that there needs to be—like you said—rules that are very clear and show an understanding of the genre. For most people it's either creepy because it's surreal, or it just doesn't 100% work.

In the short story, the threat is a group of teenagers who are possessed by the spirits of the dead. In the movie, I wasn't sure if the teenagers were possessed or reincarnated or just ageless monsters. At first, I thought they only existed in the head of the main character, because he's so tormented by his past—but then his wife and son are able to see them too and be hurt by them . . .

The director admires his creation on the set of *Sometimes They Come Back*

The way I approached it was that these guys have *literally* come back. They are solid ghosts. They are ghosts walking around in human form, in the same way that I believe angels and demons walk around in totally human form. These guys to me really were flesh and blood and could hurt other people.

I saw a lot of those kinds of teenagers (violent '50s greasers) when I was growing up—they picked on guys like me with long hair. Those guys in real life were scary enough. Now to say that they can come back from the dead, hurt other people in your life, and do things that nobody else would believe they can do—I mean, they can tear off their own faces!—and if you get into a car crash with them, they're going to walk away and you're not. They were solid when they needed to be solid but they could disappear when they needed to not be there.

So there really were no rules for them as monsters . . . That's what makes them scary.

Yeah, maybe so. The old cop was the only one who gave Tim's character any kind of explanation. There really was no mythology outside of that.

Maybe that's even what Stephen King was thinking. Maybe he sat down to write the story and asked himself what he was really scared of in his life. He thought of kids like that who acted as if the rules didn't apply to them, and then he took it to the next level—where the scientific laws about life and death and the passage of time—didn't apply to them. How scary would they be then?

It's not a figment of the character's imagination that they are back. They are literally back. Where do they live? Do they eat? You can dismiss all those rational questions because, when you see them, they're back simply to torment you and harm people you know. That's why they exist.

[At this point, our conversation is fortuitously interrupted by the sound of a distant train horn.]

To this day, I can't hear a train horn and not think of *Sometimes They Come Back*, because that's something that I purposely put in the film. Tim Matheson hears that sound almost the second he gets back to his hometown, and it has a haunting quality to it. When I was growing up, that was always a reassuring sound—it meant somebody was going somewhere and life was going on. My idea was to take that sound and make it part of a dark memory—make it deeply troubling because it's associated with his brother's death. One of the cool things about making movies is to be able to take things like that and turn them into something else.

To me, that's something that a good movie should do—or good music, painting, sculpture, whatever. It mixes with life. People say, "I cannot go into the water because every time I think of *Jaws*." Or, "I can't take a shower when I'm home alone because I think of *Psycho*." Powerful horror movies twist a normally non-threatening thing into a scary lifelong impression, and it's wonderfully cool to be able to do that.

I have learned, after many years and many films, that I can personalize a lot of things because of my love of the genre or because I have had some experience in my life that connects me to the world in the story. I can take somebody else's material and

Brooke Adams, Tim Matheson and Tom McLoughlin on the set of *Sometimes They Come Back*

somehow fuse it with my own sensibilities. In fact, I often feel that it's more interesting to take on other people's material and try to find my own way into that universe, as opposed to drawing exclusively from my own experiences. Kubrick once said he loved using other people's writing because it allowed him that first time discovery, that exciting first impression. Then, as a director, you've got to get everybody thinking and feeling in the same direction.

Which seems like it would never work. But there must be something universal about certain patterns and symbols that makes good stories resonate for a lot of different people with different backgrounds and experiences. Like the train horn—maybe the sound is comforting to a lot of people because it's a subconscious cue that life goes on. I feel that way about airports—all the coming and going . . .

Yeah, airports are a hotbed of emotion. Having spent so much time in them over the years, I can say that I get energized in environments like that. It helps me to focus—just like being on a movie set. I love working in situations where I'm surrounded by a lot of people. For some people it's distracting, but not for me.

You like being in the eye of the hurricane . . .

I don't like focusing on doing things solely for myself. I love being part of something bigger. Whenever I've gone into states of depression, it's mentally and physically debilitating. That's the worst kind of death—you're alive but you can't do anything. To me, that's scarier than anything else—the idea of being on this planet and not being an active part of the world around you. I really learned this lesson again when I had children. I found I wanted to make sacrifices to see them happy, to see them light up and feel secure.

It's the same thing when I'm working as a director. When I do something that allows an actor to shine, I'm so happy that I was able to help make that moment happen. Maybe I was the one who said yes to casting them in the picture. Maybe I was the one who said, "What would happen if you were saying that to your father instead of your boyfriend?" Sometimes I don't even know where the idea came from, but the result is amazing. The other person gets it and runs with it. To have that level of participation—to help create something that goes beyond my individual life—is amazing. My greatest dream is that certain films I've done might have a lasting effect on people after I'm gone.

It's a Wonderful Life was absolutely life-changing for me. So was *Rocky*, because it came out during a period in my life when I felt like I was never going to be able to direct, and was never going to achieve any of my dreams. Seeing [Rocky] pull himself up on the ropes—that image stayed in my mind every time I got rejected, every time somebody said, "No, we don't like your script. No, we're not going to hire you for that." Sometimes I felt so defeated, and then I remembered that image. The down-and-out guy trying his best just to get through—and the fact that he is still standing at the end—really was a powerful influence on me. As filmmakers we can make a difference if we focus on things that not only entertain, but inspire.

Rocky is a story about survival in a tough, gritty, depressing and often debilitating world. In contrast, Stephen King's short story ended on a very dark note—the main character summons

The McLoughlin family on the set of *Sometimes They Come Back*

Shane's first industry job, on *Sometimes They Come Back*

the spirit of his dead brother in order to survive, and after that he is forever cursed. The movie, on the other hand, gives the lead character a choice about his future. He can go to heaven with his brother or stay with his wife and son in an imperfect, painful world. How much of that ending was your idea and how much was already in the script? I can't help noting that, when you made that movie, you were a pretty young father . . .

What was going on in my life at that time was actually very dramatic. In 1990, my dad was dying. We knew it was just a matter of time. My daughter was born during that same time, so I had all these incredible emotions over birth and death going on simultaneously.

At the same time, I was working on my friend Steven Banks's show, *Home Entertainment Center*, which was a pilot for Disney. That was fulfilling a childhood dream for both of us; we both wanted to work at Disney. Then Universal gave me [as producer] an order for twenty episodes of a TV series called *They Came from Outer Space* and twenty episodes of *She-Wolf of London*. So I was trying to get directors and writers for those episodes while creating the pilots. I ended up kind of letting go of both series, and never was happy with the end results.

And then Dino offered me *Sometimes They Come Back*, so that was being prepped during this same period. I've never had that much on my plate at the same time—life, death, two TV series, a four-camera pilot at Disney, and a feature film. The thing that was of primary importance was my wife and unborn daughter—making sure that the pregnancy was okay and that I was a part of that.

When I was first told about my dad's illness, it was horrible. I was at the hospital in Culver City, standing in a hallway with a doctor and my family members, hearing that his cancer had spread throughout his brain and that there was nothing that could be done. I'm standing there with the doctor—and I still can't even believe I said this: "No, there *is* something you can do. I've filmed scenes like this. There is *always* something that can be done." And he said, "In the movies, maybe . . . but this is reality. I'm sorry." And I'm still going, "No, we're going to figure out something."

He said, "You can certainly get another opinion, but I'm telling you—this is just the way it is." I went home and cried, both over the news and because I couldn't figure out what I could do about it. I wanted to control the situation like a director. I had so much work that I *was* controlling at that time . . . but how do you save your father from dying?

My father was very quiet and shy and I know he was scared about what might be on the other side, but he wouldn't talk about it. He wouldn't talk about how much pain he was in. I was trying to do whatever I could, knowing that the clock was ticking. We did a lot together. I took him to see a David Copperfield show . . . I did anything that I could to make him feel loved. The fact that I was so busy and couldn't spend all of my time with him made me feel incredibly guilty. There was so much I wanted to learn from him about his life. I had so many questions and I knew it was just a matter of time, a very short amount of time, before he'd be gone.

I had to first pull myself away from the two TV shows, because you can't suffer over something that seems meaningless compared to life and death in your own family. But Steven Banks is my best friend and I wanted to be there 200% for him on his show. So that was a challenge.

Then the script for *Sometimes They Come Back* didn't quite work. Dino didn't think it was emotional enough and I agreed. So he brought in Tim Kring, and we forged these emotional connections between Tim Matheson's character and his son and his brother. We set up the idea that he'd lost his brother when he was the same age that his son is now, and that set up the ending.

Finally, my lovely daughter Hannah was born. I made sure that my dad got a chance to hold her. Then, in the middle of rehearsals for Steven's show, I got the phone call saying that my dad had died. Unfortunately, the funeral was on the day we were taping the show in front of a live audience. I was lucky to have a very cool assistant director who did the rehearsal blocking for me so that I could go to the funeral, but then I had to return to the studio for the taping.

I was feeling guilty the whole time. I wasn't with my family, but thankfully they understood. And I knew that my father would tell

Tom and best friend Steven Banks

me not to sit and be miserable over him. "Go to work. You're lucky. You're fortunate." I knew that's exactly what he would say. I somehow managed to get through Steven's show, and I believe it was literally the next day that I had to get on a plane to Kansas, to start prep on *Sometimes They Come Back*. There was no time to mourn or grieve. This huge, long story is to explain that all of that emotional baggage is what I walked into this movie with . . .

Now, if ever a movie had some kind of curse, this was it. I'm not exaggerating. Every day, something went wrong . . . and not small things. I'm talking about major things—people falling down on set, ambulances coming and going, the entire transportation department walking off, leaving all the trucks at the last location. Every lighting setup took two or three hours instead of the hour that was budgeted. And it was one of the coldest winters they'd ever had in Kansas. When we were shooting the scenes in the railroad tunnel, it was so cold that we were all in constant pain.

One day, Tim Matheson was doing a scene in there. He was sitting down on the ground and, just as he got up, a boulder—probably two feet by two feet—fell down from the top of the cave and landed right where his head had been thirty seconds before. It was a miracle he didn't get hit . . . On another day, Brooke Adams fell and twisted her ankle, so we were behind a day . . . Then we had an actor who had a heart attack just days before his big scene.

He begged and pleaded with us not to replace him because he hadn't worked in so many years. I couldn't say no. So he came and, sadly, had a really tough time remembering his lines. But we both hung in there. We had to use huge cue cards and shoot the scene in sections. He was very embarrassed about that. After all that, when the footage came back the next day, we found out that someone in the camera department had exposed the film for the wrong stock, so the whole thing was purple and grainy. This movie was just one horrible thing after another.

Towards the end of shooting, some local asked, "How's your movie going?" And I said, "Well it's been a little rough—we're eight days over schedule." Which for a low budget movie like this is absurd. Thank God Dino is a producer from the old days and

Tom with actor Robert Rusler

he would just call me and say, "So are you giving me a goddamn good picture?" I'd say, "Yessir." He just dealt with the overages, because he understood it wasn't anything I was doing [that was causing the problems]. We were victims of one bad circumstance after another. Then this local person says, "You realize you are shooting on Indian burial ground." I said, "Oh bullshit." He said, "You can look it up." So I did, and sure enough that railroad tunnel was not supposed to have been built. Years ago they literally dug up an Indian burial ground to create that tunnel.

So was the movie cursed? Who knows? I was willing to accept any explanation at that point because anything that could go wrong had gone wrong—starting on day one, when it snowed six inches during a time of year when it never snows. From that first day, we were behind schedule . . .

Did you tell Stephen King about all of this?

Never did. Should have.

Sounds like something he would have written into the story . . .

And I'm just giving you the tip of the iceberg. There were so many personality conflicts . . . The production crew had been pulled from places across the United States and everybody seemed to hate each other. The [working] climate was like: "Can we just get this fucking thing done and over with?" Some departments were sabotaging others.

I have this unbelievable story from the cemetery shoot. We had a soundman who was, shall I say, *overly intense* about his job. If anything messed up the sound, he took it too seriously and would get into people's faces—because to him, sound was everything. We had these huge lights with these balustrades that were buzzing, and he felt it was a problem. It's three o'clock in the morning in a cemetery, so even the crickets are quiet, and these things had a buzz that really bothered him, so he kept asking for the gaffers to move the balustrades. But they wouldn't do it. I don't know if they were just being difficult or if it really wasn't possible. But this guy decided he was going to do it on his own. He started moving things, a cord came loose and hit something, and [simulates the sound of an electrical shock] all the lights in the entire cemetery went out.

We were moments away from doing the huge emotional scene with Tim, and then we had to stop to wait for someone to fix the generator. I don't remember how long it took, but I remember we were chasing the dark. I was terrified that the sun was going to come up before we could finish the scene. We just barely made it . . . All because some sound guy was pissed off about hearing a buzz that we could have easily been fixed in post. That just epitomizes the experience of making this movie. We were lucky to get this thing finished at all. I'm amazed that the film works on *any* level.

One thing that I'm incredibly proud of is the score by Terry Plumeri. He hadn't done a lot of movies, but I took a chance on him because he had such passion. We had very little money and he was going to find a way to make this score work and sound big. He created a fabulous orchestral score that was much better than the usual synth score you have to settle for on a film like this. I remember that [editor] Charles Bornstein and I were temping our early cut with a very haunting music by Georges Delerue from *The Escape Artist*. I didn't want Terry to rip that off but I wanted something that was like that. I spent a lot of time with him, plucking out notes—making him keep rewriting. I was obsessed. He was obsessed. We finally came up with two wonderful themes that we kept repeating throughout the film. I felt like Terry really gave the movie its soul.

And Tim [Matheson] did such an amazing job. That was one of the best casting choices in my life. I was so blessed to have him. He's the kind of person I would like to be, in an ideal world. I was really impressed with his manner, the way he handled things, how charismatic and funny—he just has all the qualities I wish I had. And because I identified with him so closely, that movie did become much more of a personal journey for me.

I was also extremely fortunate to get Brooke Adams, who I've loved since *Days of Heaven*. And the boy, Robert Gorman [who plays Matheson's son in the film], was amazing. He came in for the casting session and was the only one who played the scene as if all the props were in the room with him. Most child actors will just read the lines of the character, but he acted it out with imaginary props—as if he had a real belief that he was looking at those things or looking at someone else in the room who wasn't there.

So I was very lucky in these ways. Regardless it was still very difficult to put all the pieces together and make that movie work. I always say there are two kinds of movies. There are the movies you make and there are movies that you survive. Thank God I do the second kind very, very seldom. But that was a survival movie.

I just tied myself to the helm and said, "I'm going to get to shore or go down with the ship."

I assumed that you must have had much more creative control over that film because the ending seems so personal. In the final scene, Tim's character chooses the future over the past— he lets go of his brother and chooses his wife and son—and at the same time you were letting go of your father and embracing your new daughter. That final scene also seems to be about choosing reality over fantasy . . . and, as it turned out, this was your last fantasy-oriented film for a while . . .

It's about love—losing somebody that you really love. And now that I think about it, the older brother really was like a father-figure to the young Tim Matheson character. I wasn't conscious of that at all at the time, but maybe because of all the emotional issues that were going on, I had a much deeper personal connection to the end of the movie than I realized.

In most ghost stories, you've got to somehow resolve the spirit's conflicts so that they can move on. Once they move on, you know you're never going to see them again. I was choosing life over death.

Anytime I've had dreams of my father or my mother, I'm aware in the dream that they are dead and I'm dreaming. But I don't want the dream to end because I've got an opportunity to be with them in that realm for a certain amount of time and it's so wonderful. It's a bizarre thing to sit here and talk about it or intellectualize it, because in a dream you're not supposed to be aware that you're dreaming. How does that work? I really do feel the same emotions that I would in life if I saw them again. If they suddenly walk through the door, I'm like, "Don't leave yet . . . I have so much that I want to ask you. We need more time." It's interesting how the mind works.

I guess I think of dreams as "movies." Some have a great ending and some have a horrible ending. Sometimes the film breaks and you don't get to the end.

Tom fulfills his mother's dream for him in a (unused) cameo for *Sometimes They Come Back*

I have one more thing that I'd like to talk about before we take a break. I understand you were at one point attached to a sequel to *The Birds* **. . .**

Did they end up making that project into a sequel?

There was a sequel on Showtime in 1994, called *The Birds II: Land's End.*

When I was involved, they were calling it *The Birds 3-D*. CBS was going to do it. It had a huge production company behind it, and they were going to do a marketing tie-in with 7-11, where people would go to 7-11 to get the 3-D glasses. They even talked about a sponsorship deal, where the commercials would also be in 3-D. It was this huge innovative gadget/gimmick.

The writer I worked with on that was Robert Eisele, who wrote *The Great Debaters*—a really nice, smart guy. When the two of us first got together, a script already existed but it was too derivative of the original. We went back to the short story that Hitchcock had used, which was cool because it all took place in a cabin. It was about one family, trapped alone, and they heard on the radio what was going on everywhere else. We knew [the producers] weren't going to go for something that simple, but we wanted to create that sense of claustrophobia. So we were in sync about what we wanted to do. And the producers said, "No, it's got to be massive, with birds flying into traffic and all this shit." And I'm thinking, *That's not scary*. So eventually we both left the project. I guess it ended up on Showtime? I never saw it.

If you tackle this kind of job, you should be able to say to yourself, "I can make a really great standalone movie that will maintain the spirit of the original." Robert and I both walked away because we saw that it was not going to be that.

It sounds like you were on the right track, because that sense of claustrophobia really is what works about the original Hitchcock film. You have this huge apocalyptic canvas— international crisis—but the story is carefully grounded in the reality of a handful of characters. It boggles my mind to

think that the financiers of a sequel or remake wouldn't recognize that.

All it takes is somebody's twenty-two-year-old assistant to say, in passing, "I just saw the third *Star Wars* and there's this awesome sequence where . . ." And that sticks in some executive's head as he's reading the script or looking at the dailies, and then he says to himself, "You know, this thing just isn't *big enough*." What they add is not even their idea. It just seemed like a good idea to them at that particular moment. A lot of times, you've got 200 random people telling you how to make the movie . . . and everybody has completely different ideas, depending on what film they just saw or what *Variety* says is making money *this* week.

As a filmmaker, you have to try to figure out which notes are actually good ones and which are just coming from people who need to justify their paycheck. Of course, if you dismiss the *wrong* note, you'll hear: "Well, do you know whose note that was? That one actually came from The Man himself, and if *he* says something you've got to make *that* work. You can forget all the other notes . . ." "But these other notes are actually good . . ." "No, forget them!"

The bottom line is we're all trying to make something good, but you can't be in sync with 200 people. That's why it's a miracle—really a miracle—whenever any movie works from beginning to end. When that happens, I always sit through the credits, as does most of the audience, because you just don't want to leave the presence of that movie. Why go back to reality? We're in magic time here.

PART IV: MEN & WOMEN

Real-life monsters / The Luminol scene / Alison's legacy / A Radio Shack future / The female version of Taxi Driver / One of God's true children / The battle for ambiguity / Directing Kirk Douglas / Coppola's advice

FILMOGRAPHY

IN A CHILD'S NAME (CBS, 1991)
DIRECTED BY TOM MCLOUGHLIN
TELEPLAY BY BILL PHILLIPS AND CHARLES WALKER. BASED ON A BOOK BY PETER MAAS.
STARRING VALERIE BERTINELLI, MICHAEL ONTKEAN, CHRIS MELONI, DAVID HUDDLESTON, LOUISE FLETCHER
   True story of a woman's fight for custody of her murdered sister's child.

SOMETHING TO LIVE FOR: THE ALISON GERTZ STORY (A.K.A. FATAL LOVE) (ABC, 1992)
DIRECTED BY TOM MCLOUGHLIN
TELEPLAY BY DEBORAH JOY LEVINE.
STARRING MOLLY RINGWALD, MARTIN LANDAU, LEE GRANT, PERRY KING
   True story of a young woman who became an AIDS activist after learning that she was infected with HIV.

THE FIRE NEXT TIME (CBS, 1993)
DIRECTED BY TOM MCLOUGHLIN
TELEPLAY BY JAMES S. HENERSON.

Starring Craig T. Nelson, Bonnie Bedelia, Richard Farnsworth, Jurgen Prochnow

A family struggles to stay together in a future where extreme global warming has created chaos.

Murder of Innocence (CBS, 1993)
Directed by Tom McLoughlin
Teleplay by Philip Rosenberg. Based on a book by George Kaplan, George Papajohn and Eric Zorn.
Starring Valerie Bertinelli, Stephen Caffrey, Jerry Hardin, Millie Perkins

True story of a woman's descent into madness, culminating in a killing spree.

The Yarn Princess (ABC, 1994)
Directed by Tom McLoughlin
Teleplay by Dalene Young
Starring Jean Smart, Robert Pastorelli, Dennis Boutsikaris

A mentally handicapped woman fights to retain custody of her children.

Leave of Absence (NBC, 1994)
Directed by Tom McLoughlin
Teleplay by Betty Goldberg. Based on a story by Polly Bergen.
Starring Brian Dennehy, Jacqueline Bisset, Blythe Danner

A man leaves his wife to have an affair with a dying woman.

The Lies Boys Tell (a.k.a. Take Me Home Again) (NBC, 1994)
Teleplay by Ernest Thompson. Based on a novel by Lamar Herrin.
Starring Kirk Douglas, Craig T. Nelson

A dying man convinces his estranged son to drive him to his childhood home.

JOURNEY (CBS, 1995)
DIRECTED BY TOM MCLOUGHLIN
TELEPLAY BY PATRICIA MACLACHLAN, ADAPTED FROM
HER OWN NOVEL.
STARRING JASON ROBARDS, BRENDA FRICKER, MAX POMERANC,
MEG TILLY

A grandfather tries to connect with his introverted grandson after the boy is abandoned by his mother.

Tom on the set of *Sometimes They Come Back*

Your work in the horror genre seems like a jumping off point for the stories you told in the 1990s. Your next group of movies is based very firmly in reality and each one is essentially about conquering some kind of real-life fear.

My way of looking at my career—and I can't be truly objective because I'm still in the middle of it—is that the beginning was about the kind of movies that I loved as a kid and still love: gothic horror, screwball comedies, Capra-esque fantasy. The horror stuff was about fears related to death and the afterlife and the supernatural. Then, when I got into the TV movies, it became more about real-life monsters that don't just die and go away: serial killers, AIDS, global warming, mental illness . . .

Instead of dealing with fantasy horrors, you're dealing with everyday horrors that exist in the world around us, and in human nature . . .

Yes. I used to believe that we all are born morally intact and then somewhere along the way we could get corrupted. If you do something horrible—if you hurt somebody or kill somebody—then I figured you're going to lay awake at night, unable to rest, feeling horribly messed up . . . wandering the streets, wondering if people can tell that there's something wrong with you. I figured that's your punishment. You're going to suffer.

Now I realize that people who are capable of doing those things are also capable of convincing themselves that they didn't do it. Total sociopath behavior. Now that's scary! Because what's to stop somebody from doing awful things if they truly believe that there's nothing wrong with what they're doing? Sociopaths can justify what they're doing. They decide it's okay to rip someone off if that person has more money than they do, or that it's okay to treat someone like an animal because they're ethnicity makes them "inferior." In life, you meet people who completely believe those things, and you try to get through to them but you can't. And sometimes it gets worse as years go by.

There is a monologue in *Mississippi Burning* where the Gene Hackman character is trying to explain to Willem Defoe why people are racist, because Willem Defoe just cannot understand it. His character is telling this story about when he was a boy. He was driving with his father and he noticed an old black man who owned a horse. The black man could use the horse to plow his field, whereas the boy's father had to do it by hand. Hackman says, "Even as a boy I could see that my father was not happy about this guy having a horse. I remember a few weeks later that horse mysteriously died." Later he saw the black man plowing the field by hand and he looked at his dad, and he knew his father had killed that horse. He could see it in his eyes. And he could see that his father knew that he knew. And his father said, "Son, if you're no better than a nigger, what good are you?" Some people need to feel that they are somehow superior to somebody else, just to have some twisted sense of self-respect. The black culture was so hated in that part of the country at that time that his father actually *believed* that he was better. It was bred into the culture.

Kids learn those things from their parents. They watch their fathers beat their mothers, and they think that's what a man does. Then those boys, when they get a girlfriend, think they can "own" a girl, and that they have the right to hit them. And the girls allow it because they've been around that kind of thing too and, for them, it's culturally acceptable. This is my long-winded way of saying that those kinds of monsters are deeply imbedded in so many people's lives. We deal with them on a daily basis—from the cops and politicians who become corrupt because they're given too much power to the lover who suddenly betrays you. The most interesting thing to me is trying to understand the subjective point of view of those monsters, instead of just telling the facts. I want to see the world, cinematically, through their eyes. That makes the story far more emotional for us as viewers.

That takes a lot of digging. A lot of times, it means delving into people's childhoods . . .

With storytelling, you have to decide where you want to begin the tale. Usually you begin at the worst incident in a person's life so that you grab the audience's attention—like the opening of *Sunset Boulevard*, which begins with the dead man's narration. So we literally know, through the whole movie, that he's going to end up dead in the swimming pool. What we want to know is how he got to that point.

How did you get involved with *In a Child's Name*?

After *Sometimes They Come Back*, CBS offered me this miniseries starring Valerie Bertinelli. To be honest, I don't watch much television. I very seldom follow TV series and I find it impossible to watch movies with commercial breaks. So at the time, the TV world was something that I was completely divorced from. Along came this script based on a Peter Maas book, about a woman who was trying to prove that her sister's husband killed her sister. The main thrust of the story was about a baby that was going to be

raised by the murderer's parents. It was the classic "somebody stole my baby" story. That wasn't something that I felt I could identify with or emotionally connect with. But then I thought it would be an interesting challenge. I wanted the chance to tell a true story based on actual people.

There was also a scene in the movie that really appealed to my dark side. Louise Fletcher and David Huddleston [the actors playing the parents of the killer] are in the bedroom where the murder happened, and the killer has cleaned up so well after the murder that nobody has found any traces of blood in the room . . . until the forensic investigators use Luminol.[15] When I got to that sequence, the horror fantasy part of my brain kicked in. I didn't just want to show a little blood. I wanted to make this a blood

---

[15] A chemical that causes trace amount of blood to glow green

bath—almost like what I did in *Jason Lives*, with buckets of blood covering the walls of the cabin where one of the girls was killed.

Basically what happens is that the two characters go in and put the baby in the crib, then turn off the lights. Gradually you start to see this green glow appear on Louise Fletcher's face. She looks around and we cut to individual shots of all these hand smears and splatter marks on the wall, but instead of blood it's Luminol, which is a glowing green color. Then the camera pulls back and you see that the walls are covered. You never see any red blood, and obviously you haven't seen the murder, but you can imagine how bad it was. We ended up putting that scene at the conclusion of the first night [of the miniseries], which was a Sunday night.

On Monday morning, it seemed like everybody was talking about it. I walked into the 7-11 and somebody was talking about it; I went to the dentist and somebody was talking about it; it was in the newspaper . . . and then the phone calls started coming in from people saying, "You scared the shit out of me." The film kicked ass on Tuesday night [when the second half aired] in terms of ratings, so that proved how many people nationwide had been talking about it. The second night was the highest rated television movie of the year.

I had no idea that it would get that kind of reaction. In fact, I apologized to the producers when I handed in my cut. I said, "I'm sorry. I don't understand this genre. I just did what I could." And I almost got fired over that scene with the Luminol. The network executives were asking themselves, "Why did we hire a horror director? We're going to have to re-shoot this scene." I wouldn't re-shoot it.

When I've talked to people over the years, they always say, "*In a Child's Name* . . . Is that the one with the green stuff?" That's what they remember. That's what kept them awake. That image made such an impact. I met Kim Basinger three years later and she told me, "I didn't fall asleep until three o'clock that morning." Anybody I came across that saw this thing, they'd get this look of horror on their face when they realized . . . "*You did that?*" It got to them because they weren't expecting it. It's exactly what we've been talking about—the audience got so wrapped up in the characters and the realism of the story, that they were really shocked by this horrible, horrible image. The combination of all these elements created one hell of a reaction.

And that was only the mid-point of the miniseries.

When audiences first saw the shower scene in *Psycho*, they thought, *If they're showing this now . . . How much worse is it going to get?* In the same way, *In a Child's Name* teased people. It made them want to see more.

But then the second half didn't have a moment to match it. That horror element was just a bridge between what plays like two different movies: a murder mystery and a courtroom drama. Did you, on some level, approach the miniseries as two separate movies?

I had to look at it as a cohesive whole, but I also learned pretty quickly that with TV movies you really are doing a series of shorts. We needed a cliffhanger at every commercial. These things have to be very carefully structured. You have a certain amount of time for the first act, second act, third act . . . They follow a very, very rigid format. You have to build to something at the end of each act, and the standard technique is to move in on a close-up of one of the characters at the end of each act. Then the music swells and you cut to the soap commercial. I did not want to fall into those clichés. If I was going to work within that formula, I wanted to do something different that had a more visceral impact.

So I had to look at it as a whole. I knew it had to build to something at the end of the first night that would make audiences want to come back the second night. And even though the second night didn't have anywhere nearly as many action sequences, I had to find moments that would deliver visually . . . like the scene where the Michael Ontkean character, Ken Taylor, is escaping from jail. I kept looking for ways to make this seem more like an independent film and less like a TV movie.

Basically, if I'm given an opportunity to make a movie, I'm going to make the best piece of cinema that I can possibly make, and put as much of myself into it as I can. Scorsese talked, in his documentary on American movies, about the "director as smuggler." If you have a low enough budget and the producers are only concerned with the production schedule, you can smuggle in all kinds of ideas, moments and theories, to make a film full of personal contributions. On big studio pictures or big network shows, everything is micro-managed and so many people are going over every detail that you can't get away with that as much. You have to deliver what is expected for the genre . . . but when I get scripts that are basically TV movie formulas, I work as hard as I can to turn them into something else.

When shooting ended on *In a Child's Name*, we had nine days to edit a four-hour movie together. We had two editors working on it in different rooms and I was jumping back and forth between rooms. It was very intense. When I watched the cut with the producers, I was very disappointed—so it was a great surprise to me when the movie got such incredible reviews and through-the-roof ratings.[16]

Did you approach *In a Child's Name* differently than your previous films because of the fact that it was based on real events? How much artistic license could you take with the story?

In my mind, I divide my projects into "movies" and "films." For me, *One Dark Night*, *Friday the 13th*, *Date with an Angel* and *Sometimes They Come Back* are movies. They exist in a "movie realm," where everything is mythic or metaphorical. When I made the leap into true-life stories, with *In a Child's Name*, I had to try to figure out what I wanted to say and how to express it without fictionalizing real-world facts.

---

[16] *Variety* writer Laurence Vittes said, "Although it is derived from a conventional miniseries formula [. . .] *In a Child's Name* is a dazzling demonstration of the television art" displaying "an unmanipulative, unblinking style reminiscent of New Wave programs like *Twin Peaks*." He concludes, "Regardless of ratings, the style, production qualities and nearly flawless execution of *In a Child's Name* will doubtless make it a rewarding subject for film students for years to come."

On one level, you want to stick to the facts . . . but a lot of times the facts are not dramatic enough, so you have to add elements or take away elements to heighten or streamline the storytelling. With *In a Child's Name*, it helped that the movie was based on Peter Maas's book. When I read the initial script, I remember thinking, *That's not very exciting* and *that's not very cinematic*. I went back to the book and started highlighting things in there that I thought could be more visual, and then I went to the producers with my notes and said, "Can we do this and this and this? It's in the book . . ." It all came down to a legal issue. If we follow the book, the author bears responsibility. If someone sues us, we can say, "It was in Peter Maas's book and we bought the book . . ."

Of course, there's always a disclaimer at the end of every movie that says: *If there's any resemblance between this and anything real, it's a coincidence*. No matter what you say up front—"based on a true story" or "based on real events"—there's that legal disclaimer so that you can take artistic license with the storytelling. I think the viewing public is caught between wanting a compelling story and wanting to know that the things they're watching really happened. These movies are always a *dramatic interpretation* of real events and real people. We have to build conflicts within the characters and between the characters, and then resolve those conflicts dramatically. It's not just facts and information. You need elements that are cinematic.

I'll give you an example. With *In a Child's Name*, the Valerie Bertinelli character's family is Catholic and very close-knit, very loving. So I went with a warmer color palette when we were focused on them. Their house is filled with pictures of their family, and the camera shots were connected and moving all the time. In the set design, we used a lot of brick, to convey history and stability. For the murderer's family, I used a very cool palette—cooler blues, grays—and a more static frame, with more space in the frame to show isolation. There were absolutely no pictures on the wall; no warmth. That was the beginning of looking at this story as a film. It wasn't a movie, although the Luminol scene is certainly something out of a movie—it's a very Hitchcockian scene.

Tom with cast members portraying the Silvano / Cimarelli family on the set of *In a Child's Name*

But it had a greater impact because it was juxtaposed with so much realism . . .

When you know you're doing a real story, you try very hard to play by the rules of real life and to be true to the real people. You want the story to be theirs. You also want it to be believable. When things didn't seem real to me, I would suggest new dialogue and just improvise the scene with the actors. Then, once we all got more comfortable with the scene, we'd bring back the words in the script. Suddenly the performances seemed more connected to what was on the page.

Capra did that too. Except sometimes he didn't bring the "real words" back. He just re-wrote the dialogue on the spot.

John Cassavettes and other independent filmmakers will say, "Here's the scene and you're the actor, figure it out from there."

But when you're dealing with a TV network, you can't even change a comma in the script without approval. You're working with producers who say, "We cannot change anything unless we get the network's okay." And I've learned over the years that you never have enough time to get the okay. Sometimes I just take a chance and shoot a scene two different ways. I always have to do what makes the scene ring true for me. That's not about asserting my ego. It's a matter of finding the best way for an actor to convey what they need to convey and make the scene believable. I had to take another "somebody stole my baby" TV movie and make it fresh, and make the characters distinct and honest.

We had to do that for *both* families, because both sides believe they are right. Even the Taylors, the David Huddleston / Louise Fletcher family, believed they had God on their side. They had their church, their minister, and a group of people who reassured them that they were doing the right thing: "You are the grandparents. These people are trying to take away *your* son's baby." Meanwhile, they were in complete denial about the fact that their son was a killer. One of the main themes that I have running through my work is bad parenting creates bad children . . . and then those bad children can grow up and hurt *your* children.

There's a great moment in *In a Child's Name* where the killer is reciting a prayer and he can't get out a line about his soul. It's as if you're suggesting that he doesn't have a soul. Was that your idea?

I'm not sure where that came from. I remember talking to Peter Maas, who said that the killer wanted to bury his wife and perform a sort of religious burial for her, and that he attempted to recite a psalm but didn't know all the words. He only knew the beginning of it. He couldn't remember the rest, so he ended up just saying "forever and ever, amen." In reality, it was just a case of a guy who didn't know the words. But I like your interpretation better. Because that's the thing—he was always [devoid of conscience] . . . He really did drive around with her body in his trunk. He really did go to his ex-wife's house afterwards and have sex with her. And she saw nothing in his behavior that made her think anything was wrong.

All this reminds me of something that Wes Craven has said. In his films, he always comes back to the idea that a person's childhood environment fundamentally shapes who you are as a person, for better or worse. He says that's where monsters come from. He's even referred to Freddy Krueger as "the ultimate bad dad," an authority figure whose sole purpose in life is to torment children . . .

To me it's still about children hurting children. Even as adults, sociopaths are still thinking and behaving like children. They're still getting back at the schoolyard bullies or dealing with unresolved issues with their parents—and they're hurting real children in the process.

It's interesting that Valerie Bertinelli, who played the protective mother figure in *In a Child's Name*, went on to play serial killer Laurie Dann in *A Murder of Innocence*. How did you cast her for *In a Child's Name*?

Valerie was already on board when I was hired as director. In general, the casting process was all about finding good actors that the network would approve, because the executives wanted to have final approval on every person in the movie. There were a lot of fights over a lot of actors. Getting Louise Fletcher was an amazing coup. And she was great because the sweeter she was in that role, the more frightening she became. David Huddleston—same thing.

The big find was Chris Meloni [who plays Jerry Cimarelli]. I had a casting director who was dead set on him. Junie Lowry, who's a very highly respected casting director, brought him back three times until finally I finally broke down and hired him. And he turned out to be one of the best actors I've ever worked with. Chris and I just clicked. I could talk to him in shorthand and he intuitively got what I was saying.

There are a lot of wonderful actors in *In a Child's Name* . . . Karla Tamburelli, Tim Carhart, John Karlen, Carolina Kava,

Vinnie Guastaferro, Joanna Merlin, and my lovely Nancy . . . They all just really bonded as a group of actors as well as the characters. I really lucked out.

After *In a Child's Name* was a big hit, were you inundated with directing offers?

It was that lucky streak that some people have when they first come out of film school and they've made a short that everybody is excited about. They get their first big feature and if it works, they can ride that wave for quite a while. I had been able to make a few films and now I was in demand. I went from total obscurity to being one of the top five directors in television movies . . . which was not quite what I had envisioned for myself. I wanted to be doing features, genre movies—but I was in a situation where I was getting all the best TV movie scripts, and I couldn't ignore that.

One of the scripts that was being pushed the hardest was a CBS property called *The Fire Next Time*. It was very expensive global warming movie, produced by Robert Halmi, who was responsible for a number of high-profile miniseries on TV during that time period. His investors had very deep pockets. He reminded me a lot of Dino [DeLaurentiis]—he was one of those great movie moguls in the old school sense. I read the script, and it was an overwhelmingly huge story that would need to be filmed in a number of states, with a lot of production resources.

At the same time, *Something to Live For: The Alison Gertz Story* came in. It was a much smaller piece with a really good script. I loved the fact that it revolved around one character. At first I thought, *I really didn't know much about this world.* I wasn't sure I was the right person to do a "woman's picture" like this. What I did know was horror. I remembered the scene in *The Exorcist* where Regan has to go through this horrible battery of tests. *Something to Live For* has a similar sequence. She's disoriented; she's confused; she can't understand why these horrible things are happening to her or why she's sick. I knew right away how I wanted to shoot that. I used a lot of subjective camera to put the audience in her head, so they could feel the high fevers, the confusion, all the needles and tests and horrible things that she had to go through.

The script by Deborah Joy Levine had so much emotional weight that I basically said to Halmi, "I'm going to do this one first. It's only seventeen days in Los Angeles, and then we'll get back to work on the script for *The Fire Next Time*." That was shocking to everybody, particularly Halmi. Much to my surprise, he did wait for me. I really didn't think he would, but he did. So I did *Something to Live For*, then started on *The Fire Next Time*.

The first half of *Something to Live For* is all about trying to figure out what's wrong with her. Was it harder to tell the second half of the story, once she knows she has AIDS?

In the second half, the main issue becomes: *What do you want to do with your life now that you know you're dying?* The new conflict was about acceptance. She's saying, "Alright, I have AIDS . . . Why can't I still have a boyfriend? Why can't I still try to have a normal life?" That conflict provided the emotional punch of the second half.

Was that the story that the real Alison Gertz wanted to tell—the secondary conflict?

Yes. The original script was called *Alison*. Just *Alison*. We thought that was great. Especially since Elvis Costello had a song called "Alison." Molly Ringwald [who played Alison Gertz] said, "You've got to get that song." But since it was an ABC TV movie, they needed a title that sounded like a TV movie—so it became *Something to Live For: The Alison Gertz Story*. That title presented it not as a movie about somebody dying of AIDS, but as a movie about someone who's determined to do something meaningful with their life. That's why the real Alison Gertz was on the cover of *People* magazine.[17] That's why she was newsworthy—because she survived for a really long time. Right up until her death, she

---

[17] July 30, 1990–Vol. 34, No. 4

was still going to schools and speaking out about safe sex. To me, Alison was a real hero.

When she came to the set, I remember she looked me in the eye and said, "Thank you. This is my legacy." She died about six weeks later, but she knew her story would live on. I've had so many people tell me that they saw the movie in sex education and health classes. And it won an award from the Department of Health and Human Services in Washington D.C. because over so many viewers called the 800 number that appeared after the movie aired, all of them seeking information on AIDS. (Remember this was 1991.) So from that standpoint, the movie actually saved lives. That was the last thing that I expected. It was only my second TV movie, and I chose to do it mainly because I thought of it as an emotional modern-day horror movie.

I remember seeing *The Ryan White Story* on TV when I was a kid, and it affected me because Ryan White was about the same age when he got AIDS. I have to imagine that young women who grew up watching Molly Ringwald in *The Breakfast Club* and *Sixteen Candles* were personally affected by *Something to Live For*. How did the producers manage to get her on board?

It was a labor of love for everyone involved. We didn't have much money to do it, so the actors basically worked for scale, or a little above scale. And I'm talking about Molly Ringwald, Martin Landau, Perry King, Leigh Grant. All incredible actors. They wanted to help tell this story.

After *Something to Live For*, you immediately went to work on *The Fire Next Time* . . .

The Fire Next Time was extremely challenging on so many levels. First off, we had to do casting here in Los Angeles, then we had to do additional casting in New Mexico, Louisiana and Pittsburgh. So I had to keep flying from place to place for local casting calls, all the while trying to get everything together in L.A. with the script and the crew.

Tom with Molly Ringwald, making *Something to Live For*

Tom, Martin Landau and Nancy McLoughlin on the set of *Something to Live For*

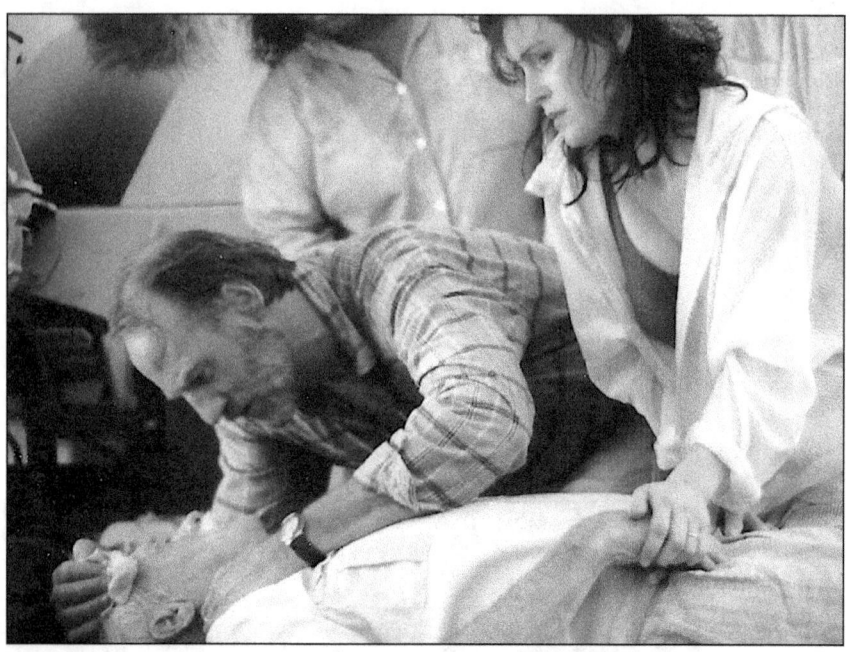

Richard Farnsworth, Craig T. Nelson and Bonnie Bedelia on the set of *The Fire Next Time*

The good thing was that I had two great leads: Bonnie Bedelia and Craig T. Nelson. Bonnie's amazing in that she can play so many different types of characters with such intelligence and strength. Even in her most vulnerable moments, there's still an incredible sexuality about her. She never loses that femininity. She would have made a really wonderful 1930s, 1940s screen actress—a Barbara Stanwyck type, but even sexier in a lot of ways. She is a force to be reckoned with, and when she and Craig got together—there was a strong chemistry there, and sometimes I just had to get out of the way because I had these two actors who were such strong actors and personalities.

Craig had reservations about me being the director on this movie. He had worked with some great directors, and I wasn't the Howard Hawks / Sam Peckinpah kind of guy that he'd usually want for a tough, dramatic picture like this. So I had to do everything I could to convince him that, although I'd never done this type of picture before, I had done my homework and I honestly did understand these kind of movies and I was determined to make this good.

On the first day of shooting, we were out on the Mississippi River doing the opening scene on the shrimp boat, where Craig is talking about how bad the shrimping business is becoming . . . Craig takes acting very seriously. He's always questioning whether there's something more that he could add to a scene, and I'm one of those directors that will keep going as long as the actor feels he's got another way to try it. So we kept going until there was literally no more time. Unfortunately we just hit one of those walls. We reached the six hour mark and had to break for lunch. Craig noticed that the A.D. kept whispering in my ear between takes and he finally said, "What's going on?" And I said, "He's concerned about the lunch, but don't worry about it. Let's keep going." So we did another take and I thought it was really good. And I said, "Alright, let's move on." He said, "You don't want to do another one?" I said, "No, I think that was good." He said, "You really do, or you just need to stop because of lunch?" I said, "No, I really think it was good." But I could tell he didn't believe me, and we didn't have any kind of working relationship yet. We hadn't built up any trust. That's the key word in any relationship with anybody in this business. Many actors, because they're so vulnerable and sensitive regarding their craft, want to make sure that you did not walk away before they came off as good as they want to come off.

The next day—or maybe even the same day, I can't recall—we were doing the scene where the hurricane is approaching. We had a wind machine going and this local character actress was projecting as loud as she could, because that's the tendency when you're working with one of those things. You instinctively talk louder because the wind machine is so loud. Because of the wind machine, I knew we were going to have loop the dialogue so I didn't worry about it too much. Craig pulled me aside and said, "What do you think about this woman's acting?" I said, "I think she's doing a good job." He said, "You think so?" I said, "Well, she's not Meryl Streep. We have to loop this scene anyway. I think it will be fine." He said, "It just seems kind of big . . ." I said, "Well, it is big, but don't worry. I'm going to go over this in the looping session and it will be fine." I was thinking to myself, *She really isn't bad.* But Craig seemed to be looking for things that weren't working for him, so I at the same time I was thinking: *Okay, that's strike two for the director.*

On the third day, we had this huge scene at the Red Cross Center with about five hundred extras, all in futuristic costume. This is the scene where Craig and Bonnie Bedelia find each other again, and then he has to explain to her that they've lost everything. He didn't renew the family insurance, so they've lost everything in the hurricane. It's a huge moment between these two people. They're relieved that they've found each other alive, but they're also learning that they've got no place to live, no money; everything is gone. So I was watching his performance and, for my taste, Craig was really pushing the emotion too far. The way he was going about it just did not ring true to me, so I kept going in and giving him notes. But it still was too big. He started to get more and more upset with me, until finally he just snapped: "Look, what is your problem with the scene?" I said, "To be honest with you, it's just coming across too melodramatic." And he glared at me, like I had just called him some kind of racial slur. He said, "Melodramatic?" I said, "Yes sir. We need to bring it down a bit." He kept glaring. "So my acting is melodramatic?" I'm thinking, *Oh shit.* Then I started back-peddling. I said, "No, it's *heading towards* melodramatic . . ."

After that he did bring it down. Everything worked in the next take. But that was strike three. So at the end of the day, we were wrapping up and the Unit Production Manager came to me and said, "Mr. Nelson wants to see you in his trailer." I said, "Yeah, I could see this coming." So I walked into his trailer, and Craig was pacing like a panther. And Craig is a *big* guy. He said, "You know what? I don't think this is going to work. So I've called my agent and I'm going to quit this picture. I just can't take this." And I said, "No, no—look, you're more important to this show than I am. You're the star. If my working methods don't work for you, then I need to leave." "No, no, no—I'm leaving! I've already made the decision—I'm leaving!" "You can't, you just can't." He said, "I can and I am." He was so angry. He felt like I was more concerned about staying on schedule than taking care of my actors. In his mind, I wasn't trusting him and so he didn't feel that he could trust me. I don't know how I managed to get this in but I said, "Give it one more day. If tomorrow doesn't work for you, one or the other of us will quit. Maybe both of us, I don't know. But if you could just hold off until tomorrow . . ."

So I came out of the trailer and the UPM was standing there, biting his nails. He said, "What just happened?" I said, "Basically I just bought myself one more day."

The next day we were at the same location, shooting a family scene with Craig and Richard Farnsworth—who I absolutely adore. He's like the grandfather that we all wish we'd had. It was a dream come true having him in that film. We were rehearsing this scene and it was almost lunch time. My A.D. came over and told me, "We're getting close to lunch." And I had this moment of inspiration. I turned to him and I said, "Look, let the UPM and everybody else know that I have to do something. Whatever happens, just realize I'm doing it for the sake of the movie."

So we're rehearsing the scene and the A.D. yells, "Tom, we really have to break for lunch." And I just went into a tirade. "You know what? Fuck the lunch! We're rehearsing here! When we're done, we'll have lunch! Are you okay with that?!" "Well, I just . . ." "ARE YOU OKAY WITH THAT?!" "Yeah, okay, fine." And I turned back and saw Craig do one of those [pulls his fist down in a celebratory manner]. From that point on, we were good. He just needed to see that I was concerned about the actors and the work. I always am, but he just needed some strong proof. I won't say that we didn't have a few more skirmishes along the way, but after that we began to truly understand and trust each other.

Up until then, I'd never had that kind of argument with an actor. Maybe because I was always working on smaller projects. *Something to Live For* was so much about the emotional content that it was easier to focus exclusively on the actors. With *The Fire Next Time*, I had to work on this huge canvas. I had a great Director of Photography, Shelly Johnson, and we wanted a lot of big, wide shots, so we carried a crane from state to state. That's unheard of on a production like this—dragging a crane from Los Angeles to New Mexico to Louisiana to Pittsburgh. Somehow I convinced Robert Halmi that it was a worthwhile expense. In the end, it was a great experience. It taught me so much as a director. Unfortunately, my A.D. Jonathan Zimmerman got fired when we started to fall behind in New Mexico. He's a terrific A.D. and it wasn't his fault. He took the bullet for me. The show was extremely ambitious.

How long was the shoot?

I want to say it was forty-five or forty-six days, which for something like that is very difficult. With travel days, it was quite a long period of time. And we had a lot of crazy things happen. We'd show up on the location and none of the set pieces would be there. Somehow, something was mis-communicated. The guy who was supposed to be in charge [in the art department] ended up leaving the show and his successor didn't get the information . . . And anytime there was a setback, it cost us quite a bit. And the schedule left no room for error. We had to finish in one place on time because all the plane tickets had been booked for the next day, and we had to start shooting in the next location on a specific day.

At the same time, there were some very complicated setups that went amazingly well. We closed down a bridge in Pittsburgh during rush hour traffic, so that we could shoot the Canadian/American border scene with all those extras. I think we were able to pull that off because of some sort of questionable connections. I saw all these tough-looking guys under the bridge in suits, just talking, and then suddenly I had the bridge. The same thing happened when we shot in the French Quarter on the weekend. Again, somebody talked to the right people and it all came together.

Let's talk about the script. *The Fire Next Time* is not exactly fun-loving, light entertainment. It offers a very bleak vision of the future.

Although it takes place thirty years into the future, in my mind it was a Radio Shack future. Instead of having incredible high-tech toys, like something out of *Blade Runner*, they had affordable devices that help them simply survive day-to-day. Most of the technology is retro-fitted, because they're trying to save power but still make things look cooler. I was really fortunate that we were able to get the services of Syd Mead, from *Blade Runner*. He was a futurist who worked with an artist to create a lot of these things, and he was really amazing. I was so grateful just to be in his presence, throwing crazy ideas back and forth. We had a great time.

And it paid off. Fifteen years later, all of the gadgets in that movie seem believable . . . except for the pay phones.

We were trying to be conservative. We sort of did what the silent movies did in the 1910s—Chaplin's in particular. They would dress up actors more like it was the 1890s, to give viewers a sense of familiarity.

In *The Fire Next Time*, we tried to introduce things that were relatively new when we were making the movie. The cars were difficult, because we had to get the latest models and then retrofit them in a way that made them look old but still recognizable—because the car company would get upset if we made them unrecognizable. We tried to come up with little tricks to make them look different. With the truck, we put these Venetian blind things in the back window to block the sun. Some of those things looked pretty cool. I wish we could have gone a little further. Syd had tons of ideas.

There were other gadgets in that movie that we need now, but haven't invented yet—like carbon-allotment cards . . . I think the movie is probably more interesting to watch now than it was in 1993, because people are starting to seriously think about these things as more than science fiction.

The DVD keeps getting re-released with new cover art. I don't know what that means, other than somebody's finding a way to keep selling it. The place where it really took off was in Australia, because global warming is such an important issue there. The kids there *do* have to put on that high-end sunscreen.

Maybe they also recognize the *Mad Max* aesthetic.

Maybe. Another interesting thing about the production was the hurricane. Hurricane Andrew hit Morgan City about six or eight weeks after we left. We were watching the news and saw some of those folks who'd been extras in *The Fire Next Time* standing in the same Red Cross staging area where we shot. It was chilling to see the fiction turn factual.

I think what made the story interesting was the fact that, in a future where there are so many problems, the biggest villain was the weather. That and the idea that when people are suffering and have lost so much, they can help each other and make the best of it. In that scene at the end of the first half, all these people are on this barge going up the Mississippi and the thing that brings them together is the music . . .

The Cajun music?

Yeah. It certainly wasn't the kind of cliffhanger that we had in *In a Child's Name*, but I really wanted to go for that *Grapes of Wrath* image, with all these homeless families heading to an unknown future together. I had a very specific shot in mind, with the bridge and the orange sun that was clouded over with smog and smoke.

It's interesting that you keep coming back to images of weather. You talked about something similar on your commentary track for *Friday the 13th*. You said that Capra suggested putting natural elements into a movie, like you did with the wind and the rain in that film, to make the action and the drama of the story seem bigger. As a viewer, I'm aware of weather in just about every scene in *The Fire Next Time*. Except toward the end, in the utopian upstate New York community . . .

That was the section where I was most concerned about the story being dull, because the conflict was so internal at that point—mostly between Craig and his wife, when he was feeling jealous of Jurgen Prochnow. It's not as interesting as the sections where they have to get out there and fight the storm, or fight to get their daughter back.

But it was such a bleak movie that it was nice to have that reprieve. The same thing is true later on the Amish farm. Life gets back to basics in those scenes. The characters are just trying to respectfully co-exist with the rest of the world . . .

I think what writer James Henerson did very nicely was to get back to basics. There was so much of what people go through in life—birth and death, parents and kids fighting—but all set against this huge backdrop. Craig was great as the bullheaded father. One of his best scenes is the one where this group of eco-hippies is taking his daughter from him. The scene rested on his shoulders, and on the actress who was playing his daughter Linnie [Ashley Jones]. My recollection is that this was one of her first acting jobs, but she had such a great quality when she looked at him and said, "Daddy, this is what I want." As a father, I know now what I didn't know then—what Craig obviously knew and put into that moment. There are times when you have to let go. If she really is truly happy, I don't want to drag her away . . . but how can I accept this?

Plus it was a young Paul Rudd that she was leaving for. Maybe if Craig's character knew how big a star Paul Rudd was destined to be, he wouldn't have been as reluctant.

You must have won over Craig T. Nelson at some point in the shoot, since he was willing to do another movie with you (*The Lies Boys Tell*) a year later.

Craig actually asked for me specifically on that, because he was thrilled with the way *The Fire Next Time* came out. And by the time we got to the end of the movie, we really had bonded. I love Craig. When we worked together it was very intense, but then we could be very lighthearted away from the set. A lot of people don't realize that Craig is a comedian. He once had an act with Barry Levinson and Rudy DeLuca. And his comic side would always come out between takes and after hours. There was one night where he went into this hysterical routine and we couldn't shoot because *everybody* was laughing too hard. At that moment, I

Ashley Jones and Paul Rudd on the set of *The Fire Next Time*

Nancy McLoughlin in *The Fire Next Time*

remembered the third day on *The Fire Next Time* and thought, *Wow, how far this relationship has come.*

When we began shooting the Amish scenes in *The Fire Next Time*, things started to really lighten up. That was a great role for Nancy [McLoughlin], who played the pregnant Amish wife. That scene where she's having the baby is an exact recreation of what I remember her going through with our first child. She did a really great job. When the shooting was over, I remember I did not want to leave that farm. It was every bit as tranquil there as (hopefully) it was in the movie. I thought: *Why can't life be this simple?* The way the Amish lived and the way they communicated showed how easy life can actually be. It was such a breath of fresh air in so many ways.

That's what gives the ending so much power—Craig's character is willing to go back out into the chaotic world and start over, instead of staying on the farm and letting his family go. It's very much like the choice at the end of *Sometimes They Come Back*.

I think this film would have been really interesting on the big screen. The story could have been pared down into a two-hour structure. It's the simple family dynamics that made it so worthwhile . . . right down to the Charles Haid character, the rich uncle who was financially exploiting the global warming situation. This guy is selling himself and the future, and he had that hustler quality. His brother could see right through him, but his nephew thought he was really exciting because here's a guy who isn't trying to hold onto old ways.

He's a man in control of his destiny.

But he's also arguing that the future's not a bad thing. That had a very interesting quality to it. For me, the strongest message of the whole movie is stated in the opening title card: "For our grandchildren." The whole time I was making this movie, I was thinking: *We are making this movie as a piece of entertainment now, but the truth is that this is what's very likely going to be happening one day.*

And the current generation is embodied in the Farnsworth character, who says "we were the last generation that had a chance to turn the tide" . . .

I have to tell you one of my favorite Richard Farnsworth stories. We had to do a ton of looping for this film. There's hardly any line in this thing that wasn't looped, because we had these young rock n roll sound guys that didn't really know how to record dialogue. Everybody had to come in for looping.

So we brought up Farnsworth from his ranch. He comes in and I say, "Richard, what's going on?" I'm expecting to hear about the next movie or something—the usual Hollywood talk. Instead he

Craig T. Nelson, James Henerson and Richard Farnsworth

pauses and says, "I have this new baby fawn that was just born on my property. She's the most beautiful thing." And that was it. *That* was what was going on. That's what made Richard so wonderful. He was just a salt-of-the-earth kind of guy.

He was great in the film. It was also nice to see Louise Fletcher, as the leader of the militant group operation on the U.S.–Canadian border.

Louise Fletcher was a great blessing as an actress. When she said to the little boy Jake, "Come over here and sit next to me," she seemed so motherly . . . but with all those cold militant guys standing around her, it was really kind of creepy.

Your next project, *Murder of Innocence*, was another very intimate, very personal film. It's also very different stylistically, because it's told from a perspective of madness. There's a lot of attention to unsettling details . . .

The first time I saw a Fellini movie in the early '70s, I said, "That's exactly the feeling of what I saw at the mental institutions when my mother was sick." Fellini would have the actors look right into the lens and say things in Italian or French (or gibberish), and later it was looped in English. I knew that it was looped, because it was such a terrible match to picture, but there was something even more surreal about seeing somebody say one thing and hearing something completely different. It had a subconscious effect on me. I found myself really connecting immediately with Fellini movies for that reason. And the same thing with the films of Luis Buñuel.

A lot of the details in *Murder of Innocence* are like that . . . they're just a little bit off. Like the scene where Valerie Bertinelli is vacuuming the hardwood floor . . . In context, that's a really unsettling image, because it makes you realize that she's not all there.

I kept trying to think like a normal person who was short-circuiting. There's a logic about her actions, but it's a different kind of logic. Like putting the laundry away when it's still wet. She thinks she's doing the right thing. She doesn't realize she's left out a step. And then there was the pure cinema aspect of it—presenting a shattered mind by using shattered images. The editing was staccato. No dissolves. No fades. It was all just CUT CUT CUT because that's what was going on in her mind.

When people ask what movie I'm most proud of, I often say *Murder of Innocence*. It guess in a way it's my female version of *Taxi Driver*. It is a realistic descent into madness. She's just trying to figure out who she is and where she belongs in life, and unfortunately she's the victim of schizophrenia and manic depression and obsessive compulsive disorder.

When I sat down with Laurie Dann's actual husband Russell, I was surprised to find that he was such a normal guy. He got into a relationship with Laurie because he thought she was genuinely attractive. In the beginning, he noticed little things about her that made him think, *Well, she's a little screwy,* but he kept getting pulled back into the relationship because she was really passionate and sexual too. As she got darker and darker, he tried to get explanations from her parents, but they at first said, "You're just imagining things." Then he slowly started to learn about some of the things that happened in her childhood.

I created some of the details of her psychotic behavior as we went along, but most of it was in the book [*Murder of Innocence: The Tragic Life and Final Rampage of Laurie Dann* by Joel Kaplan, George Papajohn, and Eric Zorn] and in the script [by Philip Rosenberg]. It was a great script, but a difficult one to say yes to because of the shooting of the children at the end.

I like the way you stylized that shooting—it all happens inside Laurie's head. As much as we dread seeing those kids get shot, somehow it's even worse being inside her head in that moment . . .

I had to come up with a way to do that scene before I could say yes to the project. Only when I said yes would Valerie say yes. CBS wanted us to do another movie together, and they felt like this one would be really intriguing. But every time I read the script, I got to that scene and said, "I can't do it." Then I finally figured out what that scene was really about . . . I had been trying to figure out how anybody could shoot children like that if they really loved children. At that point, children were the only people that Laurie Dann could connect to, so why would she do that? Then I realized that she could do that if there was something in her childhood consciousness that made these children frightening to her. I came up with that visual device of her clenching her hand as she's pulling the trigger. She's not even aware of what she's doing in those moments. It's like a reflex. Once I came up with that, I said, "Okay, I can do this thing." Then I had to talk Valerie into it. I explained to her, "You're never going to see the kids and the gun in the same shot. It's all going to be fast, panicked cuts juxtaposed with what's going on in your head."

There also seem to be some horror influences here. The flashbacks have a *Bad Seed* quality to them, and I noticed that the kids in Laurie's car (the ones she's babysitting on the day of the shooting) had very distinct blond haircuts, sort of like the alien kids in *Village of the Damned* . . .

That was a happy accident. When you're casting, your subconscious picks up on those things. I just thought there was something a little odd about those two. There was also a little boy in the film with red hair and braces. He appears at the bottom of the slide and he had this menacing grin. I didn't ask him to grin like that. He just put on this cold-looking grin, and Laurie interprets it in the film as malicious. In her fragile mind, that grin became the most terrifying thing in the world.

It's also a sad story on another level because Laurie Dann really was a very attractive girl—and many people sort of dismissed her strange behavior because she was attractive. They said, "Oh, she's just going through a phase or something." Roman Polanski's *Repulsion* had that same quality. With Catherine Deneuve as the disturbed woman, the audience is conflicted: *I'm attracted to her but I'm also afraid of her and repulsed by what she's doing.*

How did you know that Valerie would be able to inhabit that mindset in *Murder of Innocence*?

I didn't, to be honest with you. What I knew about Valerie was that she comes in with an open mind, and she *totally* commits to every moment. If you ask her to bring a particular emotion to a scene, she does it. When we were doing *In a Child's Name*, she'd put on headphones and listen to music—something that meant something to her—to get into the right place in her mind. But I don't recall her doing that on *Murder of Innocence*.

I suspected that there had to be something in her past that she was drawing from for her performance. She was always pretty secretive about what her process was and where she had to go to get these feelings. We had a few conversations about it, particularly for a scene where I was shooting incredibly tight on her eyes. When you get that close, the eyeball itself doesn't convey emotion but the area around the eye does . . . and I could see her pulling in feelings and then letting them go. I have no idea what she was drawing from, but I certainly know it was scary. She would go from dark to light to confused. Once we did those close-ups, I realized there's some stuff inside her that I don't think anybody knew she had . . . and she could tap into it.

Valerie Bertinelli in *Murder of Innocence* (CBS, 1993)

She could turn it on and off?

She could turn it on and off—and that was great, because there are a lot of actors who have to bury themselves in their characters and alienate everybody else during the process. To this day, I still say she was one of the greatest actresses I've ever worked with. In our working relationship, we had an intimacy that was so important. She became like my sister. We would talk about things that are usually taboo topics with anyone that you haven't known for a long time, and that intimacy allowed her to be vulnerable onscreen. When she came onto the set, she'd say, "Tell me what you want me to do and I'll try to get there." She never said, "Well here's how I see the character . . ." She would never do that. Valerie was always ready to go for it. The trust and love was very strong.

In her book, she talks about how absolutely terrified she was of playing Laurie Dann—because of what might come out of her. One incident symbolized the whole experience. We were doing a scene where she's walking down the street, collecting leaves. I was talking to her and these two black crows were squawking at each other real loud. We looked up and these two birds just collided, and one of them came straight down and landed on its back in front of Valerie. Its beak opened and blood poured out. And she went, "Oh my God." To her, this was an omen.[18]

Were you rolling on that?

No, we were still rehearsing. I promptly blocked it out of my mind because my initial thought was: *Oh God, don't let her have any reservations about committing to this part.* For the entire show, we both knew that we were treading on really emotionally dangerous turf. Despite that, she still went head-on into the role. When she's supposed to be sweet in the movie, she was so warm and childlike . . . because that's Valerie. So when you see her go dark, it's all the more unsettling. In certain scenes, she exerted a kind of power that seemed almost demonic.

Tell me about casting the other roles.

Stephen Caffrey, the actor who played her husband, came in to read for the part and he was terrific. Since I had met the real-life husband of Laurie Dann, I had a sense of what I was looking for. The actor didn't meet the real husband. Sometimes that's safer,

---

[18] In her autobiography, *Losing It–And Gaining My Life Back One Pound at a Time* (Simon & Schuster, 2008), Bertinelli writes that they looked up when they heard "an ear-splitting squawk that I swear to god sounded like someone saying 'Fuck off!'" Afterwards, she decided "I don't want to be this woman anymore." She says that that the role "took me as far away from myself as I'd ever been . . . My job was all about showing emotions, yet in real life I went to great lengths to avoid them, which put me in conflict with myself." (see pp. 157-158)

because then they won't try to imitate. But I could suggest nuances based on my sense of the real guy. The rest of it was just about finding the best actors here in Los Angeles. It's always great when you're casting here, because you get to see so many talented people. If you've got the right casting person and they're really tuned in, the casting sessions can be one of the most exhilarating parts of making the film.

I was really excited to work with Millie Perkins. She is still as lovely as she was as a young girl when she starred in *The Diary of Anne Frank* (1959). And I remember she was so attached to her character [Laurie's mother] in my film. She's such a sensitive actress that she really struggled with one particular line. When her daughter is surrounded by the SWAT team, she says—and this is an actual quote—"Maybe it's best if Laurie doesn't get out of this alive." As a mother, Millie kept saying, "I can't believe I'm saying these words." I said to her, "Whatever this does to you, you have to get there—because this is what Laurie Dann's mother really said." I completely understood what Millie was having trouble with. This was such a hard thing to say, but she *had* to say it.

I also cast my wife and son in the scene at the end, where Laurie goes berserk in the classroom. Nancy plays the teacher and Shane is the boy who gets shot. That film, for me, visualized my greatest fear as a father. It became almost like Michelangelo's *Pieta*, with a mother holding her son in her arms. Nancy hated that I asked her to do that. For me, it released some kind of deep fear. For Shane, it was just a fun thing to do.

Soon after *Murder of Innocence*, you did another story about a mentally-challenged mother and her children. In *The Yarn Princess*, the main character played by Jean Smart (Margaret) seems like Laurie Dann's antithesis.

All Margaret wanted to do was love her babies and take care of them and never lose them. Laurie wanted to be close to children, but she eventually felt threatened by them so maybe that's why she attacked them. Doing those two movies back to back was amazing, because they were truly like flip sides of the same coin. One was cold, dark and shattered. The other was warm, loving and poetic.

Nancy and Shane McLoughlin in *Murder of Innocence* (CBS, 1993)

With *The Yarn Princess*, I was working from was my personal belief that there are many adults in this world who are childlike, with hearts that are pure. They are truly God's children, because God is the only one that truly protects them. The rest of the world has a hard time dealing with them, and the legal system in particular. The legal system is not going to let somebody like Margaret raise her own children . . . even though nobody could ever be a better mother than this woman was.

You've mentioned that the Jean Smart character reminds you of some of the best qualities of your own mother. She's not "normal" by society's standards, but that's part of what makes her such a good mother. In this case, her mental illness makes her more supportive of her children's creativity . . .

In the scene where Margaret and her kids are talking to the social worker, the social worker says, "Your mom lets you draw on

Jean Smart, Luke Edwards and Bradley Pierce in *The Yarn Princess* (ABC, 1994)

the wall?" And Margaret says, "Oh yeah, look what he made over on this wall." She was like a little child and a proud mom at the same time. To her, the walls were the same as a piece of paper. She didn't care about walls—she just wanted her kids to have a space where they could create. Then there's the scene where she talks about finding a rat in the underwear drawer: "He's got a little home in there." And she names him Mr. Rat. I think part of me would love to be like that, to be able to cruise through life focusing on the simple things. And Jean was amazing in her ability to embrace that character and convey her excitement over those simple things, and to be 100% there in everything she said and did. She was stellar.

The same thing was true with Robert Pastorelli [who played Margaret's husband Jake]. When he did the mental breakdown scene, it was frightening to be in that room with him. He was supposed to get close to the mirror with his fist and let the breakaway rig break the glass . . . but he smashed that mirror and cut his hand. He went to that dark place and he couldn't hold back. He was that kind of actor. You clearly see it in the work, the way he committed to every moment. He could smile and it would make you smile. He could go crazy and you would step back . . . even though you knew he was just acting. He had that unique gift. So seeing Jean and Robert work together was just dynamite.

I loved throwing myself totally into *The Yarn Princess*, which was so different from *Murder*. I shot-listed the whole thing before I started and I knew everything I was going do, so I had more time to spend with the actors because of all that prep work. My A.D. Bob Wilson was on top of everything. Every day was so well planned—because we really had to work around the kids' hours. Young actors have very short days, so you have to get the shots with them right at the beginning of the day. All these boys were a blessing. They all worked together so well, and they were so believable.

The Yarn Princess—like In a Child's Name, Something to Live For, and Murder of Innocence—is based on a true story. Do you usually get into reality-based movies assuming that people know the story or do you assume that people are coming to it without knowing anything about the story? Ideally, do you want the viewer to interact with the films more as fiction or nonfiction?

I'd prefer for people not to come in to the movie having read the book and expecting it to be exactly as written. A movie can't do justice to all the details in a book. A movie has to stand on its own, in a ninety-minute adaptation of the story. Hopefully it will have an interesting point of view. That's sometimes hard to do in television because there are many network people who want the story to be overly clear and so you have to tell the story from an omniscient perspective. I really like a sense of ambiguity, but

Blythe Danner and Brian Dennehy in *Leave of Absence* (NBC, 1994)

anytime I try to go for ambiguity, it's a battle. Not that I haven't gotten away with it a few times . . . like on *Leave of Absence*.

Leave of Absence was based on a true story, but that wasn't advertised. It was based on Rex Harrison, and Polly Bergin carried that story around for years before it was scripted and made into a movie. In this case, there was quite a bit of artistic license, but the premise was simple: A man leaves his wife for another woman when he learns the other woman is dying. After she dies, he wants to come back to his wife.

Leave of Absence ended on an ambiguous close-up of Brian Dennehy. He's just totally fucked up his life. He loved Jacqueline Bissett [who plays his mistress] and he also loved Blythe Danner [who plays his wife]. At the end of the day, he loses both of them. And there he sits in a friggin' sushi bar, drinking his sake, and thinking, *Now what?* I liked the ambiguity of that "Now what?" He didn't seem sad. Instead, he seemed like he was even slightly by the irony of his fate. I loved that. And I somehow got away with that. Brian was brilliant.

Did you tell Brian Dennehy what to think at that moment?

No. I was aware that Brian was making the transition from actor to director. It seemed to me like he was a little bored with acting. He'd ask me, "What do you have in mind for this scene?" And I would tell him and he'd say, "Alright, fine" or "I don't see it like that. I think it's . . ." When we got to this final scene, he said, "What do you want me to be emoting here?" And I said, "Nothing. I just want to bring the camera in close. And whatever happens happens." So he just sat there. As the camera moved in on his seemingly emotionless face, he made this little smirk . . . It was subtle and very right.

My interpretation of Dennehy's expression in that final moment is that he was amazed that life could still surprise him. It's true that he's caused himself and his wife a lot of pain, but it's also true that he's more alive at the end of the movie than he was at the beginning.

I like that. I think there's still the possibility that he could get back together with his wife one day, because he really is not a womanizer. He had to pay such a high price—his wife and his daughter both felt betrayed by what he did—but I think it's true that he was doing more than just having an affair. It was something, like you're saying, that made him feel alive again. That happens to a lot of men and women. The routine just becomes unbearable. "I've got to do something to break this." And as damaging as an affair can be, it's worth it at that moment because they just can't live with themselves if they don't do something.

And then it's a question of whether the other person can accept that. And whether or not they *should* accept it. That's a pretty complicated question—not the kind of thing you usually get in a movie of the week.

It got really good ratings and did incredibly well in the reviews, so I was happy. Most people saw the finished film as a very clean piece of storytelling, and they empathized with Brian's character.

This was the first in a group of films where you directed some of cinema's top leading men. Next up was *The Lies Boys Tell*, which featured Kirk Douglas. What was it like working with him?

He scared me. I mean, forget that he's Kirk Douglas, *The Actor.* He's just intimidating as a person. He'd say [does a Kirk Douglas impression with gritted teeth], "If you make me go down these fucking stairs one more time . . ." I'd say, "I'm sorry, the camera jammed." Then he'd say, "That's not *my* fault." There were times when I could see his fist clenching up and I thought, *He's going to cold-cock me. He's going to knock me from here to Mississippi . . .* Then I will have this great story about the time Kirk Douglas knocked me out on set. He was a no-nonsense guy. He knew his job and he did it. He is a star.

Kirk came ready. He would go over his lines again and again, and he would do the exact same nuances and the exact same gestures every single time. I tried to suggest changes, but whenever I did that, it turned into a war. That was just the way he acted. That was his style, and he didn't have enough faith in me to break from that. He'd spent too many years doing it the way he did it, and he didn't want to give the director too much control. He came from the "star system" in Hollywood and he'd produced so many of his own movies. He figured nobody knew Kirk better than Kirk. When you're dealing with that kind of legendary talent, you're just along for the ride. He had already made his creative choices.

Kirk Douglas on the set of *The Lies Boys Tell*

Now although he really was a force to be reckoned with, it was an amazing experience. I constantly kept saying to myself, "That's Kirk Douglas." He's so mannered and so easy to imitate—all the things that a movie star is supposed to be. A person can say a couple of words [in his voice] and you know immediately "that's Kirk Douglas." Working with him was great. Occasionally I would get a compliment from Mr. Douglas: "Now *that's* a good idea that you *finally* gave me." That was the greatest compliment I could get.

***The Lies Boys Tell* seems like a natural fit for you at this period in your career. For the first half of the '90s, you were making movies about family dynamics. You'd just done two movies that allowed you to draw on your relationship with your mother. Now along comes a movie that's about a father/son relationship, where the father (played by Kirk Douglas) is part of that same stoic generation that your father came from . . . Coincidence?**

I didn't think about that. *The Lies Boys Tell* was based on a really interesting book about a father and son who don't get along. The father decides he wants to die in the bed he was born in, and he needs to be driven across the country so he can accomplish this. He chooses his hippie/deadbeat son because they disagreed on so many things in life. On that road trip, they reconnect and both find the love that they need back in their life.

The book [by Lamar Herrin] was purchased as a vehicle for Kirk Douglas and Michael Douglas to do together. Kirk was attached and Michael was planning to do it, but then when the film was green-lighted Michael was already doing another movie. Kirk still wanted to do it, so the producers decided to look for another actor to play his son. They brought in Craig T. Nelson, and he wanted me as director. I came in, met with the producers and got the job. We had a script by Ernest Thompson, who had won the Oscar for *On Golden Pond*. It was a huge compliment to me that I was going to be able to direct a script from that caliber of writer, with these two wonderful actors.

Now there's something I want to say about TV movies. A lot of people think that with TV movies you basically take whatever you're given. I was blessed that after I did *In a Child's Name*, I was able to choose from a number of projects that interested me—based on the way I was feeling at a particular time. I did go through a period of being estranged from my father. That was over by the time I made this movie, but I was still haunted by that period when I couldn't really connect with him. So there are some things from my life that made their way into the film.

You said that when your father died, you suddenly realized that you had a lot of questions that you'd never get to ask him. That's what this movie is all about—Craig's character is getting an opportunity to connect with the father he lost years ago.

It's a wish-fulfillment fantasy for me, but played out in a completely different arena. It's a bit of a dark story because you know Dad's going to die. But it's also a screwball comedy character piece. Basically it's two men struggling with their last chance to say something to each other.

I tackled that same theme when I did a play called "Bullpen," written by Steve Kluger. It was about bunch of baseball players who are warming up for a game, and they all know that one of the guys is about to get cut from the team. They don't know who it is, but they know one of them is going to get cut. So all these guys start opening up and saying things to one another that they've never had a chance to say or could be open enough to say. We had some terrific emotional scenes because it really addressed issues that are hard for guys to talk about with other guys. The characters cared for each other, but for years had done nothing but tease and rag on each other's faults. Now they're trying to resolve a lot of stuff, all within the period of one game.

The Lies Boys Tell had the same kind of setup. The characters know that a lot needs to be said in a short amount of time. Kirk's character needed to talk about the way things used to be. He had ignored the way the world works for so long that he really was bothered that things had changed so much. And we needed the romance—when his character visits a woman from his past—to soften the edges. The whole thing had that homespun, nostalgic quality. I brought as much Capra to it as I could bring. If it had been a feature, I think it would have been one of those features that people really talked about—because I think you can't help but love spending time with these characters. The best stories I have from that movie are my various adventures with Kirk.

We shot the movie on the outskirts of San Jose, and we were all staying at a hotel in downtown San Jose. Every morning I was awakened by the phone at about 6:30. "Tom, it's Kirk. Are you up?" "Yessir, yes I am." "Why don't you come down here and let's go over today's work?" "Yessir, okay." I'd get up, get dressed as fast as I could, splash some water on my face, try to sneak out of the room so I wouldn't wake Nancy and the kids, and go down the hall to his room.

Kirk had already been up for two hours. He'd had breakfast and he was full of energy. He'd say, "I just want to go over today's work. See what you think. See if you're okay with it . . . as the director." There was a thinly veiled message in that statement: *You better not have a problem with it.* But he was respectful enough to say, "I just want to make sure you're okay with it."

So I would read the other character's lines and he'd go through the scene. He would always do it in grand Kirk Douglas style, and

Tom, producer Patricia Meyer, and the principal cast of *The Lies Boys Tell*

then say, "What do you think?" I'd say, "Yeah, it's good." "Any comments?" I'd make a few minor suggestions and he'd say, "No, no, no. Anything else?" "Well . . ." I sort of learned that I pretty much had to love it the way he gave it to me. At the end of this early morning session, he'd say, "Okay, I think it's a good scene. Today's going to be a good day, don't you think?" And I'd say, "Yessir, I do."

A few hours later, I'd arrive on set and the A.D. would say, "Mr. Douglas would like to see you in his dressing room." I'd say okay. Go over and knock on his door. "Yeah, what's up Kirk?" "Tom, I just thought we should go over today's work. Go over these scenes. Just see what you think, see if you're okay with it." "Um . . . We already did . . . sir." "What do you mean we already did?" "This morning, when I came into your room . . ." "We didn't go over *these* scenes today." "Yeah we did." [more forceful, gritting his teeth] "*We didn't go over* these scenes *today*." "You're right, sir, I'm sorry . . . that was yesterday, I'm so sorry. Yeah let's go over today's scenes." "I just want you to take a look and see if there's anything . . ." And then we'd go through the exact same routine.

I quickly realized that sometimes he had a short-term memory problem. On the other hand, he could regale you with stories about his first job, his relationship with his father, the first time he saw Michael perform at the West Side Jewish Theater . . . and how horrible he was when he wouldn't give him [Michael] a compliment afterwards . . . all in incredible detail. But short-term things just . . . fell right out. At the end of the day, when it got dark and we were heading into that twelfth hour, he'd say, "Well, I guess I'm done for the day." And I'd say, "No, we've got another hour and two more scenes to shoot. " He'd say, "No, *you've* got two more scenes to shoot." I'd say, "Well . . . you're in them." "No I'm not." And off he would go.

Well, he was getting up at 4 a.m. every morning to go over his lines . . .

Yeah. He was on a set clock. That was the old Hollywood studio system routine. They didn't work these insane eighteen-hour days like we do now. They got up early, worked on set all day, and came home at night.

I'm glad you weren't directing him in a horror movie, or something that took place mostly at night . . .

He'd never do that anyway. We had to take a much later call [time], and convince him there was no way we could cheat the night scenes day-for-night. He always seemed to be surprised: "That's a night scene—really? Isn't there any way you could shoot it during the day?" He really did get me thinking about whether or not there was a way I could get around shooting at night.

He would be very adamant about doing things a certain way. Normally when you have scenes where a character is in bed and other actors are standing around them, you have to keep moving things around and angling the actors to get the proper coverage. When we were shooting one of the bed scenes, I said to him, "We can get a much better angle if you could just turn this way." "Why?" I started to explain, "Because the camera . . ." He stopped me and said, "Look—the money is on this face, not on the goddamn black box." He always referred to the camera as "that goddamn black box." He made it clear that I had to live with a slightly cockeyed angle, or move the goddamn black box—because he was *not* going to move. He did what felt natural to him and the black box just had to deal with it.

My biggest thrill was watching him and Craig T. Nelson play off of each other. Craig had so much respect for Kirk and he exuded an incredible love for him as an actor. They really did have fun together. I remember one day we were shooting a driving scene and they started singing "Whale of a Tail" from *20,000 Leagues Under the Sea*, incredibly loud. I thought, *It just doesn't get any better than this.*

You must have felt the same way about working with Jason Robards in your next film, ***Journey.***

Jason was absolutely the consummate actor. No complaints, no attitude. Would do as many takes as you want. Always asking, "Are you happy?" Always had a sense of humor about the proceedings. And he could deliver these astounding moments as the character. He never planned them, but just allowed them to happen.

That also describes Robards's character in ***Journey.*** **As tough as he is, he's willing and able to adapt and conform to whatever his grandson needs. He doesn't expect the kid to adapt to him.**

Exactly. Jason, as a New York stage-based actor, doesn't have the kind of "movie star" persona that Kirk Douglas has. But whatever he does—whether it's a starring role or a smaller character part—has so much emotional weight and truth. As an actor, he's committed to every word, and he can convey so much without having to say *anything* . . .

It's the experience behind the eyes.

Exactly. He's so down to earth that you can talk to him like an average Joe, but you'll catch a glimpse of this man who has *worlds* of experience. One day he went into a story about how he basically

Jason Robards and Brenda Fricker in *Journey* (Hallmark, 1995)

took Lauren Bacall away from Humphrey Bogart and they went off and had an affair. He always told stories like that with such simple honestly. It wasn't bragging. He was just sharing a story that was part of his life.

Brenda Fricker was also quite unique. She had this ritual . . . On the first day of the shoot she came over to me and said, "There's something I do with every director on the first day. I press a silver coin into his hand." And she gave me this silver Irish coin. Then she said, "I have to tell you the truth. I lost me husband, I lost me boyfriend, and I only agreed to do this movie because I need the money, so I don't know what you're gonna get. But give me enough Guinness and I'll get through it." And you know, she was solid as a rock.

The best Brenda moment was with Meg Tilly. We had a scene where Meg and Brenda confront each other out in a field. We had already staged the scene, but then a big, dark cloud came overhead and we had to readjust the lighting. When Meg came to the set, she said, "Wait a minute, why are we shooting it over there?" I explained to her that we had a lighting issue. She said, "Well, I'd rather do it next to this tree." I explained why we couldn't, because we'd be shooting the wrong way and the light was going to change. Then I turned to my D.P. and said, "Right?" He said, "Yes, that's going to be very harsh on her. It's not going to make her look very good." Meg said, "I don't care about that. I just really feel like I need to be next to this tree." Brenda's standing a short distance away, smoking a cigarette, watching this situation unfold. And I've got a crew of eighty people standing there, listening to us go back and forth.

In all fairness, I should have talked to her first. I should have worked that out before I had the whole thing lit. And of course I was careful after that, because certain actors really do want to be part of the staging and the blocking. With this particular scene, the difference just seemed too miniscule to me. So we went on for what felt like twenty minutes. "What if?" "No." "What if?" "No." "Well, can't you?" "No, we can't." Back and forth, back and forth. Finally, out of absolute frustration, I turned to Brenda Fricker. Here's this Oscar Award winning actress, standing here watching the director fighting with his actress. I said, "Brenda, what do you think about this? Does this make any sense to you?" She just looked at me and said, "I'd bloody well tell her to fuck off." Everybody broke up laughing. I looked at Meg and she said, "Okay, let's do it." Brenda saved my ass in that moment.

Was Meg Tilly channeling her character's stubbornness?

Meg really knew what she wanted. Her character was a woman who kept leaving her children behind with the grandparents as she went to try and find herself. She would get involved with men for a while, then come back, then leave again with another man. She would not sacrifice her own freedom for her kids. She just had not grown up. One day, early in the process, I was talking to her

Meg Tilly in *Journey* (Hallmark, 1995)

about this character, and I said, "How do you think she rationalizes these decisions to herself?" And she looked at me and said, "What do you mean how do I *rationalize* it? Am I supposed to drag these kids with me to a motel? And if I meet a guy that night, what am I supposed to do with them then? It's even worse if I have them there with me!" She continued with this impassioned response because she had inhabited the character 100%. She argued it so convincingly, and that's what makes her a great actress.

When I would talk to her about her own kids, she was just as strong. She talked about how, if her kids failed in school, she'd let them fail. "It's their responsibility," she said. Suddenly I thought, *God, she really is an amazingly strong personality and a strong mother.* And after she did this movie, she decided to stop acting and become a full-time mom.

Maybe she had too much trouble juggling her life as an actress and her role as a mother. How have you managed to be both a family man and a filmmaker?

A huge part of my life is the fact that my wife is an actress. I always try to see if there's a role for her in the movies I direct. If so it's wonderful for both of us. Plus it helps me to treat the movie as an extension of my life. When they were little, my kids were often in the background some of some scenes. As they got older they had dialogue scenes in some of my movies. I always tried to connect my family to my work.

The first time I met Francis Ford Coppola, I asked him if he had any advice for an aspiring director. His response was, "Keep your family together. That's the most important and the hardest thing—making your family part of this." Obviously, I took that to heart. Once I had the success with *In a Child's Name*, I built it into my contract that if someone wanted to hire me, they also had to provide first class tickets for my wife and my kids. My price was higher than some other directors because of those extra requirements, but for me it was mandatory. I turned down projects where the producers didn't want to meet that requirement. But this decision really helped to keep our family together.

Shane learned to ride a bike on a movie set. Hannah took her first steps on a movie set. All those things are huge moments that I would have missed had I not made them part of the process. Some people say, "How can you keep your sanity when you're constantly balancing film *and* a young family?" Well, there were times when it took a toll on my sanity—having to be focused at work, then focused enough to also deal with personal issues at home.

And it's not a nine-to-five job where you get to come home at the end of the day and then deal with your family life. Everything overlaps.

Everything overlaps. If Nancy's feeling insecure about her work that day, it's not like I can just say, "Look, I don't want to hear it right now" . . . although there were times when I did say that, and

The McLoughlin family at Paddington Station in London, 1995.

times when I wasn't the best husband, because I was an exhausted, grumpy director who just didn't want to talk to anybody about anything. I just wanted to chill. And then oddly there were other times when our family issues mirrored aspects of the show, and gave me ideas at midnight that I might not have come up with if I was just sitting alone in a hotel room, going over the next day's shot list. So there's good and bad. But the most important part is that the family stayed together.

I remember when Hannah was very young, maybe three or four years old, she and Nancy were in downtown San Francisco. They were discussing something when suddenly Hannah looked up at the tallest skyscraper and declared, "If I fell from up there, my daddy would catch me." She then continued her talk with Nancy, which had nothing to do with this statement. Nancy told me later

The McLoughlin family at Paddington Station in London, 2005.

that Hannah had said it as if this "fact" had suddenly entered her mind. She just shared it, then returned to the previous topic. To know someone feels that secure and trusting of you is such an indescribable feeling. The deep sense of responsibility I have for my children is a true blessing. I never want to lose that bond.

PART V: MORE MYTHS & MONSTERS

Ghosts and innocents / Arthur Conan Doyle, Harry Houdini and the power of imagination / Yes, Burbank, there is a Santa Claus / "Survival movies" / Exit elves? / Meeting Marlon Brando / A Hawksian love story / The return of The Exorcist / Tone wars

FILMOGRAPHY

THE TURN OF THE SCREW (A.K.A. THE HAUNTING OF HELEN WALKER) (CBS, 1995)
PRODUCED AND DIRECTED BY TOM MCLOUGHLIN
TELEPLAY BY HUGH WHITMORE. BASED ON A NOVEL BY HENRY JAMES.
STARRING VALERIE BERTINELLI, ALED ROBERTS, FLORENCE HOATH, DIANA RIGG
  A nanny believes that the children she is caring for are becoming possessed by ghosts.

A DIFFERENT KIND OF CHRISTMAS (LIFETIME, 1996)
DIRECTED BY TOM MCLOUGHLIN
TELEPLAY BY BART BAKER.
STARRING SHELLEY LONG, BRUCE KIRBY, BARRY BOSTWICK
  A woman struggles with her father's insistence on being Santa Claus, 365 days a year.

FAIRY TALE: A TRUE STORY (ICON, 1997)
DIRECTED BY CHARLES STURRIDGE.
SCREENPLAY BY ERNIE CONTRERAS. BASED ON A STORY BY TOM MCLOUGHLIN & ARTHUR ASH.

Starring Peter O'Toole, Harvey Keitel, Florence Hoath, Phoebe Nicholls
Two young girls convince an entire country to believe in magic.

"Leaving L.A."—Pilot (ABC, 1997)
Directed by Tom McLoughlin
Teleplay by Nancy Miller.
Starring Chris Meloni, Melina Kanakaredes
A day in the life of Los Angeles coroner's investigators.

The Third Twin (CBS, 1997)
Directed by Tom McLoughlin
Teleplay by Cindy Myers. Based on a novel by Ken Follett.
Starring Kelly McGillis, Jason Hedrick
A criminologist falls for a younger man while investigating his killer clone.

Behind the Mask (CBS, 1999)
Directed by Tom McLoughlin
Teleplay by Gregory Goodell
Starring Donald Sutherland, Matthew Fox
True story of a doctor who is saved by a mentally ill patient, and subsequently becomes his closest friend.

Anya's Bell (CBS, 1999)
Directed by Tom McLoughlin
Teleplay by David Alexander
Starring Della Reese, Mason Gamble
A socially awkward boy and an elderly blind woman become friends, and draw each other out of their shells.

"The Others"—"Theta" (CBS, 2000)
Directed by Tom McLoughlin
Teleplay by Fred Golan
Starring Julianne Nicholson, Gabriel Macht, Melissa Lahlitah Crider, Jeanette Brox
Three young paranormal investigators help a demonically-possessed teenage girl.

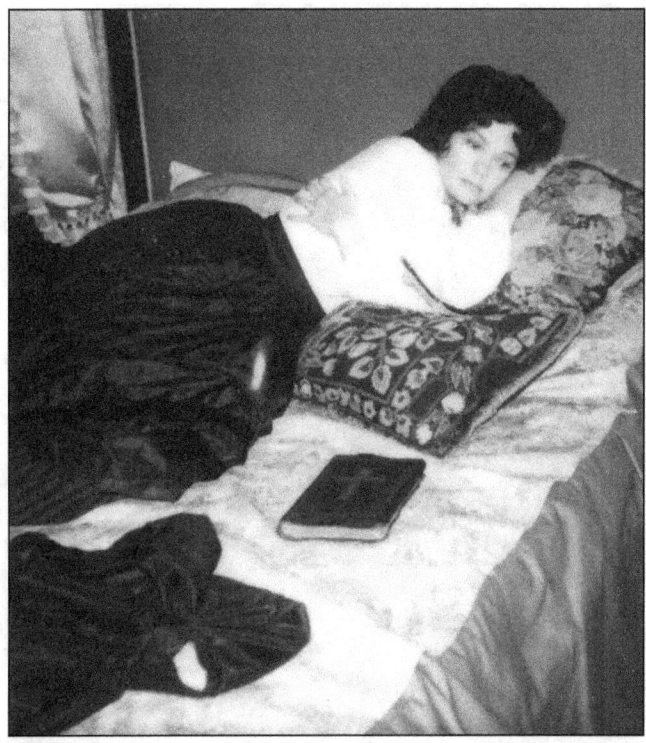

Valerie Bertinelli as Helen Walker

In 1995, you got back to your horror roots and made an adaptation of Henry James's ghost story *The Turn of the Screw*.

That was a thrill because I am a huge fan of *The Innocents* [Jack Clayton's 1960 film adaptation of the same story]. I didn't think I could make a better adaptation than that, but I took the chance to try a different approach to the story. I wanted to make the kids more sexual, which I thought would be really creepy, and I wanted to enhance those Victorian gothic details—to embrace James's combination of love and fear.

Basically CBS said, "We'll do it if Valerie Bertinelli plays the governess." I said, "That won't work. I'm not going to ask her to do an English accent—because even if she did it brilliantly, nobody would buy it. She's *America's* sweetheart!" They eventually convinced me that the character could be an *American* governess. Valerie did a terrific job, but I don't think she ever felt 100% comfortable doing a period piece.

Tom and Nancy McLoughlin with Alec Roberts and Florence Hoath

I focused a lot on the kids. They were incredible young actors. The boy Alec Roberts [who played Miles] was amazing. When he smiled, I could see this old soul inside of him. To me that was fascinating. And Florence Hoath [who played Flora] was so smart and so captivating. They really did seem like adults in some of their scenes—like when Miles kisses the governess and then sits back on the pillow and gives her this smug, seductive look. I couldn't tell him to give that look—I can't even remember what I said to him or what he was thinking—but he got it. And it was very creepy.

The Henry James novel works because it effectively puts the reader into the governess's head. It's a document of subjectivity. Did you approach the film the same way—telling the story from her perspective?

What *The Innocents* did so well was convey that *this is absolutely happening*. The ghosts are *absolutely real*. There's no gauze on the lens to make you wonder. There's nothing dreamy about their appearance. Likewise, I tried to keep the coverage really simple. What you see is what's really there. It only got more stylized toward the end of the movie, when Quint is coming down the stairs. In that scene we take the governess's now maniac perspective, but overall the ghost scenes were more objective.

The first time we see a ghost in the film, it's only a fleeting glimpse. Later, the ghosts are featured much more prominently. In general, do you think it's more effective to feature the ghosts or leave them somewhat to the audience's imagination?

I did not want to make a moment out of that first scene with the face in the glass. Thinking back on it now, I should have made it even shorter. It should have been so fleeting that she thinks it could have been her own reflection. It's just a tiny pebble in the water. Those moments build and build to the point that, in the end, we completely believe that Miles is being completely corrupted and that the governess has to save him. Ultimately, I always go back to what Capra said: This is a people to people medium. If you care about the people, you go along for the ride. I wanted the audience to be totally invested in all these characters, no matter how surreal the circumstances.

You crafted a much more visually elaborate final sequence than the one in *The Innocents*—with these wildly impressionistic shadows and Quint looking like Nosferatu.

I was never happy with the ending. It never got as big, emotionally, as I wanted it to be. I tried a lot of in-camera effects that weren't as successful as I'd hoped—like when the room starts to get dark.

What I had in my mind was shadowy fingers going up the wall and across the ceiling. Even a decently-rendered CGI effect would have done the trick, but there was no budget for that. There was so much pressure to get through everything as quickly as possible that I really didn't have a chance to refine.

What I think worked well was the death of Miles. If you haven't read *The Turn of the Screw*, I don't think you'd expect him to die—so that sequence is a real shock. We originally temped the sequence with Beethoven's *Moonlight Sonata*. To me the familiarity of that piece enhanced those images much better than any original composition ever could.

After so many years of making reality-based stories, is it hard for you to go back to horror?

Horror, to me, *is* more challenging now. The easy thing to say is that audiences have seen so much horror that it's hard to shock them these days. I don't believe that, because movies like *The Sixth Sense* and *The Others* can still work. The audience can still get just as invested in the story and still be just as surprised by the outcome. The challenge is getting audiences to get emotionally invested, so the first thing I always look at is character because the characters are what pull *me* into the story.

I also loved shooting in England. A lot of the crew members had worked on the classic Hammer horror movies. Tony Imi was my director of photography, and we lit the movie like one of those old Hammer films and tried to make it feel like it had been made during that particular time. Because Valerie was an American in England, there's that "stranger in a strange land" quality. When we got to the actual haunting, I wanted to convey a sense of hollowness. I wanted to emphasize the idea that she's lost in a big place that she doesn't know very well, and it's all disorienting. That was the tone.

The greatest thing that can happen to a director is to read a script and know immediately what the tone of the movie needs to be. Then your goal is to maintain that tone through prep, through the shoot, and through post—right down to the ending credits—so that it feels cohesive. Even if you're trying to achieve different emotional content within different scenes, the story as a whole never moves away from that basic tone and point of view that you, as a storyteller, bring to it. That's the ideal.

***Fairy Tale: A True Story* is similar to *The Turn of the Screw* in that it asks the audience to suspend their disbelief in the supernatural. How did you get involved with that one?**

It started when I went to Paris to study with Marceau. My trip to over there was one of the most emotional experiences of my life. I'd just left everything and everyone I knew—my girlfriend, family, friends, the band. I got to Paris and I was about to check into the Hotel Des Arts in Montmartre. I walk in; I'm exhausted; I haven't slept in two days; I'm trying to get the concierge to understand me. Then I hear a voice: "Hey, are you American?" I turn around and it was Albert Ash. He was from Fresno, California. A few years later, he became part of the L.A. Mime Company.

Now cut to two decades later and I'm a filmmaker, Albert came to me and said, "Did you ever hear about the true story of the two little girls who photographed fairies?" He had this idea of doing a TV series about "myths, truths and the greatest cons in history": Bigfoot, The Loch Ness Monster, and this story. I was trying to get out of television, so I said, "What about doing the fairy story as a feature?" We met many times and talked out the story over a period of months. I thought we should bring the mother into the story, and that the girls should plan this con not just as a lark, but for a better reason. In our story they do it because Elsie's brother, who recently died, really did believe in fairies. They wanted to give Elsie's grieving mother a sense that she could perhaps connect with her son, through his beliefs.

Albert wasn't confident enough to write the script alone. He wanted us to do it together, but I was directing a lot at that point and didn't have the time. But we wanted to pitch it around town. So we worked out the story, got some pictures and put together a presentation, and started presenting it to pretty much anybody that would listen. Albert did most of the pitching because he's so animated. I would try to keep certain things grounded while he

Tom and Albert Ash as Dufus and Big Al

would go off on details, so we made a very good pitching team. We always got the same response: "Well, this is interesting . . . Sweet story, but it's got three problems. It's about girls. It's a period piece. And it's British." I remember one person said, "If you change it to boys and set it in present-day America . . ." We were like, "Boys and *fairies*?" They said, "Well, then, maybe it can't be fairies. How about tiny aliens?" We were hitting one brick wall after another.

One of the toughest things in Hollywood is pitching something really original. If there's not already something out there like it, then most people can't see the potential. If you go in and say "It's sort of like *E.T.*" then they might be open to it. No one was connecting with our story. Finally, after almost two years of taking it around the industry, we pitched it to Wendy Finerman, who had a deal at Paramount. We only knew her from *Hot to Trot*, the talking horse movie. So we felt we had pretty much hit bottom.

Afterward, she mentioned that she had seen my film *The Yarn Princess*. She asked me how Jean Smart had prepared for her role, and I said that we went to a place up in the Sylmar area called Tierra del Sol and visited with some of the mentally-challenged people there. She said, "Oh great, because I'm doing a movie right now about a mentally-challenged man. I think I'll take Tom up there." I didn't think much about it at the time. About a year later, along comes *Forrest Gump*—produced by Wendy Finerman for Paramount.

Much to my shock, she contacted me and said, "The next movie I want to do is *Fairy Tale*." Suddenly we had this amazing opportunity. I had been willing to make the movie for four to six million dollars, and try to find some cheap way to do it—maybe as a co-production with the BBC or something. We knew we had to do it in England. We knew we need English actors and we knew period shooting would be expensive, so we figured we'd have to really minimize the locations and the spectacle. Now suddenly it was going to be a thirty-two million dollar movie with an Academy Award winning producer attached.

We looked for the best writer we could find for this kind of material. My lawyer Alan Wertheimer represented Ernie Contreras. He was brought in and we thought he was the right choice to write the screenplay. By this point, we were regretting the fact that we had not written the original screenplay. Even if it had to be rewritten, we would have been more strongly attached to the property. So, word to the wise out there: *write the screenplay yourself*. It will help you down the road when your dream project becomes a reality.

Now I'm going to these meetings at Paramount with Sherry Lansing, the head of the studio. She couldn't have been nicer about the project. At the same time, I had just been given the green light on my adaptation of *The Turn of the Screw*, after years of trying to get it off the ground. So I said, "Sherry, it's going to take a while to get the script in shape. So I'm going over to England for seven or eight weeks to shoot. The good news is that I'm going to be casting girls for that project, so I can pre-cast for *Fairy Tale*." She said, "Great." I took off for England. Then the tide turned. Paramount wanted a "name director" for their thirty-two million dollar film.

Lasse Holstrom was approached to direct. He read the script and loved it. I had to make a phone call to Paramount and say, "In the contract, it stipulates that I'm attached as director." But the fine print said that I would get to be a director, a writer *or* producer. I was thinking that I'd get all three credits, but the wording was "either/or." Ultimately it came down to someone saying, "If you want this movie to get made, you can't stand in the way." For me, that was a major heartbreak. This was a story I was really looking forward to doing. It was a longtime passion and I knew I could bring something wonderful to it.

That said, one of my favorite movies is *My Life as a Dog* [directed by Lasse Holstrom], so if anybody was going to take the reins, I was thrilled that it would be Lasse. From that standpoint, I said, "Okay, I want to see this movie get made." I licked my wounds and moved on.

In the meantime, a movie called *The Indian in the Cupboard* was released. Beautiful movie, very well done . . . but it did not make much money. Then Warner Brothers released *A Little Princess* by Alfonso Cuaron—another childhood fantasy with a period setting—and it didn't make money. Suddenly the thirty-two million dollar budget for *Fairy Tale* became eleven million, and Lasse was smart enough to know that all these special effects that he'd planned would not be possible on that kind of budget. So he left the project.

The great fear was that the whole thing would fall apart. I began lobbying to come back as director, and there were some discussions about me doing it. Then Mel Gibson stepped in to produce the film. The new deal was that the movie had to be filmed by an exclusively British cast and crew. So once again I

Florence Hoath in *Fairy Tale* (Paramount, 1997)

was out. They started looking for a British director and hired Charles Sturridge, who had done *Brideshead Revisited* and the *Gulliver's Travels* miniseries that Robert Halmi produced.

He shot a pretty straight-ahead movie. There was nothing terribly inventive about his coverage, but he is an artisan and he surrounded himself with the best of the British crews. They had a visual effects company that really wanted to break new ground with the fairies, and it was actually quite amazing what they pulled off. I was able to get Florence Hoath, who I had worked with on *The Turn of the Screw*, in the movie and of course she was brilliant.

It was also a huge honor getting Peter O'Toole to play Sir Arthur Conan Doyle. And Harvey Keitel. At first, I thought: *Harvey Keitel as Harry Houdini?!* But he pulled it off. I think I would have emphasized Houdini even more. When I used to pitch the story with Albert, one of the selling points was that the story would work for both boys and girls. I wanted to give Frances a little bit of a tomboy quality. I think the finished film was a bit distancing for boys, but girls and their mothers adored it. So did the critics. I don't think it got one bad review. Everybody seemed impressed that it was such an adult look at childhood; very respectful and very classy. I credit Charles Sturridge for that. I also thought it was cool that Mel Gibson gave himself a little cameo at the end. Most people didn't catch that.

Sherry Lansing, being the incredible Hollywood executive that she is, kept me involved in the process the whole time. Even though I immediately went on to do another movie, she called me up to share the box office numbers when it opened. She talked about their plan for their upcoming week, and how they were going to change the publicity. She was very committed to making it as successful as possible. The movie opened very well, but it dropped 50 or 60% the next week. It did not have the legs we all hoped it would. We were definitely ahead of the curve on fairies becoming a popular subject. Now Tinker Bell is a superstar.

Watching *Fairy Tale* today, I can't help comparing it to the magical realism of *Pan's Labyrinth*. Both movies are very firmly grounded in a historical setting, but the supernatural is seamlessly integrated into that reality. In *Fairy Tale*, you've got World War I, Sir Arthur Conan Doyle, Harry Houdini . . . and then you integrate myths and the supernatural. That's a delicate balance.

All of those historical details were added during the process of getting the movie made. The thing that made me want to tell this story was the idea of kids conning adults. This is a story about how a child's beliefs can be so strong that even a brilliant man like Sir Arthur Conan Doyle can be convinced. After the death of his son, these little girls gave him hope that there's something more to life than what we see every day . . . and something more *after* life.

When my father was a magician he saw Houdini's final performance in Detroit, so I grew up hearing stories about Houdini. He was a hero to me, and I loved the idea that he was a skeptic *because* he was a magician. He was a master of illusion, so it was easy for him to debunk people's claims about the existence of ghosts or fairies or anything supernatural. Then Arthur Conan Doyle, a man he admired for his brilliant mind, said that he believes these girls were telling the truth about the existence of fairies. Houdini had to decide how important it was to expose the truth, and possibly hurt someone he respected.

Ultimately, Houdini decides that what the girls are doing, they're doing for a good reason. This is a theme that I come back to again and again in my work. If people are coming from a place of love, trying to do something that helps other people, then I can't fault that person. They may not be doing what they're doing in a particularly moral or honest way, but their basic intentions are good. Of course, the flip side of that are murderers who convince themselves that they are right and that the acts they commit are a good thing. They convince themselves they have a good reason for killing someone.

In our original storyline outline, *Fairy Tale* was bookended by scenes of Elsie and Francis as old women. It opened with a BBC film crew coming down the road in Cottingsley, and Elsie and Francis nervously wondering whether or not they should reveal the truth after all these years. They did in fact do a BBC interview in which they finally confessed. In the interview, they revealed how they'd made the wings move and everything. Then at the end of the interview, someone said to Frances, "So you don't truly believe?" She responded, "Well, there were fairies . . . it's just we couldn't photograph them. But they are still out there." Elsie sort of looked at her, like, "Please, can we just let this thing go?" But she wouldn't . . . which I thought was great.

We wanted to end the film with a scene that takes place after the BBC crew has left. The two ladies are having their tea, and Frances says, "Can't we just go out to the garden one more time? Just to say goodbye . . ." Elsie figures this is something she needs for closure, so they walk out there and Frances says, "It was magical, wasn't it?" And as they walk, we start to see these strange lights appearing . . . We don't *show* anything. We leave it up to the viewer's imagination, and let them believe what they want to believe. Albert's original title for the script was "The Golden Afternoon," like the song from *Alice in Wonderland*. That was the aesthetic we wanted—that rich, beautiful, late-day sunlight that could seduce you to believe in magic.

Once again, so much in that movie is very personal for me. It's very much about my belief that believing in magic can help a person overcome pain . . . and my belief that sometimes when you've told a story for many years, the story becomes its own truth.

That reminds me of what Bruno Bettelheim[19] said about the importance of having magic and mystery in life . . .

For better or worse, I've infused that belief system into my kids. They believed in Santa Claus for the longest time. And the Easter Bunny, the Tooth Fairy, real fairies, leprechauns . . . I loved creating those fantasies. The visitations by Peter Pan and Tinker Bell were legendary in our household.

If we were on location, staying in a hotel somewhere, and one of my kids lost a tooth, when they woke up in the morning there would be a silver dollar under their pillow and a path of glitter (fairy dust) trailing away from their bed. One time I made a trail of glitter from Shane's hotel bed, across the room, under the door, down the hall, into the elevator, through the lobby and out to the street. For some reason, the hotel staff allowed me to do that. They got into the spirit of it. When he woke up, he followed that path all the way outside and looked skyward. He smiled because he was glad the tiny creature got out okay.

Once when we were in Ireland, he went searching the woods for leprechauns with one eye closed. He'd learned that secret technique from Darby O'Gill and the Little People. And every Saint Patrick's Day, we left out whiskey for the leprechauns. We set a box trap to try and catch them and get their gold. Of course we never caught them, but the leprechauns would always leave odd trinkets or notes of Irish wisdom . . . Nancy and I went WAY overboard. [laughs]

To this day, I wonder whether I messed up my kids' sense of reality. Maybe. I wonder, *Will that be a good thing for them in the future? Will it make them more creative?* Right now, they both absolutely love how unique their childhood was. Whenever I apologize and say I think I went too far, Shane says, "Dad, those

---

[19] Bruno Bettelheim (1903–1990), child psychologist and author of *The Uses of Enchantment: The Meaning and Importance of Fairy Tales* (1976)

Shane hunting leprechauns outside of Donegal, Ireland

"So come with me, where dreams are born, and time is never planned."
—*Peter Pan*

Shane with Peter Pan in Hyde Park, London

were some of the best times of my life." But I think sometimes it's hard for him and Hannah to let go of childhood because it was so magical. When I was a kid, I had to create all that on my own. I guess most of us do. As a father, I must have unconsciously thought it would be ideal to grow up with someone you trust creating the magic for you. I loved being the magician. I loved creating all those illusions and seeing the kids respond with such open hearts. For me, there really can be something magical in life. I don't think I'll ever stop believing in that.

It gets back to the basics of religion. Collectively, we've never gotten away from the idea that there is a God and that there are things in this world greater than ourselves, whether it's fairies or ghosts or people with special powers. I do believe that we mere mortals can make fantastical ideas real through the power of our imagination and belief.

When people ask me if I believe in ghosts, I always feel like I have to define "ghost" before I can answer the question.

Yeah, because if you say, "Yes there are ghosts and demons," people immediately assume that you mean something specific. We say "ghosts" because the phenomena pre-dates our scientific studies of energy, what we see with Kirlian photography. Once we figure things out scientifically, we'll use another term to define the phenomena, instead of "ghosts" or "spirits."

***A Different Kind of Christmas* fits into this conversation too. You talk about creating a world of fantasy-illusion for your kids, and how that might affect them as adults. That's more or less the backstory for *A Different Kind of Christmas*, which is about a grown woman whose father thinks he's Santa Claus.**

That was another longtime passion piece. There was a man named Robert George who lived about five blocks from here [in Glendale, California], who believed he was Santa Claus, and he felt that Christmas should be 365 days a year. He drove around town in a red Cadillac, yelling, "Merry Christmas!" I found out

The real Mr. and Mrs. Robert George, with Shane and Hannah McLoughlin

about him from a story in the local newspaper. The headline was: *Should Santa Claus be shut down?*

Now maybe he was a little *un-normal* . . . but so what. He was helping people. If a kid had a terminal disease, you could bring him or her—at any time of the year—to sit on Santa's lap. People donated toys to this man, so that every kid who visited his house would walk out with a toy. It was amazing we have this fantasy character in our neighborhood. He was one of those unique individuals who make life worth living. I love him and his Mrs. Claus, Stella.

Bart [Baker, the screenwriter of *A Different Kind of Christmas*] took that idea and said, "Well, what if you were this guy's son? Would you try to convince him that he's NOT Santa Claus?" It was a little bit of a *Miracle of 34th Street* thing. We took the script to CBS and got it set up. Then a new regime came in and said, "We're not going to do your Christmas movie, but would you like to instead do a new pilot of this series called *Touched by an*

Angel?" I said no, took the movie to Lifetime and they said, "Well if you can change the son to a daughter, then we'll do it." So we did. Martha Williamson did the rewrite, then became the writer and showrunner of *Touched by an Angel*. Had I chosen to do the pilot of *Touched by an Angel*, I'd be very rich today, like Martha. Oh well.

One of the first actresses who read the script was Shelley Long. I didn't think there was any chance she was going to do it, but she thought it was great. Then we cast Eddie Albert to play the Santa Claus character—not realizing that this poor guy was in no condition to do it. By the end of the first day, we could see that it wasn't going to work. Carol Newman, the producer, said, "I'm bringing in somebody else to play the role." I asked who, and she said, "Bruce Kirby—Bruno Kirby's dad." I was incredibly nervous because I'd spent years developing this project and now we were blindly recasting the lead roles. But I didn't have any choice. We needed somebody on a plane who could start *tomorrow*.

In comes Mr. Kirby, and he couldn't have been nicer. He couldn't have been more of a team player. He was absolutely the right choice. My daughter Hannah is a scene with him. She's the little girl in McDonald's who says, "Don't I get a toy with that?" She was about six when we shot that. I did not want her to do it, but I was convinced (by my former assistant Melissa, and my wife) to let her come in and read, and I said, "Fine—but she has to come in with all the other actors and read." She only gets the part if she gives the best read. And she did.

This is the first of two Christmas movies that you did. Since *It's a Wonderful Life* was such a profound influence on you, I'm wondering if you feel that building stories around the holidays adds extra emotion to a story?

Yes and no. The thing that I thought was great about this particular story was that it's a classic show business story about being a celebrity's kid. Shelley Long's character hated the fact, in her childhood, that all the other kids gravitated toward her because Santa was her father. She was so embarrassed. She wanted to disassociated from her father altogether. I saw that happen with

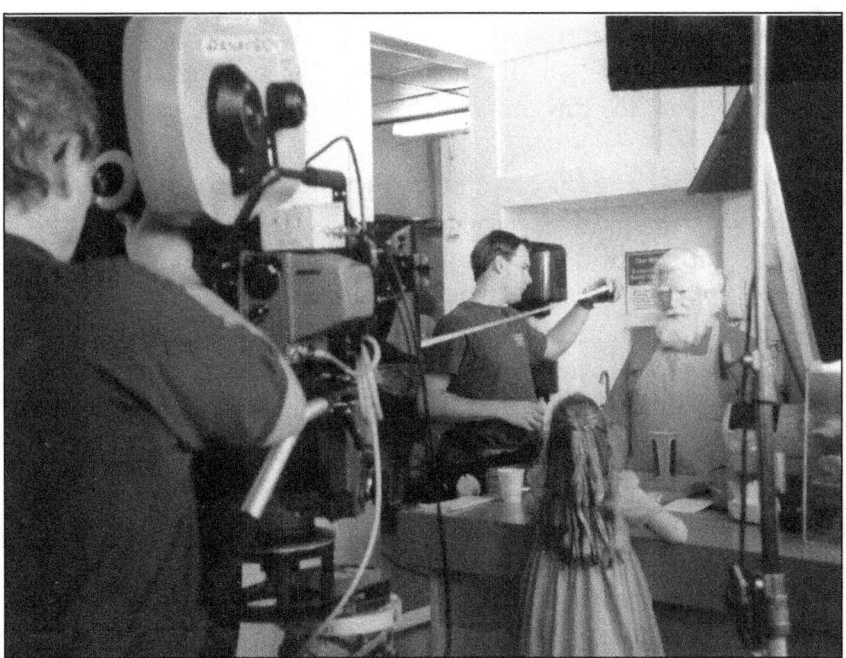

Bruce Kirby as Santa Claus in *A Different Kind of Christmas*

Hannah McLoughlin in *A Different Kind of Christmas*

my son Shane at a certain point, when he decided that he didn't want to be labeled "the director's son." On set, he felt he was only known as "the director's son." He had no identity other than that.

The Shelley Long character wants to avoid all the embarrassment, but she's struggling with her decision to cut herself off entirely from her father. How can you deny your parent something that is so much a part of them? Her father wasn't doing anything wrong. He just had a unique calling, to say the least . . . and maybe he was letting his celebrity go to his head a little bit. On top of this, her feelings about her father are compounded by what happened on the day her mother died. This was all based on the true story. The real Robert George went to the hospital to be with his wife when she was dying. The hospital staff asked him if he would mind going down to the children's wing and play Santa to the kids there. When he came back, his wife was dead. He never forgave himself for not being there when she died.

There's a choice that appears again and again in your movies. The father has to choose between heaven and earth, fantasy and reality . . . like Tim Matheson at the end of *Sometimes They Come Back* or Craig T. Nelson in *The Fire Next Time*. Is that a dilemma you relate to personally?

It's my *Peter Pan* syndrome, I guess. I've always loved that quote from J.M. Barrie's book: "To die will be an awfully big adventure." It's not that I'm morose, but I do remember my mortality every day. I'm not afraid of death, but when it comes I don't want to have any regrets. I feel like there are so many things I need to do before I die. I want to make a film that *really* has a positive effect on people's lives. A movie for all those like me, who don't ever want to surrender that childlike feeling of discovery. A film to deeply believe in.

It's an amazing power that great movies have—because they're speaking to you in the dark, speaking intimately to your subconscious. When I go see a movie, I try to surrender myself to it with a totally open mind. Usually, when the movie ends, everybody is talking and getting up to leave, while I'm still sitting there. I love

Hillary Swank, Chris Meloni, Nancy McLoughlin and Billie Worley on the set of *Leaving L.A.*

being transported into another world. Even if it's not a brilliant movie, I appreciate that fact that the movie got made and that it worked on some level. There are almost always good things about every movie. I look for those things and just try to appreciate them. I'd like to feel that there are films I've done that might fall into that category of having a lasting effect on audiences.

Was the pilot for *Leaving L.A.* a passion project?

Definitely. It was Nancy Miller's dream and I was so blessed she brought me on board. *Leaving L.A.*, which was originally called "Exit Elves." Nancy wrote the script, and it's hands-down one of my all-time favorite scripts. I adored it's great, dark sense of humor.

The pilot is sort of like *CSI* crossed with *Six Feet Under*—before either of those shows existed.

A year or two after ABC cancelled *Leaving L.A.* (because Michael Eisner didn't think a show about forensic crime was entertaining), the script for *CSI* came to me and Nancy Miller. I read it and said, "Wait a minute . . . This is a pilot for CBS?" I didn't think it would get picked up, because it was so much darker than what we'd been doing—and there was no humor. So I passed on directing it. Nancy Miller passed on it as well. Of course the show has proven to be enormously successful, and now it's okay to do shows about dead bodies and the people who deal with them.

Nancy Miller now has another show on, *Saving Grace*. She's had a number of shows in between. She also created the series *Any Day Now* that ran for four years on Lifetime. I was asked to do the pilot for that, but I stupidly took a Showtime movie that fell through. My wife Nancy played the mother of Annie Potts's character for the 1960s. They dressed her up like an astronaut's wife with the big hair and the heavy eye makeup. She played this Southern racist who was raised to believe in segregation. Then they aged her to play Annie Potts's mother in present day. Thankfully she's moved beyond that racism, regrets the way she acted in the sixties and is trying to get on with what's left of her life. It was a great part for Nancy, and she did a terrific job with a really challenging role. Nancy Miller's series tackled so many incredible subjects.

Tell me about casting *Leaving L.A.* You had some great character actors in there.

I pushed for Chris Meloni [from *In a Child's Name* and *Something to Live For*]. Everybody loved him. Lorraine Toussaint cracked me up when she came in. She has this wonderfully dry sense of humor, and we had an instant rapport. Hillary Swank was an amazing find. I thought her first read was terrible, but she came back a few days later , having reworked the material, and she blew everybody out of the water. And Anne Haney.

God, I love and miss her.

We shot the pilot with Lisa Rinna in the lead. She was great. But then ABC decided to shoot the entire thing a second time because they wanted Melina Kanakaredes as the lead. The first time you do something, it's fresh because you're creating things on the spot. The second time, you're constantly thinking: *Should I change this?* We had the same script, same lines, same actors (except for Lisa), and more money . . . but the freshness, the discovery, and the instinct were gone. For whatever reason, ABC aired the pilot on Saturday, which is ratings graveyard night. After about six episodes, the show was pulled.

How did you get involved with *The Third Twin* miniseries?

That was the first time I worked with Jaffe/Braunstein Films, and I have done a number of movies with them since, including *Odd Girl Out* and *Not Like Everyone Else*. They're great producers. Somebody must have been pretty adamant about getting me to direct *The Third Twin*, because my agent asked for everything and they gave it to me. I wanted to fly my family [to Toronto] for the shoot. The kids got a real summer vacation at a huge lake house. The highlight for them was the rope swing on the tree. It was a picture-perfect summer for them and Nancy.

Less so for me. I wasn't familiar with the Ken Follett books, but I knew they were incredibly popular and remain so today. When I finally sat down and read the book, I was impressed with the writing. The screenwriter, Cindy Myers, did a terrific job of boiling it down, but it's sort of like a Stephen King adaptation—so much of the success of the book was in the way the story was told, and when you take away that voice, it just isn't the same.

Casting was the first major challenge. The main character was written for a woman in her late twenties. I was picturing a Jennifer Jason Leigh type, somebody who is feisty and intelligent. Eventually Kelly McGillis was cast. I thought she was a great actress, but not quite right for this type of character. I tried to suppress that opinion, because a lot of actors are capable of many types of roles once they're finally given the opportunity to play them.

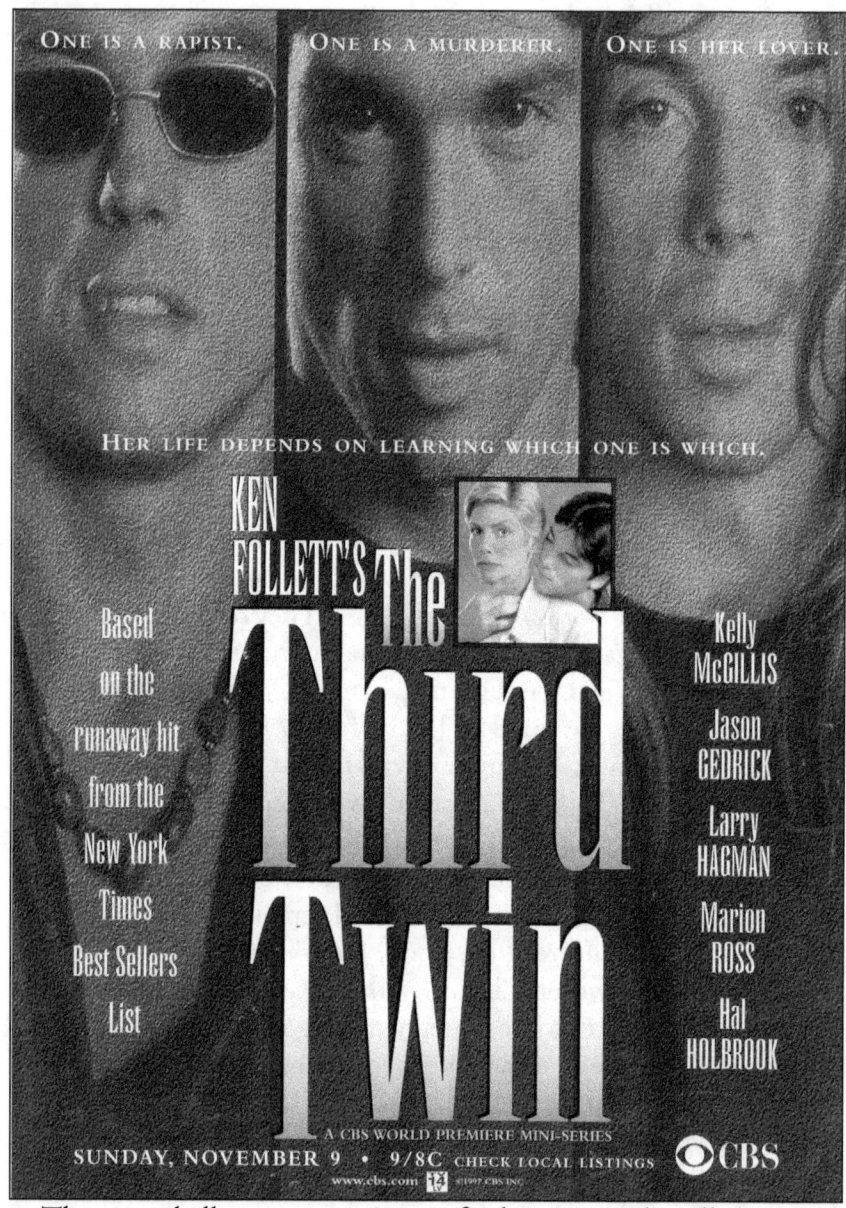

The next challenge was trying to find a guy to play all the clones. After a series of interviews, we cast Jason Gedrick. He had just done *The Last Don* with Joe Mantegna, and that made him a major CBS favorite. I knew he had done some good work, but I was nervous because this guy had to play five very different characters who were physical clones.

Sounds like a scheduling nightmare, if nothing else.

Needless to say, I wanted to have plenty of actor rehearsal time. I knew that the movie would only work if there was strong chemistry between the male and female leads. Two weeks before shooting, Jason got the measles. So forget rehearsal. I had to start shooting all the scenes with Kelly McGillis and the other actors to buy time while he recovered. Once you're in the middle of production, at least on a TV movie this big, it's really hard to start developing a rapport with actors and also keep the show moving quickly to stay on schedule and budget. I never had a chance to get fully engaged with the actors on this particular piece.

It's one thing to sit down with an actor when you have time to work through things. If you have taken the time beforehand to talk about the character and come to a consensus on an approach, then you're both open to try things on the set. It's another thing entirely when you didn't get that time and you're in the middle of a scene, on the second or third take, and suddenly the actor stops and says, "I don't know what I'm doing." I was grasping for some basic human truths that would allow the actor to get through these moments, but these were not realistic situations that either of us could relate to. I was constantly struggling with how to emotionally tell this story. I wish I could have done what David Cronenberg does and build the whole thing around bizarre set pieces, but the script was locked and we didn't have the kind of budget that would allow us to create new scenes.

There are two kinds of movies. There's the kind that you make, and then there's the kind that you survive. For me, this was a survival movie. I loved the people I was working with, but I didn't feel confident in my own ability to turn this thing into something really special. Even in post, I felt that way. Don Davis composed a very interesting, unique score—but I felt like I kept trying to put sizzle where there was no steak.

It's a film about nature vs. nurture, but the nurture element seems underrepresented. The strongest nurture element in the story was the subplot about the relationship between Kelly's character and her father, played by Hal Holbrook.

There were two things about this film that I really responded to. One was working with Hal Holbrook, who lived up to every expectation I had of him, and then some. Such an enormously talented, sweet, wonderful man. Also, the convention of twins was fun. I loved bringing together all these people who were twins in real life, including our producer Chris Sacani. She's an incredibly talented woman who had been working for Jaffe/Braunstein for years. When we were putting together the twins convention, she said, "Do you want me to fly my sister up?" I said, "There are two of you?! Yeah, that would be great!" And it was.

There were a few other sequences that I enjoyed directing, like the fight with the two clones in the bathroom. Basically I had the *From Russia with Love* fight in my mind—the one with Sean Connery and Robert Shaw on the train. I was excited to create that kind of fight in a claustrophobic environment, but with the same actor fighting himself! I had it storyboarded. But unfortunately it was shot on the very last night and we had to change the set locations twice, so it was really rushed.

There were some other blessings that came out of *The Third Twin*. I met Kwame Parker, who was my assistant on the show. We continued working together for a few more films. Then he went off to become a producer on a number of huge films, but we have remained close friends. I also learned that whenever I'm making a decision about my next project, I have ask myself: *Am I doing this just because I want to make a movie? Or am I really passionate about this?* If I'm not passionate, I know I shouldn't do it.

If I'm not mistaken, the next thing that came along for you was a chance to work with Marlon Brando . . . Wasn't he supposed to play Dr. Shushan in *Behind the Mask*?

After *The Third Twin*, I hit a wall. In retrospect, I knew I had done that movie for the wrong reasons, and I made a very conscious decision to say no to things that I wasn't passionate about. Around the same time, I was being pursued by an agent at the William Morris Agency. I had been with CAA for nine years and I loved my TV agent there—Bruce Vinocour. But a lot of movie agents had come and gone. In all fairness to them, they had a right to get frustrated because I would go to meetings for feature film projects and we would get the ball rolling. Then suddenly the project would get put on hold, I'd get offered a TV movie and decide that I wanted to work instead of sitting around waiting, so I had to pull out of the feature film project. At that point my film agents would say, "Obviously he doesn't want to make features. He wants to make TV movies." That wasn't it. I just wanted to make *movies*, period. Either I could sit around for the next three months to a year or more just talking about it, or I could go off and actually make a film and get paid for it and, in the process, get better at the very thing I want to do. Every time you make a film, you get better at your craft. You find out what you can and can't do, and that hands-on experience is very important.

Because I felt like I had hit a wall, I was open to a change. With great reluctance about leaving CAA and a great hope that this was going to help me get back into the world of feature films, I signed up with William Morris. There was one particular agent at William Morris, Steve Glick, who was very excited that I was now there. He was their television movie guy and he said, "If you ever want to come back to TV . . ." I said, "Not right now." And for a year, I didn't work. I took meetings, made a lot of phone calls, and wrote a script called *If You Knew Me* with my friend Tony Reitano. It was based on a book that I had personally optioned. I thought it was a good enough character piece that I could make it as a little independent film for a few million dollars. At one point, I had Mary Steenburgen involved. A lot of people were interested, but never enough to generate the money to get it made.

Eventually, after I'd turned down a number of TV movies, I got a call from Steve Glick. He said, "Would you do a TV movie if it had Marlon Brando in it?" I said, "Are you serious?" He said, "He's going to do a movie for CBS and they're interested in hiring you to direct." I thought about it for a day, then called back and said, "What's required?" He said, "Read the script and then you'll meet with Brando." I figured: *This isn't an offer you get every day.*

The script was based on a true story that actually happened in Culver City, my home turf. The main character was a doctor named Robert Shushan who ran a business that employed handicapped people. One day Shushan had a heart attack and one of his janitors there, a guy named James Jones, found him in his car and pulled him out. After that Shushan became like a surrogate father for him. It was basically a male love story, which I thought was really fascinating.

I started wondering, "Could Brando really play Dr. Shushan?" I started talking to every living director who had ever worked with him, and they all said the same thing: "Run—do not walk—from this situation! You'll have great war stories, but he will kill you! He doesn't like directors. He is his own boss. He gets paid a million dollars a week, and he will push you over schedule so that he can get prorated for those extra days . . ." I decided it would be worthwhile to take the meeting regardless. At the very least I could say I met Brando.

So I headed to Brando's house. He lived off Coldwater Canyon, on this private road that leads to three different gates. One went to Warren Beatty's house, one went to Jack Nicholson's house, and the other went to Brando's place. Brando's home was really very simple—white walls, modern, 1960s-style house. When I got there, [producer] Stan Brooks was already there, along with the writer/co-producer Barry Morrow, Brando and his housekeeper . . . and his large dogs. When I walked through the door, Brando got up and warmly greeted me. He was dressed in black, which reminded me of Orson Welles. He had this huge coffee table filled with sushi and a ton of other Japanese appetizers.

I became instantly overwhelmed, standing before The Godfather and Captain Kurtz. It wasn't until I sat down with him that I really got a sense of the power he had. He had so much charisma. The meeting lasted almost three hours. Basically, he held court the entire time. I would ask a question, he would start to answer it and then he would veer off onto all these other subjects. I was thinking, *Maybe he's really lost it.* At the same time, the things he was saying were brilliant. He was like a genius who would lose his story point, and then suddenly he would be totally back on track, answering precisely. Then he kept repeating, "Eat eat eat. I got all this fuckin' food here."

He brought up so many stories about his past. "Fuckin' Robert

Evans, that's why I'm so fuckin' fat today is that fuckin' asshole." And then suddenly he'd shift into the details of all the sexual encounters he'd had over the years. This meeting was taking place right after the Bill Clinton / Monica Lewinsky scandal, so he said, "What man in this room wouldn't take a blowjob from Monica Lewinsky?" And everybody sort of laughed nervously. He pointed at me and he said, "You would." And I said, "No, I don't think I would." He glared at me. "You wouldn't take a blowjob from Monica Lewinsky?" I said, "I don't think it'd be worth it." He turned to the others and said, "What's with this guy?" I kept trying to make my case, "Well, I'm happily married . . ." He said, "You're an asshole. Marriage has nothing to do with it." I was actually worried that I had alienated him because I didn't want a blowjob from Monica Lewinsky.

At one point I said, "Marlon, I've got to ask you a question. I am a huge Chaplin fan and you worked with him on *A Countess from Hong Kong*. There are stories that you guys didn't like each other . . ." He said, "No, no, Chaplin's a genius. Fuckin' genius." Then he said, "Did you ever see the movie *City Lights*?" I said, "Yeah, about fifty times." Then he proceeded to dissect, shot by shot, the last scene in *City Lights*—the whole encounter between the tramp and the blind girl. He recited the title cards as if he had just seen the movie yesterday. That movie must have made a major impact on him, for him to be able to pull up all those details . . . and to act it out the way he did. At that moment I thought, *There's no place I'd rather be right now than sitting here watching Marlon Brando do Chaplin.*

I kept trying to steer the conversation back to the film [about Shushan and Jones], but he wasn't interested. He didn't really want to discuss it. I only remember him saying one thing about it. He said, "I see this guy Shushan having fingernail clippers . . . He's always cutting his fingernails, what do you think?" I said, [confused] "Yeah . . . okay . . ." Later, after talking with more people who had worked with Brando, I learned that he had gone from being an actor who pulled from his own experiences and his own understanding of life, to being an actor who didn't want to learn his lines and always needed a prop, a wig, a piece of wardrobe . . . something to help him find his way into the character.

From everything I was told about working with him, I knew I was going to be jumping into a hornet's nest if I agreed to do the movie. But I figured: *What the hell, let's see.* So I signed up and went up to Toronto to start scouting locations. We got the production offices all set up, and then we got a phone call from CBS that Brando had pulled out. Why? He decided that he didn't want to play Shushan. He wanted to play Shushan's son and he wanted to ride around on a motorcycle as this character, throwing toilet paper to the poor. The head of TV movies at CBS said no to his idea, and that was that. I think he just wanted out, as he has on so many other films. I think he was deeply insecure about playing someone who was just a regular guy. Anyway, we closed down the offices, came back from Toronto, and I figured that was the end of it.

When Brando was attached, Vincent D'Onofrio was going to play James Jones. Sean Penn was interested in doing it if D'Onofrio fell out. Chris Penn came to the office and met with us about another role. I also got a call from Pam Grier, who was willing to work for scale, just to have a chance to work with Brando. People were coming out of the woodwork to be in a movie with Brando. Nobody considered the fact that it would be very difficult working with him.

Donald Sutherland, who worked with him [in *A Dry White Season*], told me that Brando wore an earpiece so that his assistant could read his lines to him. In the old days he had cue cards all over the place, but now he felt it was better to have somebody read him the line. He would hear it for the first time just before he said it. Donald said that was incredibly difficult to deal with—because, while the other actors were delivering their lines, Brando was having his lines fed to him. He wasn't even listening to the other actor. And his hearing was going, so he had to turn up the volume on his earpiece so that it was loud. The other actors were having trouble delivering their own lines, because they were now overhearing his incoming lines. Despite all of that, everybody in town wanted to work with him.

Anyway, once Brando pulled out, all the other actors jumped ship. We were back to square one. We had to find actors to play both Shushan and Jones. Eventually the script made its way to

Donald Sutherland. I thought he was a great choice for Shushan. I've always been a fan of Donald's work and I thought he would be really wonderful. But he'd been playing darker roles during that time period, so the folks at CBS were worried about whether he'd be likable. Stan Brooks and I basically assured them that he would be. We said, "Think about his role in *Ordinary People* . . . He can do anything. He's an incredible actor." We eventually convinced them.

Somehow the word must have reached Donald, because during the first few days of filming, he went out of his way to say, "I know they questioned my likability, but I know I can make this guy likable." He requested that we not schedule any of the scenes at the beginning of the movie on the first few days of the shoot. He said, "Schedule those toward the middle, because I need time to find the character and I don't want to be struggling to find him right at the beginning of the shoot. Once the audience knows who he is from those initial scenes, the other scenes will just fly by." And he's absolutely right. It's so crucial that you really establish the character right away, because that's the viewer's gateway into that world. I've used his advice on every movie I've done since then. Some people think the best thing to do is to shoot the scenes in order, to keep track of the character arc, but I now believe it's more important for the actors to spend some time in the shoes of their character before shooting those introductory scenes.

Once Donald was on board, we still had to find an actor to play Jones. That was not an easy part to cast. The real James Jones was very off-putting in several ways. He was loud and aggressive and funny-looking . . . but in the movie he had to be sympathetic. Eventually, we got hold of Gary Sinise, who was interested in the role. I was pretty much begging him to do it, because I knew he would do a great job. After a few days of talking, he said, "Look, Tom, I would love to do a part like this, but you guys start shooting in two weeks. That doesn't give me enough time to prepare." That was the bottom line. He just couldn't take on a role like that without having more time to define the character for himself. I had to respect that.

Les Moonves [president and CEO] at CBS decided that the role should go to Matthew Fox. I thought that was the most insane idea I'd ever heard, because at that point Matthew hadn't

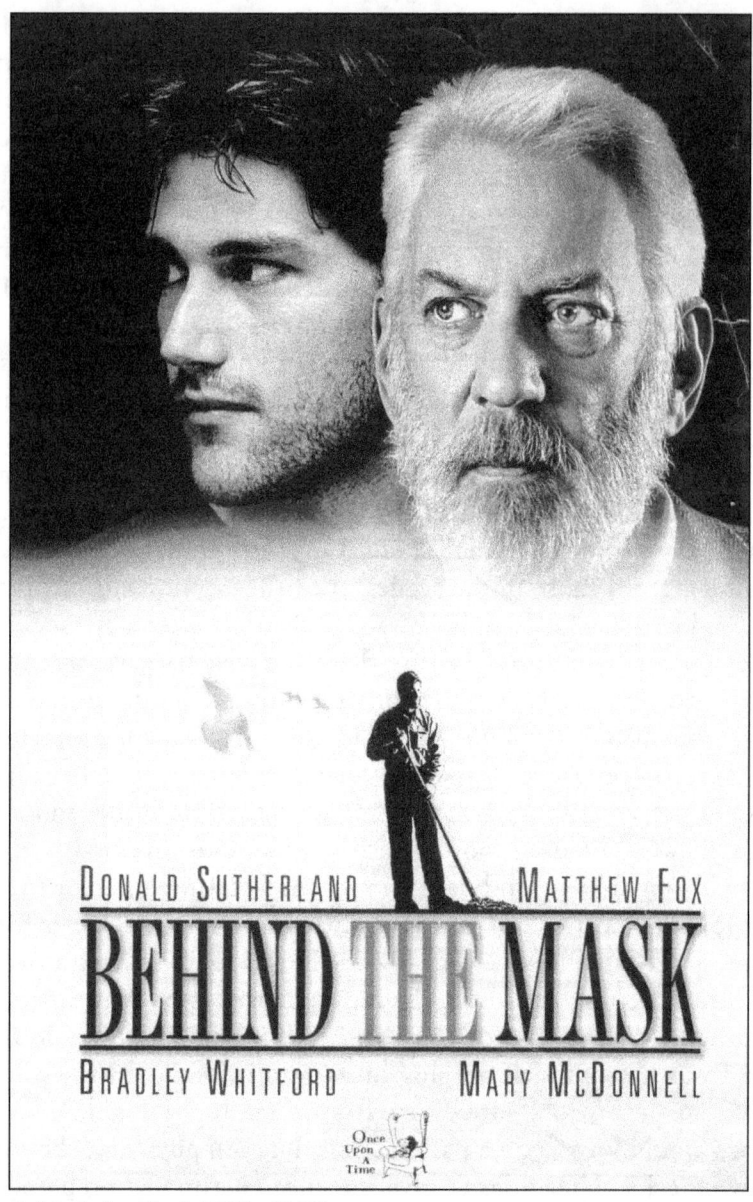

Behind the Mask (CBS, 1999)

done much other than "Party of Five." He was a model before that. And this was a part that Gary Sinise and several other very accomplished actors didn't even want to attempt because it was so difficult. To make matters worse, Matthew would still be shooting "Party of Five" while we were shooting this movie. He'd have to take flights back and forth to Vancouver to do this role. Also, Matthew Fox is a very handsome guy and he was going to be unrecognizable as Matthew Fox in this role—hidden behind the stringy hair and missing teeth. But, like it or not, we needed a James Jones and now we had him.

I met with Matthew in advance, because I wanted to have some degree of confidence that I could get this performance out of him. He couldn't have been nicer. He said, "I don't know if I can do something like this but I really want to try." He said he really wanted to be an actor's actor, and I admired that. I asked him to meet with Shawn Nelson, an acting coach that I knew really well who has worked with a lot of great actors. He coaches the same way I like to direct, so I knew we'd be on the same page. Matthew was willing to do that.

Then we had to cobble his [character's] look together, without having much money for special makeup. I called in a big favor to Rick Baker, to get him to make the teeth. Adding the extra weight and the beard was more difficult—especially because we were working with somebody that people recognize. We got nailed in a few reviews over Matthew wearing a wig and beard.

Once I had my leads, I started casting for all the other roles. When we started shooting, I still didn't have a wife for Donald. It was a Tuesday and we had to start shooting the wife scenes on Thursday. Finally, just before lunch, I got a call that we were going to get Mary McDonnell. I thought she would be great. I told Donald, and he gave me kind of a strange reaction. As I was heading to lunch, someone said, "Mr. Sutherland wants to see you in his trailer." So I went in and he was sitting there, still wearing his hat and his overcoat and holding his umbrella from the scene we'd just completed. He should have been out of wardrobe and going to lunch, but instead he was just sitting there. He said to me, "Do you think this actress is the right choice? This is not who I imagined . . ." I said, "Really? You don't think she's a good actress?" He said, "No, no, no, it's not that. She's just too young. I'm going to look like her grandfather." I did my best to reassure him: "I don't want you to be uncomfortable. Whatever we need to do, we'll make sure she doesn't look too young."

Their first scene together was the hospital scene, right after he's had his heart attack, and she was amazing. At the end of the scene, I went up to Donald and I said, "Well?" He said, "Shushan would marry someone like her. She's perfect. She's great." That was a huge relief. Donald and Mary just seemed like they were bonded, and chemistry is always the most important thing.

Once we had Mary McDonnell, we were off and running. Matthew was amazingly committed. Somehow he was able to make those flights from L.A. to Vancouver, fulfill his commitment to "Party of Five" and to us without anything ever going wrong. There were a couple of days where I really pushed him hard. One day he broke down and said, "I just don't know what you want." It was not my intention to break him down like that, but once he was in that vulnerable state, I started rolling and went right back into the scene again and that take ended up being in the final cut. He really did a great job.

Another great thing about the film was that we cast mentally-challenged people in some of the minor roles. They were so excited to be a part of it. We were risking the possibility of falling behind schedule because whenever somebody would too overemotional or too hyper or whatever, we had to stop and that slowed down the production. We had a guy that threw up every day at the same time. He just went off like an alarm clock, so we had to make sure that we always had somebody around to clean it up. Once we knew what was going to happen, we planned for it. We didn't lose any time. They were a real blessing to have on set. So loving and fun.

Are you happy with the finished film?

Yes. I think we kind of captured what [Howard] Hawks always did so well, the male love story. As much as these kinds of relationships exist in life, a lot of people are not comfortable seeing the softer side of male characters. There's a scene where Donald meets his son for lunch and he's telling him a joke, and his son appears so uncomfortable while he's listening. He's just waiting for his father to get to the point. It demonstrates that they just can't get comfortable with each other, even in the smallest

The cast and crew of *Behind the Mask*

moments, like a joke. Donald came up with that, and I thought it was a brilliant addition.

I think the dynamic is different when it's female to female, or female to male, but when you put two guys together, intimacy can have a very strained quality to it. If one of those people is mentally challenged, it makes it even more difficult. In this case, Shushan is dealing with James Jones, who is like a little kid in an adult world. James gets loud and aggressive and there's no way of knowing how violent he might become.

My favorite scene is the one where Jones brings Shushan to his neighborhood. The rest of the movie is about Shushan teaching Jones how to fit into society, how to be normal. In this scene, Jones explains that he has to act a little strange—he has to act like the Wolf Man—to keep from getting jumped in his own neighborhood. It's a role reversal . . .

People actually did call the real Jones "The Wolf Man." That was his nickname . . . That scene was part of the true story. There were so many interesting aspects to that man. He knew he wasn't normal and he knew he was never going to be, but he wanted a normal connection to his father. He wanted his father to be proud of him, and because of that he really did understand the estranged relationship between Shushan and his son. What makes the story work is something very basic: that desire we all have for our parents to be proud of us for who we are and what we're doing with our life.

One of the best reviews that I've ever received on any movie was for *Behind the Mask*. Ironically it appeared in *Variety* the day *after* the movie aired, so it didn't help the ratings, but the reviewer just loved everything about it. Producer Stan Brooks still has that review, blown up and hanging on the wall in his office. It was one of those reviews that you'd like to put on a t-shirt and wear around town. I believe all of us who worked on *Behind the Mask* felt very proud of the film.[20]

The very best thing about the whole experience, for me personally, was the actor/director relationship that I had with Donald. It was unlike any other film I've ever done. At the end of every day, he'd always say, "What are you doing for dinner, governor?" And I'd say, "I'm having dinner with you." We had hotel rooms right down the hall from each other in Vancouver, so I would go to his room every night for dinner and we would go over the next day's work. Basically, Donald's main technique was to cut lines from his own dialogue. He always said, "I don't want this guy to be redundant." He never touched the dialogue that belonged to the other actors, but he felt that he personally could act certain things better than he could say them. It was all about economizing the character. He's a master at that. A brilliant actor and craftsman.

. . . which, because of your background in mime, you must have loved.

---

[20] "It will be tough to better this network telepic in 1999, a poignant little gem that proves to be the best kind of weeper, earning its tears with meticulous plot construction and the kind of brilliant performances rarely on display in broadcast primetime. It features no women in jeopardy, no ticking time bombs, not a single assassin, just a simple human story told with uncanny eloquence. Bravo." —*Daily Variety*

Sure. But it's more about pure cinema—moments that are universally understood. The tough thing about doing network television is that you're supposed to run every change by the network executives. Luckily, Stan Brooks was very supportive of our process. He said, "You guys do what you have to do to make this thing shine." And Donald was so involved in the process. That's something that he always does. If people fight him on it, they have an unhappy working relationship. If there was something that I felt we needed, he was always open to exploring it. Every so often I would convince him to try something he really didn't believe in—always with the understanding that if it wasn't working in the edit, I'd cut it out. He trusted me.

What about the real Shushan and Jones? Did they like the finished film?

Shushan was understandably very excited that Brando was going to play him, then disappointed when Marlon changed his mind. When he came to a screening, he said he felt very honored by Donald Sutherland's portrayal of him. And proud of the film. James Jones, unfortunately, died about a year after the events in this story occurred. He had a seizure in his home, fell and hit his head and bled to death.

You said *Behind the Mask* got good reviews. Did that help you to land your next job?

What happened is that it pulled me back into the TV movie world. It was such a great experience, and it made me say, "Well, if I can find good character pieces like this, then I'm happy to keep doing movies for television." Ultimately, it's about making things you're proud of.

Along came *Anya's Bell*. I can't remember if Della Reese was attached to it from the very beginning, but the script was what sold me on it—for two reasons. First of all, it was set in the 1940s and I love that time period. More importantly, the story revolved around a twelve-year-old boy who had a learning disability that made him very anxious and self-conscious. The story was about two very different people and their handicaps: a sweet elderly blind lady and a dyslexic boy, who was sort of like me as a kid. He didn't want to go to school because he didn't feel like he was very smart. He wanted to escape. When I was a kid, I escaped to the movies. In this boy's case, he sneaks off to the airport to watch the planes fly off and land.

Anya's Bell has a very nostalgic quality to it, sort of like Sometimes They Come Back.

It was even more nostalgic, because the entire movie took place in the past. We had to find period cars and we had to find the right streets to shoot on . . . We shot in Salt Lake City. I'd never shot up there, so I had a great sense of discovery. This was the first time I worked with production designer Chester Kaczenski, and he managed to take a very low budget and still give us sets with amazing detail. I love Chester's passion.

My main conflict on that movie was Della. Bottom line, she told me, "I'm a singer, baby. You put the notes in front of me and I'll sing. But don't ask me to sing any different than the way I sing." My response was, "I want to make you as comfortable as possible, but at the same time I want to guide you out of total comfort and into something that's real, vulnerable and spontaneous." She didn't like that. Certain actors restrain themselves if they don't trust the director. They're afraid that you're going to make them look bad. At a certain point, she kind of stopped talking to me. Either she didn't trust me or she just didn't want to feel vulnerable. On the other hand, the boy Mason Gamble was great to work with. He was an incredibly smart young actor. It was a great cast and crew, but doing a period film really made me long to do a feature.

While I was editing *Anya's Bell*, I was approached about doing a prequel to *The Exorcist*.[21] William Wisher had written a first draft, which had too many similarities to the original *Exorcist* movie. It had a great *Sophie's Choice* opening, where Father Merrin is being confronted by the Nazis. They say, "Give us the name of the person who killed our soldier or we're going to start shooting these townspeople, one by one." And Merrin prays to God not to let this happen, but people are killed. Then the Nazi says, "Where's your God now?" I thought that opening was really powerful, and I was very excited about the idea of doing a smart, atmospheric prequel set in the 1940s.

Was it doubly appealing because you'd just done a movie set in that time period?

I didn't think about that at the time. I was excited about the possibility of doing a horror movie with *The Godfather* / Gordon Willis style of photography. And I was challenged by the idea of doing the story of the exorcist before *The Exorcist*, and answering all those character questions: *Who is this priest? What are the details of his first encounter with the demon Pazuzu?* I also knew the film could potentially be a career killer.

I started developing the project as I finished *Anya's Bell*, and I became completely ensconced in that thing for about two years. It was announced in all the trades that I was doing it. I was involved in casting and the local news stations covered our search for a black child to play the possessed boy. In my home office, I had an entire shelf filled with nothing but books on demons, possession and exorcisms. William Peter Blatty [author of *The Exorcist*] personally gave me a tape of a real exorcism that was performed in Italy.

I do think all of that had a subconscious psychological effect on me. A lot of dark things happened while I was working on that project, but I kept telling myself: "This has nothing to do with what I'm working on." Now I think there is something about walking the path of this type of demonic darkness that somehow draws dark things to you.

---

[21] On November 1, 1999, *Variety* reported: "Morgan Creek Prods. has tapped Tom McLoughlin to direct *Exorcist: Dominion*, the prequel to the Exorcist saga [. . .] Pic will be produced by [James G.] Robinson and exec produced by Jonathan Zimbert; script was penned by William Wisher [*Terminator II*, with James Cameron], based on the novel by William Peter Blatty. Lensing is slated for a spring start in Africa."

The Exorcist (Warner Brothers, 1973)

Did you talk to William Peter Blatty about the prequel?

On day one, I said to the producers, "I've got to talk to Blatty." They asked, "Why do you want to talk to him? He has no interest in seeing this movie get made." What I didn't know was that, years earlier, Blatty had made a deal with Morgan Creek to make his book *Legion* into a movie. When Blatty screened his director's cut for the producers, somebody said, "Why isn't there an exorcism in the movie? Isn't this supposed to be *The Exorcist III*?" And Blatty said, "No, this is *Legion*—not *The Exorcist III*." They said, "Nobody's going to go see *Legion*, but they'll go see it if it's called *The Exorcist III*, so you need to add an exorcism." Blatty refused and they said, "Fine, we'll get somebody else to do it." He reluctantly said okay. I don't know how the whole thing was orchestrated, but then they spent another million dollars to bring in Nicol Williamson, the actor who played the exorcist, and add an exorcism to the storyline of *Legion*.

Blatty was pissed that they owned the rights to *The Exorcist* title. It was the biggest mistake in his life, as far as he was concerned. So he looked at me and he said, "Look, I don't know you from

Adam, but I'm telling you this: If you make this movie and I don't like it, I'm going to go on every talk show and slam this thing—and you!" It wasn't even close to a veiled threat. I said, "Sir, if this doesn't come out well, I'll be slamming it right next to you. *The Exorcist* changed my life. I saw that movie, studied that movie, and went to every seminar involving anybody who worked on that movie. I could write a book on it, and the reason I got this job is because I came in with so much passion. I know it could be the death knell for my career, but I believe I could do something very cool with the right script." I guess I somehow won him over, because the rest of our meeting was wonderful. He was very supportive. Before I left I said, "I swear to you on your house—because his house was shaped like a cross—I will not do this movie if I don't think it's going to be great." In the end, that statement was the main reason I backed out. I gave the man my word.

What happened that made you lose faith in the film?

For pretty much the entire time, I was campaigning to get Caleb Carr to do a rewrite. I thought *The Alienist* was a brilliant book. When we finally got him on board, he and I had great discussions and I was convinced that his script was going to be brilliant. Then he came back with a script that was basically "My Dinner with Satan." It was so talky. I said to the producers, "I don't think this works." And they said, "So you're telling us that after two years you're walking away from the movie?" I said, "I need to get back to you on that." I called up my agent and asked what would happen if I walked off. He said, "You get nothing. They've got to fire you." I'd never been fired off of anything, so I decided to let this thing play out. The producers wanted to greenlight the movie, but I said I wanted to do another rewrite. They said, "Well, we think it works the way it is." I told them I had to believe in what I was doing, and I didn't believe in the current script.

What happened next is that they went to other directors, and a number of people responded the same way I had: "The script doesn't work." Then John Frankenheimer agreed to do it. That was really weird. I walked away from something that was going to be directed by John Frankenheimer, who had directed me as the mutant bear in *Prophecy*! I figured he was powerful enough to get the script rewritten. He was involved with it for about a year, and then he went into the hospital for back surgery and then died suddenly of some complication.

Then the script came back to me and they said, "Are you interested?" I said, "Well, let me look at the script and see where it is." *It was the same fucking script!* Not a word had changed. I said, "John was going to shoot this script?" They said, "Yeah, he was really happy with it." I said, "Well, I still don't think it works." So then it went to Paul Schrader, and I figured that Paul Schrader—because of his talent and his religious background—would make it a classic. But he didn't change a word either! Shot it as is and turned it in. Executive producer James Robinson saw his director's cut, said "this isn't scary," fired Paul Schrader, and then started looking for someone to shoot additional scary sequences for it. Finally, they got Renny Harlin. Renny decided he wanted to reshoot the entire movie with the same cast and the same D.P. So they made this thing all over again. It was exactly what I hadn't wanted to do—filled with CGI effects. I had been adamant about doing it the way they did the original, with in-camera effects. So the movie I was going to make for 18 million was made for . . . I think the first version cost thirty to forty million, and then the second version cost, I think, fifty million.

Wow. I had no idea it was that expensive. I guess that's why they eventually released both versions—because they needed to make some of their money back.

When they released Renny's version, it got panned badly.

And then everybody on the Internet was saying, "Why did they scrap Schrader's version?"

They decided to show Paul Schrader's cut at a film festival. Somebody said, "Well, it's certainly better than the other one." But most audiences didn't fall for it. They just said, "Haven't we already seen this?" I think, all together, both versions ended up making about forty million domestic.[22]

It seems to me that you channeled all of your ideas for *The Exorcist* prequel into your episode of the Steven Spielberg series *The Others*. Is "Theta" your version of *The Exorcist*?

Not consciously . . . But it came out well, I think. The directors on this series were all given carte blanche to make their episodes however they wanted to make them. When I turned in my director's cut, I got no notes. Spielberg approved without making any changes. After that, I got a call from DreamWorks, asking me to come in for a meeting. There was all this enthusiasm about what I wanted to do next. Then that guy accepted a job at another company and that was the end of my ten minutes of heat.

What was surreal about *The Others* was that I was shooting it at the same time that my mother-in-law was dying. Right in the middle of shooting, I needed to go with Nancy up to San Francisco to be by her bedside. Then go to her funeral. It was very emotional. These things put you in a frame of mind that really affects what you're doing. The line between reality and fantasy gets blurred, and somehow the emotional experience of that period in your life ends up on the screen.

"Theta" does seem very personal because it's character-based. The audience identifies with the main character because we don't know what's happening to her anymore than she does: *Is she haunted? Is she possessed? Is someone using supernatural powers to hurt her?* It's very much like the beginning of The Exorcist, where we are being pulled along by our sympathy for the main character.

I love the lead actress in "Theta," Jeanette Brox. She totally commits to what she's doing. When she smiles there's something so warm and genuine that makes you feel like you know her, like

---

[22] Boxofficemojo.com reports that the total domestic gross, as of November 7, 2004, was $41,814,863.

you went to school with her. She really internalized the pain of a character that knows this horrible secret and can't deal with it. There was so much complexity in her performance.

She's aware of the paranormal attacks on her, but she can't understand them. It was important to emphasize the literal darkness that surrounds her. When she's walking through her apartment, you can't see what's there. I added the sound of dead air, to help put the audience into this void with her. Usually in those suspenseful moments, you have music—a long violin strain, and then [a burst of staccato sound]. To me, silence is always a more effective setup. Then she gets *slammed* onto the floor and dragged down the hall. It was all done with very simple effects, but the silence and the darkness are what give the audience the psychological connection to her, and that's what pulls you into her world.

What happened to the series?

It was a show that Steven Spielberg did with showrunners Glen Morgan and James Wong. NBC greenlit it at the same time as *Freaks & Geeks* and, for whatever reason, they just didn't have faith in these two shows. They put *The Others* on Saturday night, which is where you put a show that you have to air but don't care about. Of course it didn't get the ratings needed. I thought the series was a very smart idea—to have all these different characters with supernatural gifts working together. And the young lead Julianne Nicholson is an amazing talent. I'm just waiting for her to connect with the right role and explode as a major star.

As a horror fan, I'm waiting for you to tack another stab at a horror movie. Didn't you say that you've been approached about remaking *One Dark Night*?

Yes, although I'm not sure how serious that was. With *One Dark Night*, it would be a question of finding a way to do something new. For one thing, I think I'd like to explore more of the Raymar character—the whole idea of a psychic vampire. Instead of a rubber corpse that gets rolled around the set, I'd want to set him up as a character at the beginning of the movie . . . so that

Mausoleum at Hollywood Forever (Meg Tilly in *One Dark Night*)

you think the whole movie is going to be about this guy who uses telekinetic power. Maybe we see him in an environment that's heightened—like the world of flashy Hollywood night life—so that the audience finds initially sees him as the typical Hollywood weirdo. Until he picks up a girl and takes her home and literally drains the life out of her. I'd want to really see the physical process of this. Then when he dies, he's been put into the Hollywood Forever mausoleum.

There is a part of me that really wants to remake that film, knowing now what I wish I'd known then. When I was starting out in the '70s, I was heavily influenced by the horror films that I'd seen. Now I have so many other influences from my life and a lot more experience developing characters and working with actors, and all the technical knowledge of making a movie. I do believe I could go back and re-envision *One Dark Night* and make it more like what I wish it had been the first time. It would be a rare but welcome blessing to have that chance to go back and improve things. But I would not want to lose what made it work the first time around—which was that experience of supernatural fear that I had in the catacombs in Paris.

A lot of filmmakers talk about their first film as their most personal film, because they got to spend more time developing it than any subsequent film. Does *One Dark Night* still feel like your most personal film?

My first three features are filled with many personal touches and a lot of references to all the movies that influenced me when I was growing up. I was trying to put everything into them ... which did make them personal, but I realize now that all those references weren't necessarily right for those particular scenes. What I've learned as a filmmaker is that you shouldn't make individual shots elaborate just for the sake of the shot. Everything has to be organic to the story. I look back at those films and I see that I was focusing more on visual acrobatics than telling a story. When I see a moment that doesn't work, often it's because the emphasis is on the camera movement instead of the actor.

In the beginning of *One Dark Night*—the scene where the police find the bodies in the closet—I did the three quick cut-ins, my nod to what Hitchcock did in *The Birds* [in the scene where Jessica Tandy discovers a man with his eyes pecked out]. The audience certainly reacted with horror, but I'm not sure I would do it the same way again. I might do a slow move, either a zoom or a dolly, instead. The zoom lens pulls the image towards you, whereas the dolly pushes you into the image. People argue that it has the same effect, but I don't think so. There's a subtle difference, and as a storyteller you have to make a choice.

It's hard to predict the effect on the audience, isn't it? Some people will be jolted by the three quick cuts, while other people will be too aware of the edit for it to work for them emotionally. I guess it does come down to the director's decision about what seems natural ...

It's all instinctive. We all make mistakes all the time . . . You wake up in the morning and you didn't get enough sleep and you're sitting there watching the first scene of the day and you impulsively say, "Can't we do something more interesting with the camera?" Then a month later in editing, you say, "Why did I do that?" Maybe it wasn't a great scene to begin with, so you were trying to make it interesting for yourself by changing something. Usually, it's a scene that's relaying information. It's someone talking. Whenever a scene isn't about one of the two Fs—fighting or fucking—you're going to have trouble with it. We need constant conflict, or the threat of conflict. Sex, or the promise of sex.

That's American cinema in a nutshell.

When I read scripts, I'm always analyzing the dialogue scenes. What's important is not what the characters are saying so much as what they don't say, what they may be struggling to say. The emotional underpinnings of the characters. Dialogue itself isn't cinematic, but if one person really wants to talk and the other person actively doesn't want to listen, then you've got a scene. Often I say to the actors, "Let's talk about where you are emotionally at this point in the story. Maybe you don't want to be here. Maybe you don't want to be paying attention. Maybe there's something else that has your attention. You have to look for the conflict. What's your intention? What's in the way?"

To me, those are the most interesting challenges as a director. How do you take the sometimes very mundane information and present it in a way that's interesting to watch? Too often we get hung up, especially in television, with the look of the scene instead of the emotional content. We say, "Just light them so that they look pretty, because the audience will watch a pretty face and there's really no time to try to get into very much depth with these characters . . ." In my early days as a director, I was very focused on moving the camera . . . but I think that's where we get it wrong. We pay attention to technical details instead of the tone of the story. That's the hardest thing about filmmaking—getting the tone right, and maintaining it.

Whenever a movie has an inconsistent tone, I always assume it's a "movie by committee." If there are too many producers with conflicting ideas about what the movie should be, then viewers pick up on the confusion. They sense that the story is fragmented, but they can't quite explain why . . .

As filmmakers, we have to keep being reminded of the simple rule that it's about tone. I forget constantly. I'll look at one scene and think, "This could look like *Chinatown* . . ." and then look at the next scene and think, "This could look like *The Exorcist* . . ." And you find yourself trying to shoot each scene in an interesting and unique style. Then when you put it together it just doesn't feel coherent.

TV movies have to fit into a set formula of eight-act chunks. As with episodic shows, the commercial breaks need to be cliffhangers, because you want your audience to come back to find out what happens. There are some acts outs that are truly great. They grab you and you won't flip the channel to see what else is on because you'd risk missing something when the movie comes back. That's not easy to achieve, because so many act outs are cliché and completely predictable. The audience has this sense of what you can and can't do, based on where you are in the movie. They think: *Okay, we're not even halfway through, so this guy can't die yet . . . the mystery can't be resolved yet . . . he's not the murderer . . .* They know the formula. And as soon as you go to the commercial, you can lose whatever dramatic momentum you had.

Commercials can kill the tone of anything.

If you're seeing a movie for the first time, and you're really trying to get involved, it's impossible not to be distracted by the logos, the commercials, and the fact that everything is so rushed. Most males, including myself, don't ever put the remote down. We're just waiting for that moment of emotional disconnect so we can change the channel. In my experience, women tend to put something on and stick with it. They might be doing other things, but they'll keep the same thing on because they're more interested in getting engaged in the story. Guys want to surf the channels and see if there is anything better on.

I went to a seminar once where a filmmaker—actually, I think it was Woody Allen—said that, as soon as the lights go down in a theater, your consciousness begins to float. Whatever that first image is, that's what carries you into the movie. He's always subscribed to two basic rules. (1) The opening titles are white text on black background, because you're not in the movie yet. This is just the credits, where music sets the tone. You cut to the first image and then the movie starts. (2) Each movie is ninety minutes, because that's the normal cycle time before your brain waves change frequency. I think there is truth to the idea that those of us who go to a theater to see a movie are seeking a different experience than those who stay at home and watch TV.

In a recent issue of the Writers Guild Magazine, there's an interview with Nancy Miller, in which she says she prefers watching television over going to the movies. She says she gets antsy when she goes to the movie. She grew up on television, she loves television, and that's why she writes for television. That's how she wants to be entertained. When I watch something on TV, I'm usually gone as soon as it breaks for commercial. When I go to the movies I will always stick with it—even if it's a bad movie. I'm there to see somebody's vision, and I want to immerse myself completely in that dreamlike experience. I have always loved making that commitment of time and energy to cinema. It's not about getting what I paid for. It's about opening myself up to the kind of emotional experience that cinema can deliver.

PART VI: KIDS & AMERICA

Demons from the Id / The murder in heaven / American terrorists / Christmas blues and black humor / Teen noir / Seduction, obsession, addiction / Twenty-first century witch hunting / Reality vs. docudrama / The grindhouse girls

FILMOGRAPHY

THE UNSAID (UNIVERSAL, 2001)
SCREENPLAY BY MIGUEL TEJADA-FLORES AND SCOTT WILLIAMS.
STORY BY CHRISTOPHER MURPHEY.
STARRING ANDY GARCIA, TREVOR BLUMAS, LINDA CARDELLINI, TERI POLO

A therapist tries to help a teenage boy who reminds him of his dead son.

"ANY DAY NOW"—2 EPISODES (LIFETIME, 2002)
DIRECTED BY TOM MCLOUGHLIN

MURDER IN GREENWICH (USA, 2002)
DIRECTED BY TOM MCLOUGHLIN
TELEPLAY BY DAVE ERICKSON. BASED ON A NONFICTION BOOK BY MARK FUHRMAN.
STARRING MAGGIE GRACE, TOBY MOORE, JON FOSTER, CHRIS MELONI, ROBERT FORSTER

A detective attempts to solve a decades-old murder of a teenage girl in Greenwich.

"Without a Trace"—1 episode (CBS, 2003)
Directed by Tom McLoughlin

D.C. Sniper: 23 Days of Fear (USA, 2003)
Directed by Tom McLoughlin
Teleplay by Dave Erickson.
Starring Charles S. Dutton, Bobby Hosea, Trent Cameron
   True story of Charles Moose, who led the police investigation into a series of sniper killings in Washington D.C. in October 2002.

She's Too Young (Lifetime, 2004)
Directed by Tom McLoughlin
Teleplay by Richard Kletter
Starring Marcia Gay Marden, Alexis Dziena, Mike Erwin
   A mother-daughter relationship is tested when the fourteen-year-old daughter contracts an STD.

A Very Married Christmas (CBS, 2004)
Directed by Tom McLoughlin
Teleplay by Joyce Eliason. Based on a novel by Elizabeth Berg.
Starring Joe Mantegna, Jean Smart, Charles Durning
   A husband and wife play out their post-divorce fantasies over the holiday season.

Odd Girl Out (Lifetime, 2005)
Directed by Tom McLoughlin
Teleplay by Richard Kletter. Based on a nonfiction book by Rachel Simmons.
Starring Alexa Vega, Lisa Vidal, Leah Pipes, Elizabeth Rice
   A teenage girl becomes suicidal after being ostracized by her friends.

Cyber Seduction: His Secret Life (Lifetime, 2005)
Directed by Tom McLoughlin
Teleplay by Richard Kletter and Wesley Bishop.
Starring Jeremy Sumpter, Kelly Lynch, Lyndsy Fonseca
   A teenager's addiction to Internet porn disrupts his life.

NOT LIKE EVERYONE ELSE (LIFETIME, 2006)
DIRECTED BY TOM MCLOUGHLIN
TELEPLAY BY JAMIE PACHINO
STARRING ALIA SHAWKAT, ILLEANA DOUGLAS, ERIC SCHWEIG
   A rebellious teenager is persecuted by her peers and school administrators.

THE STAIRCASE MURDERS (LIFETIME, 2007)
DIRECTED BY TOM MCLOUGHLIN
TELEPLAY BY DONALD MARTIN. BASED ON A NONFICTION BOOK BY APHRODITE JONES.
STARRING TREAT WILLIAMS, KEVIN POLLAK
   True story of a man who murdered his wife, but convincingly pleaded his innocence in a documentary film.

"SAVING GRACE"—1 EPISODE (TNT, 2007)
DIRECTED BY TOM MCLOUGHLIN

FAB FIVE: THE TEXAS CHEERLEADER SCANDAL (LIFETIME, 2008)
TELEPLAY BY TEENA BOOTH
STARRING JENNA DEWAN, ASHLEY BENSON, AIMEE SPRING FORTIER
   True story of five Texas cheerleaders who made news headlines by breaking all the rules.

You spent a few years struggling to work your way back into feature films. How did you finally get an offer to direct *The Unsaid*, a theatrical feature starring Andy Garcia?

   Geoffrey Wright was attached as director, but he wanted to turn it into more of a horror movie. At a certain point he and Andy Garcia realized they weren't going to be making the same movie, so the producers started looking for a new director and I ended up on the radar because of my agent.
   I went into a meeting with the two producers, and told them that I saw the movie as a psychological thriller. They said, "Great, but you've got to sit down with Mr. Garcia, because he's very particular about who's going to direct this movie now." I went and met with Andy at his house, and we were both sort of dancing

Andy Garcia in *The Unsaid* (Universal, 2001)

around each other, each trying to figure out what the other was looking for. Ultimately, I think what bonded us was the fact that I had a background in physical comedy. Andy lit up when I started talking about that. He's got a wonderful sense of humor, and he loves doing comedy, so the conversation started to spin off in that direction. I think at one point I even said, "Screw this movie—let's do a comedy instead," and he said, "Yeah yeah yeah!"

A few hours later I got a call from the producers saying, "We need you to get on a plane tomorrow." It happened that fast. I didn't have to go through the months of agony, wondering whether it was going to happen or not. I was used to the faster paced world of TV movies. I'd get a script on a Thursday and if I loved it, the deal was made on Friday and I was on a plane by Saturday.

Did you and Andy finally discuss your vision for the film?

Absolutely. What Andy and the producers *didn't* want was a horror movie, or anything supernatural. That was fine with me

Andy Garcia and Vincent Kartheiser in *The Unsaid* (Universal, 2001)

because I had shifted my own storytelling preferences from traditional horror to real-life psychological monsters that are far more frightening. These are the monsters that you can't always get away from . . . like the doctor in *The Unsaid* who molested [Andy Garcia's character's] son. I wanted the movie to convey the perspective of the actors, and to visualize the horrors that come from their subconscious. When Andy's character, who is a psychiatrist, is looking at [his patient] Tommy, he starts to see [his dead son] Kyle in him. He knows that Kyle is not really there, but subconsciously he is. It illustrates transference—the very thing psychiatrists to avoid. He can't stop working with Tommy, trying to help him, because Tommy reminds him of his son. It's like this case gives him this way to access his son's suicide. Then there are love stories, between Andy and the Teri Polo character, and between Tommy and Andy's daughter, played by Linda Cardellini. And the dark love story at the center of the film is between Tommy as a boy and his mother.

The title sums it up. It's a movie about relationships that are too complicated or too illicit for words. And it requires a strong commitment from the viewer—a willingness to endure

the pain that all these characters are going through. It starts right away, with the scene where Andy Garcia discovers his son's body. He just loses it . . . and you hold on that for a long time, unlike a slick horror movie that moves on very quickly. It made me genuinely uncomfortable as a viewer . . .

That had a lot to do with Andy's commitment. He felt very, very strongly that those moments had to really be painful. He called it the monk's wail, when he got into that scene—just totally letting go. We did run the risk of going too far, or pushing people away because they just don't want to watch anyone in that much tragic pain. But it was an honest moment for Andy's character. He had sensed a problem with his son and thought he had dealt with it. But it had only made things worse for his son. He had so much regret, pain and sorrow that he just caved in on himself. His marriage and his relationship with his daughter fell apart, and then he became a recluse for the next few years. As far as he was concerned, his life was over.

I wanted to do something interesting for the flashbacks where Andy is remembering his son. The normal way you would do that is to get a kid who looks like the actor and then shoot the flashbacks. I wanted to the flashbacks to look like home movies. I talked to the mother of Trevor Blumas, the actor who played Kyle, and she said she had a lot of footage of him as a little boy, and she was willing to let us use it. So my editor Charles Bornstein and I went through and handpicked those moments: the first haircut, the kid in the little stroller, looking up at the lens. All those in-your-face moments. We certainly could have gone out and shot something where we see little Trevor growing up on VHS home movies, but this was the real thing. Nothing surpasses that.

His mother must have had a hard time watching that part of the movie.

She might have. I certainly appreciated her allowing us to use those clips.

I can imagine that this is what would happen if I were in

Andy's situation: You think about all you've lost. I can see myself doing that—watching old home movies—to try and somehow cathartically deal with such a loss. I don't think those images would stop running through my mind. I cannot fathom getting up every day and trying to get on with my life. I can't even imagine taking comfort in the notion that it was God's will. I can accept it in theory, but when I think about the extreme emotional impact . . . I don't know how I could. Especially if you're a parent who cuts a child out of your life for some reason and then something horrible happened to the child. You'd have to struggle with that regret for the rest of your life. That is deeply horrible to think about.

How do you get through a film like this without getting mired in that dark headspace the whole time?

I remember twice getting very emotional while I was making this movie. One time was after my family came up to visit. When they left, I had this overwhelming sense of loss and grief beyond anything I'd ever experienced before. I didn't share that with anybody on set or even with my family, but I suddenly felt completely overwhelmed. I was weeping in sorrow. I'd never had that occur before.

Maybe it's because, as director, I try to throw myself into the minds of the characters in order to understand them and to relate to the actors. I certainly wanted a deep kinship with Andy. I also really connected with Linda Cardellini's character, who feels alone and separated from her family.

Vincent's character Tommy was a different challenge altogether. He was basically a little boy who was corrupted and confused. He witnessed something so intense that he literally had blocked it out. He had no memory of what he had seen. At the end when Andy is pushing him to remember what happened, it's pretty melodramatic, but it had to be that extreme in order to ring true . . . because [Tommy] has pushed the truth so far down into his subconscious that he really had no idea what fucked him up. Then comes the pseudo-Catholic moment when he tries to kill himself. He opens his arms in front of a train, in symbolic

Vincent Kartheiser in *The Unsaid* (Universal, 2001)

fashion. Those scenes really did require an emotional commitment, from the actors and from myself.

I was shocked by the ending. I didn't expect a mainstream film to go there, because it's such a taboo subject.

Some people figure it out early, but most people don't realize how tragic it's going to get. In the flashbacks, you see the husband attacking his wife like a madman, and you have to think that, if he's just caught her with another guy, he's overreacting. Then once you know what the circumstances are, you're likely to have different feelings about it . . . But did she deserve to be beaten to death? No.

I had a long discussions with the actress playing young Tommy's mother, about how this situation with her son might have evolved. It started with having her child in bed with her. The boy was needy. She was comforting him and one thing lead to another . . . The starved-for-affection mother justified it to herself as love. It's hard for me to believe that any parent could ever justify that, but some do. These things have and do happen. In this case, it wasn't just about sex so much as it was about an unfulfilled need for physical love that she wasn't getting from her husband.

To me, it's a movie of extreme horrific magnitude. This type of horror is beyond what you want to think a person could rationally do. And her punishment for that is so severe. As a result, this little boy grows up sexually damaged, and he's just as violent to women as his father was with his mother. He snaps, and suddenly he's acting out the things he's been trying to suppress for all those years. Maybe it's as close as I'm ever going to get to *The Exorcist*-caliber horror, at least in terms of the real human emotions at their peak. In *The Unsaid*, that one event in the past opened the psychological door for a demon to come in. It created the battleground for these characters. All that was missing was a supernatural element.

A supernatural element would have made it easier to deal with, in some ways. "*The devil made them do it.*" This is too real, even for horror movie audiences.

When the movie was over, I had a sense of a huge emotional weight being lifted off of me. At the same time, I didn't want to let it go. I was afraid it might not be successful. We were telling a complex, multi-layered story, forcing the viewer to participate in something very uncomfortable, and it evoked strong reactions.

I think Universal decided that movie was just too dark tonally to make money. Maybe there wasn't a way to properly promote it. They didn't believe there was an American audience for this kind of thriller. On the other hand, the Europeans and press overseas totally embraced it. We received a standing ovation at the Deauville Film Festival. Reviewers in France understood what we were trying to do, and they loved it. Partly because they thought it was a very European film.

The French were like, "Well, of course a boy could want to sleep with his mother. It's psychologically very natural." Here, we say, "Oh God! Are you fucking kidding me?!" It doesn't mean that those thoughts have not gone through certain people's heads. It's that they're never going to admit that out loud, or even to themselves.

You can say it in a horror film, because it's less realistic—like in your episode of *Freddy's Nightmares*. That audience will accept it under those conditions.

When we shot that scene [where the teenage boy dreams he is being French kissed by his mother], people said, "Oh God, the kid's kissing his mother!" In reality, it's just an actor kissing another actor, but people had such extreme reactions. But in *Freddy's Nightmares*, the whole scenario is so fantastic and so over the top . . . it wasn't presented in a realistic way. I do wonder what would happen if *The Unsaid* was being released today. It seems like people now more open to disturbing movies that are grounded in a deep sense of humanity.

I have one more random question about *The Unsaid*: What's the significance of 333? In the film, there's a scene where Andy wakes up and the clock reads 3:33, and you said on the DVD commentary track there's some significance to that number in your life?

This falls into the category of "strange but true" . . . For years, I always found myself arbitrarily looking at my watch at 3:33. And it always gave me a feeling of déjà vu. So in a number of my movies, whenever I had to arbitrarily pick what time a clock was going to be set at, I always chose that number. It's in "The Prophecies" and a few films. I've never really talked about it until

I recorded the DVD commentary on *The Unsaid*, which I recorded in Auckland, New Zealand, while I was making *Murder in Greenwich*.

About two weeks after I did the commentary, I got a phone call in the middle of the night from my younger brother Jim. He said, "I've got bad news. Mom's dead." I rolled over in bed and my eye went right to the digital clock and it was 3:33. That was it. That was the time that I heard that my mother was dead. What was so strange was that I had just brought up this anecdote on the DVD commentary two weeks earlier, and had said, "One day, maybe, I'll figure this out."

I experienced a complex emotional release when I heard my mother died. I truly regretted not being there, but the good thing was that she went peacefully and quickly. She didn't suffer for a long time like my father did. The hard part was that I was on the other side of the world, in the middle of a shoot. The funeral couldn't wait until I was done shooting, so I had to help make arrangements while I was in New Zealand. The really sad thing was that my wife and kids were on location with me, and we couldn't afford to fly the whole family back to L.A. for the funeral. Thankfully, Nancy was very understanding, as were the kids.

On the last day of the third shooting week, I got a car to take me directly from the set to the airport, got on a plane, flew to L.A., gained back that day and a half [because of the time zone change], came home for a few hours, then went to the mortuary to see my mother, spent some time with my brothers and sister, came back home, slept for a few hours, got up and went to the funeral, gave the eulogy, said everything I could think of to say about my mother, then went from the funeral into a car, back to the airport for another fifteen-hour flight. On the morning I got back to New Zealand, I literally went directly from the airport to the set and continued to shoot the movie. It was just like when my father died. Once again, had no time to grieve. People would ask me, "Are you okay?" And I'd say, "Yeah, I'm fine. Let's shoot."

Wow . . . I guess it's a good thing that you thrive on chaos. I remember you once told me that you enjoy being in the eye of the hurricane.

I miss being on set every day I'm not. I miss the excitement of creating. Of course I'm conscious that any number of things can and do go wrong, but I'm still happiest when I'm working. I remember one time somebody asked Steven Spielberg what the hardest thing is about directing and he said, "Getting out of the car when I arrive on set." On some shoots I have so much anxiety about getting everything done. On other shoots, I go in thinking: I know what I want to do, but if it doesn't all happen that way, *I know something else great will happen—because I have a great crew of talented people and everybody is watching everybody else's back.*

When I first met John Frankenheimer, I asked if he still loved directing. He said, "What I really love to do is fish or hunt, and that's when I feel like myself. Once I'm refreshed [by doing what I really love], then I can go and be a director." I thought to myself, *Boy, I'm not I'm not cut from that cloth at all.* I am the most myself when I'm watching movies. When I'm making a movie, I'm watching. I'm looking at the script, trying to find something really interesting to focus on . . . or I'm watching the actors, looking for those great moments and remembering them for the edit. That's the only way I know to direct. That's how I got into this. It's an obsessive passion.

If I'm not making movies, I'm going to the movies. Watching movies makes my love for what I do that much stronger—because I'm constantly learning new things, looking at things in new ways, and thinking about things that I've never thought about before. Fellini said that he didn't like watching other people's movies because he didn't want to be influenced by them. I can understand not wanting to watch somebody else's movies when you're making your movie—because you don't want to confuse your vision. At the same time, I love it when I recognize the influence of an earlier film on somebody else's film. Artists copied Rembrandt and Monet because Rembrandt and Monet were brilliant. I can't think of any piece of art or music that hasn't been influenced by someone else's work.

Murder in Greenwich seems to be influenced a bit by *Sunset Boulevard*. In both films, the main character addresses the audience from beyond the grave. Was that part of the original script?

The history of that movie is that Fox made a deal for Mark Fuhrman's book [*Murder in Greenwich*]. Somehow that deal fell apart. Then USA picked it up. What they were hoping to do was make it part of a series of films introduced by Dominick Dunne. I think [Dunne] was either going to host the series, or do book ends where he introduced and wrapped up each movie, like "Masterpiece Theater." Then that fell through. After all of that, the producer Bernie Sofronski was left with very little money to make his project, but he still was determined to do it.

Dominick Dunne wasn't going to be involved anymore, but his name stayed on it because money had been spent. And contrary to what a lot of reviewers said, Mark Fuhrman wasn't involved at all. I never met him, I never spoke with him, and he never came to the set. I don't know if he even read the script. Fuhrman is still a character in the movie, but I put more focus on Martha. Also her mother, who was so devoted to solving the murder.

It's interesting that you chose to focus on the victim instead of building the film around the investigation of her murderer, Michael Skakel.

Jon Foster completely threw himself into the role of Michael. He became a recluse for days and put himself into that very dark frame of mind. In the fight scene between him and his brother, those guys really went at it. I kept saying, "Guys, don't kill yourselves." And they'd say, "No, no, we really want to go for it." Almost all the actors in *Greenwich* pushed themselves to make everything as real as possible.

What I wanted to convey was the sense that Martha was telling the story, calling out from the grave. We had a wonderful script by David Erickson, and he had that voiceover in the script, but I wanted to *see* her talking to us. I wanted to make her presence part of the fabric of the whole movie, so I shot her monologues with a moving camera, to create a sense that her spirit was weaving in and out of the movie. Shooting the monologues with Maggie Grace [the actress who plays Martha] was the challenge, because they had not been scheduled. I had to pull her off to the side whenever I could. I'd get her into a room with a camera man

Jon Foster and Toby Moore as the Skakel brothers in *Murder in Greenwich* (USA, 2002)

and the sound guy and just let them shoot while I was setting up the next scene outside.

A lot of what we did on that movie was very instinctive. We were in the cemetery shooting the funeral sequence, and we finished up by shooting Martha's grave marker in the grass. We had all these leaves blowing across it, because I was trying to make it look like autumn in New England, even though we were shooting in the middle of summer in New Zealand. We had a warehouse full of spray-painted leaves, which the art department carried around in huge bags. When we were done, everybody was starting to pack up and bag the leaves, and I said, "No, wait, I want to do a slow move in on the marker." The producer was looking at his watch and saying, "We have to make a move. What is this for?" I said, "I don't know. I just want to shoot this thing while we've got the camera here. It'll take me five minutes. Give me five minutes and if I can't do it in that time you can pull the plug." He said, "Okay, you've got five minutes." So we shot this slow push in on the grave marker, and had a leaf blower slowly uncover it. I really didn't know what I was going to do with it. It wasn't until I got

Jon Foster and Maggie Grace as young lovers in *Murder in Greenwich* (USA, 2002)

Foster and Grace as murderer and victim in *Murder in Greenwich* (USA, 2002)

into post-production that I even remembered I had that shot. It seemed like the perfect way to start—clearing away the leaves to reveal the girl and her story. I think some of the leaves even had blood on them, because we had used them in the scene where Martha gets killed. That became the opening title sequence.

Why did you shoot the movie in New Zealand?

When they started looking for a place to shoot it, the obvious choice was Toronto. It's close to the east coast and it would have been much easier to do a period setting there and make it look like Greenwich. But there was not enough money, even with the tax breaks in Canada. It turned out that at that point, New Zealand was fifty cents to the American dollar—so without any tax breaks at all it was going to be cheaper than Toronto. Sony had a relationship with an independent production entity down there, run by Jake Rose. He convinced Sony to make the movie in New Zealand.

Bernie and I thought this was crazy. We went kicking and screaming. But Jake was right. Once we got down there, we were both completely in love with that wonderful country. Everything about it—the weather, the people—gave us this feeling that, no matter what happened, making this movie was going to be an enjoyable experience because New Zealand is such an enjoyable place to be.

When we did our first casting session down there, the actors who came in were totally prepared. They had read the scripts and worked with American voice coaches so that they could do the accents. They were extremely professional, and it was just a question of who was right for each part. I had a crew that would party on the weekends, get out all their pent up energy, then come to the set on Monday mornings, ready to work and happy to be there. Nobody complained. The crew responded to my every request with such enthusiasm—and often they'd come up with something even better than what I asked for.

I had a wonderful production designer, Michael Ralph, who loved the challenge of turning Auckland into Greenwich. Basically, we had a choice of two houses that looked right, and we used both of them—one for the Skakel house and one for Martha's house. We shot almost the entire movie in those two houses and those two yards. On the weekends, me and Michael and the Australian D.P. Mark Wareham worked out the production board. The film was incredibly overambitious for the schedule, but we were hell-bent to make it extremely cinematic. We shot some scenes with three cameras, and me and Mark were running back and forth the whole time. We tried to keep the camera moving and to make the locations as interesting as possible throughout the whole process, working within whatever restraints we had. It all came together incredibly well. The only sad thing about the New Zealand shoot was the death of my mother. It was shocking and heartbreaking to lose her, but I can't imagine a better cocoon that I could have been in at that time than making this film, with that cast and crew, in that country.

Years later, when I wrapped *The Staircase Murders* in New Orleans, I was depressed because that shoot hadn't gone well. I knew I'd shot everything I could think of to shoot, but I felt like I didn't get the movie I wanted. I shot a lot of pieces, but I didn't know how the pieces were going to come together, and I didn't have that feeling of closure that I usually get when production wraps. I was pacing in my hotel room on the wrap night, feeling like I should tear up my DGA card. Around 2 in the morning, I flipped on the TV and it so happened that *Murder in Greenwich* was on. I sat on the edge of the bed and starting watching it. It was such a blessing. It broke me out of the doom and gloom mood I was in. After that, I could go to sleep without feeling like I was the worst director in the world.

Those two movies have very different aesthetics. Even though it's nominally a movie about murder, *Murder in Greenwich* is very warm and comforting in a way. It has a lot of color and a lot of light. It's like a reassuring dream of a deceased loved one. On the other hand, *The Staircase Murders* is very cold and dark. And so is *D.C. Sniper*.

That definitely was the objective. When you watch a movie with "murder" in the title, you're expecting something dark, but I wanted to make it about life and the loss of a life that was special. Like I said, I wanted the movie to have an emotional connection to Martha. Hopefully the audience wants to see Mark Fuhrman solve the murder, because we care about Martha. Maggie was the center of the film. The heart. She was able to project that warmth and innocence and that very pure sexuality of the all-American

Maggie Grace, the All-American Girl

girl. She's not just a pretty face—she's very grounded and really connected to the work. You can look into her eyes and see that she is listening and processing everything. She really has the gift.

But some of what you're talking about is really a credit to the director of photography—Mark Wareham, who did both

Greenwich and *D.C. Sniper*, and Lloyd Ahern, who did *Staircase* (and so many other films of mine). Everything is always thoroughly planned out. I decided, before we started shooting *Murder in Greenwich*, to look at all the stock footage I could find in Hollywood of Greenwich and the east coast. Then, when I was picking locations in New Zealand, I planned around the best stock footage instead of doing it the other way around. I'd see a piece of stock footage that had fog in it, and then we would add fog to our corresponding scene. That way I could start with a huge flying vista and dissolve into a ground-level scene with our painted leaves. The scope was really important to me. It opens up the movie and makes it feel like a bigger story.

Where did you shoot *D.C. Sniper*?

That was Vancouver.

I wonder what *Murder in Greenwich* would have been like if you'd shot it there. Would it have been comparably drab?

It wouldn't have been, because we chose our color palettes. For *Murder in Greenwich*, we wanted those light colors and that feeling of the 1970s—including the drug parties and all. I was trying to create what I remember that world looking like when I was younger. Not that I'm an expert on '70s drug parties or anything . . . [laughs]

It reminds me of *The Virgin Suicides*—that same look.

Yes. She [director Sofia Coppola] did a wonderful job with that film. I love her vision.

The aesthetics of *D.C. Sniper* are the complete opposite.

I wanted *D.C. Sniper* to have this cold, blue palette. Part of it's in the shooting, but it's also related to the color timing in post-production.

That blue-gray palette conveys a strong sense of despair.

Every time I scouted a location in prep, I would figure out which direction we were going to be shooting. Then we would paint the walls. Nine out of ten people don't notice the use of those colors throughout the film, at least not consciously, but I believe it affects their impression of that world. I try to keep those things somewhat subliminal, so it doesn't pull the viewer out of the story.

What made you want to direct *D.C. Sniper*?

USA network wanted to make a movie about [Police Chief Charles] Moose and all the pressure he was under to find out who was the killer. When we began making the movie, the police of course had John Muhammad and Lee Boyd Malvo in custody, but they had not been convicted yet. The FBI had not released much background information about them. I managed to get information from people who weren't supposed to speak about the case. The more information I got, the more obsessed I became with the father/son relationship between the murderers. So I started splitting the focus of the movie because, while I thought Moose was a fascinating character and Charles Dutton turned in a hell of a performance, I became more interested in the snipers. I wanted to show what I had learned. How they could have done what they did.

John Muhammad was a very twisted father figure. This was his way of feeling in control. He praised this teenage boy [Malvo] for doing evil, horrific things. The kid needed love and this was his way of getting love. To me, that was the scariest thing about the whole story . . . Muhammad was desperately trying to be a surrogate father to this boy, because his wife had taken away his real kids. Malvo never had a father, so this fulfilled a need for him. The thing that was most revealing to me was seeing the sketches that Malvo had drawn in prison. They were artistically really good. Also some of the things he had written made me realize that this was a child who had potential, but who was used in an incredibly horrific way by his father-figure to get attention.

Trent Cameron and Bobby Hosea in *D.C. Sniper: 23 Days of Fear* (USA, 2003)

Muhammad definitely had his own agenda. As I started to hook into his story, I realized that these are the villains that are really hard to stop, because they truly believe that they're on an important mission—whether they're shooting down someone in a parking lot or crashing a plane into the Twin Towers. They believe that they're doing it for a higher purpose. They rationalize: "This is a good thing I'm doing. It's going to change people's lives. It will make a lasting impression on the American way of life." How can you fight a villain that believes they are totally right and justified?

I wanted the actors, Bobby Hosea [who plays Muhammad] and Trent Cameron [who plays Malvo], to work deeply with these characters on an emotional level, so that it wasn't just a story about two guys shooting people. I wanted to explore how they got to that point, why they were doing what they were doing, and how it escalated until they got cocky and sloppy and then were caught. I thought there was a really compelling story to be told from the standpoint of those two characters.

In the process of working this story out, I kept questioning whether there was any chance that these two guys might be found innocent. This had just happened six months ago. *Should we make sure these guys really are the real killers, before we start pointing fingers?* But truthfully, after all the research I did, I had absolutely no doubt that they were the Beltway Killers. I figured

Tom and Charles Dutton on the set of *D.C. Sniper*

out what they were doing with the walkie-talkies that were found in the car before that became public knowledge. David Erickson did an amazing job with the script [*D.C. Sniper*]. I tried to make it as much of a psychological thriller as I could, without losing track of Chief Moose's story.

Charles [Dutton] is one of the greatest actors and greatest people that I've ever worked with. He doesn't talk about the role. He doesn't intellectualize. He takes a couple of simple notes, then goes in and does his job with flawless consistency. Most of the time, he remained very private. There were hours and hours of tape [of Chief Moose], but he didn't want to try to imitate the man note-for-note. He just immersed himself in the situations and became an even stronger version of Chief Moose.

Was that the first movie you did where you had to be conscious of the fact that the audience was going to compare the movie to real life? The murder of Martha Moxley had happened decades before the *Murder in Greenwich* movie came along...

True. With Michael Skakel, all you saw in the media was an overweight Irish guy being led off to prison. And all that most people knew about Martha Moxley was that she was a pretty, blonde fifteen-year-old girl. With *D.C. Sniper*, all the details were fresh in everyone's mind. The whole country had been watching, because everybody was looking over their shoulders at gas pumps and afraid to go to Home Depot. Nobody knew how or why the killers were choosing their targets. And nobody believed that it was just one person doing the shooting. People thought it was a diabolically well-orchestrated terrorist attack.

There was a lot of freedom to create Muhammad and Malvo as characters, because all we'd seen at that point were their mug shots. The two actors worked extremely well together. Both are incredible actors. They played frightfully well the premise that they weren't doing anything wrong.

I wanted to end the movie with Muhammad and his anger—knowing that the kid had squealed and now he's completely fucked. I did not win that battle. I was required to end the movie with the sequence of Moose and his wife going to a football game. The network wanted a scene that suggested that everything is okay. I do understand their thinking . . . but to me, seeing the villain realize that he is finished is a more satisfactory conclusion. Overall, I'm incredibly proud of the film. It won two NAACP awards for Best Television Movie and Best Actor (Charles Dutton).

Your next movie was quite a change of pace. If I'm not mistaken, *A Very Married Christmas* is your only straight-ahead comedy?

Unfortunately, I think that movie was perceived as an interesting failure.

You perceived it as an interesting failure?

No, I didn't. Seems like everyone else did—the critics and the network. The film was based on a book called *Say When*, which really was not about Christmas at all. It was about a husband and wife breaking up, and how their daughter gets caught in the middle. Joe Mantegna was doing *Joan of Arcadia* at CBS and he

Joe Mantegna, Tom and Charles Durning on the set of *A Very Married Christmas*

was looking for a movie project, and the network decided that he would be perfect for this. I've known Joe for years because he's a close friend of Jean Smart's. Then we got Jean to play his wife. I was very excited to work with these two incredibly gifted actors, as well as Charles Durning [who plays the character Ozzy Larson]. I could go on and on about Charles Durning. He's such a remarkable individual.

While I was shooting, I found myself going back into some of my early influences, especially Buster Keaton. I brought all of my Keaton DVDs up to Toronto and watched them at night in my hotel room. I wanted Joe's character to be like Keaton. I said to Joe, "I want to approach this character as somebody who is really out of step with the rest of the world. He doesn't know anything about dating, so there's this awkwardness about him." And I wanted him to play out the awkwardness physically.

Normally, Christmas movies are light and fluffy. But Joe, Jean and I said, "Let's make this *real.*" When the husband and wife went at each other, it got nasty. It was a real knock-down between a couple of people who know each other so well that they're able to go right for the throat. The producer had me tone it down quite a bit in editing. Still, we horrified the network. They said, "Oh my God! This is not a fun Christmas movie. We've got to play up more comedy. At least make the music funnier." We wanted something more in the style of *About Schmidt.* The network wanted a much more sugary-sweet holiday movie.

We shot the movie under the title *Say When,* but they changed it to *A Very Married Christmas,* which we hated. We must have gone through 400 different titles trying to find something else, but CBS wanted that one. Then they sent out the press release hyping it as a heartfelt Christmas movie. Of course the critics were really taken aback when they saw it. "How dare you make a Christmas movie about divorce, and put this poor child at the center of the story?" I thought: *Wait a minute*—It's a Wonderful Life *is a movie that starts with an attempted suicide. And Charles Dickens's* A Christmas Carol *is basically a story about thinking you're dead and seeing the worst side of your humanity.* I'm not trying to say that *A Very Married Christmas* is equal to *It's a Wonderful Life* or Dickens, but my point is that some of the ugliest events in people's lives can happen during what's supposed to be the happiest time of the year.

Unfortunately, our characters are going through a divorce at Christmas. The husband is trying to escape his pain and trying to be a man. The wife is trying to redefine herself. And then there's this guy who might be Santa Claus. If he's not, then maybe he should be. There's a little touch of fantasy at the end of the movie, where Joe Mantegna wants to believe that maybe the guy really is Santa Claus. The movie isn't saying that is true, but he *wants to believe* it's true. As do we.

That's an upbeat message. Maybe people who thought it was too harrowing missed the point.

I enjoyed the movie immensely while I was making it, especially all the physical comedy stuff. I was shell-shocked when the network said it wasn't working for them. Then I learned that the exec who pitched the idea to them never read the script. They never knew anything about the complexity of the relationship between the husband and the wife.

On the set, we did occasionally ask ourselves: "Should this confrontation really be this strong? Should they be insulting each other this much?" But we always came back to the truth that if both characters aren't fully engaged in this emotional battle, then we're not committing to the reality of life. When people feel hurt, they do get protective and selfish and they lash out at the other person. There's extreme pain in that kind of breakup and that pain has to come out. I wanted that in the movie. And I don't believe we made the wrong decision. I think what we did wrong was trying, in post, to make the movie into something it wasn't. I wish the network had embraced it for what it actually was. Had the film been released as a feature, perhaps those critics would not have reacted so harshly to the darkness of the story.

You moved into a new phase of your career after that and did a series of Lifetime movies focused on teenage characters. I like to think of it as your "high school phase"—*She's Too Young, Odd Girl Out, Cyber Seduction, Not Like Everyone Else* and *Fab Five*. This was during the same period that your own kids were in high school, right?

Yes. The most recent movie I did where my family went on location and was part of the moviemaking process was *She's Too Young*. We shot that in Halifax, Nova Scotia, and my kids have incredibly fond memories of Halifax. My son Shane shot some second unit stuff on the set and Hannah did some acting. They were really part of the experience. As was Nancy. There were also family influences that affected the script. I remember two specific instances at our apartment when Hannah and Nancy got into some kind of argument. I literally took their dialogue and put it into the movie. The great thing was that when the movie aired, a number of teenagers posted on the Lifetime website: "Yeah, that's exactly how that argument would go with my mom."

She's Too Young was the beginning of tackling darker aspects of the teen world. I was trying to play out things with realism but also with a film noir style. I couldn't escape from that film noir look in those films, because to me it really reflected the subject matter. We were creating a world where the main character always suffers these feelings of alienation, loneliness and anger. And many of the girls were truly femme fatales.

Did you approach *She's Too Young* with a sense that you were getting into new territory as a storyteller?

Yes and no. On one hand, I had done films with similar story dynamics involving younger characters—*One Dark Night, Friday the 13th*, even *Date with an Angel* (where the characters are older but still act like teenagers)—so that wasn't unusual. The challenge on this was making a movie about teenagers and oral sex. I didn't know of anything on network television that dealt with that. You have to remember that this was made just after the Clinton administration, when oral sex was a hot topic in the media. If you look closely, you'll see that I named the school in the movie Clinton High.

Before I signed on, I did a lot of research on teenage sexuality, and was shocked by what I found. I talked with so many doctors who said, "You have no idea how many STD cases there are in the public schools these days . . . but it's all kept under wraps. Nobody wants anybody else to know that their kid is having sex." Halifax is probably one of the most squeaky-clean cities I have stepped into in the twenty-first century. You could fire a cannon ball down the streets on Sundays and not hit anybody. And the teenagers seemed like they had stepped out of some small town in the 1950s . . . But even at the school where we were shooting, I was hearing those same stories. There were posters on the walls about safe sex. The school clinic was giving out free condoms . . . but when I talked to the kids, they treated it like a joke: "Would I wear a condom that was given to me by a teacher at school? Hell no!" They'd take the condoms and put them on the antennas of their cars, or make water balloons out of them. One doctor told me about a school dance where all the adult chaperones stood

Megan Park and Miriam McDonald on the set of *She's Too Young*

around the perimeter of the gym, while the kids formed dance circles within that circle. In the middle, a girl would service her boyfriend while the others kept watch to make sure the parents and teachers couldn't see them. Again, this was a very squeaky-clean community. That was a huge awakening for me as a parent.

You got such honest performances out of the actors. I'm assuming that most of them were older than the characters they were playing.

Megan Park, who played the Christian girl [Becca], and Miriam McDonald [who plays Dawn] were sixteen or seventeen. I was surprised by how willing they were to act out some of those very awkward scenes. They were both so innocent, but so savvy. So many child actors grow up really fast because they get thrown into this adult world and they have to adapt. I wanted them all to think about how they would personally handle these situations.

Alexis Dziena in *She's Too Young* (Lifetime, 2004)

Alexis [Dziena, who plays Hannah] was amazing. She's attractive and sweet and has incredible depth. She was a little older than the others—about twenty, I think, but still completely believable as a fourteen-year old. I really didn't want to do the low-budget horror movie thing, where you hire twenty-eight-year olds to play seventeen-year olds. I needed them to look fourteen. Of course, today's fourteen-year olds don't look the same way a fourteen-year old looked when I was growing up. Kids mature so fast now.

The tough thing for me as the filmmaker was telling this story from all sides. I couldn't just focus on my own agenda as a parent. It's not Ward and June Cleaver sitting down and explaining things. I had to take a number of different characters with different perspectives, throw them all together and show everything—because the story isn't just about any one position. I was always in awe of what John Hughes was able to do in his "teen movies," especially with *The Breakfast Club*. He presented so many different perspectives and, even though nobody in real life is as articulate as his characters, it seemed like he always hit all the right notes.

Did the actors in *She's Too Young* improvise some of their own lines?

A lot of times actors will look at the script and say, "I'd never say that." They are convinced that the words just aren't going to sound right coming out of their mouth or out of their characters. The trick is to avoid putting too much emphasis on any particular word. When they just throw it away, it usually works. Sometimes someone will come up with something new that sounds great. Many times, I don't know if it's a new expression or if they just made it up in the moment. It doesn't matter as long as it seems organic to that character or the moment.

Are younger, less experienced actors more open to being directed than older, more experienced actors?

That depends. I've worked with many actors early in their careers who, because of some advice from a casting director or an acting coach, are very self-conscious. In general, it's easier working with an actor who understands the circumstances of the scene and is not concerned with how you're photographing them or how many takes you're going to do or how they're being lit.

I guess that has a lot to do with how comfortable people are in their own skin. In my opinion, that's what the best parts of the *She's Too Young* are about—Hannah becoming comfortable in her own skin.

One of Lifetime's stock-in-trades for a while was the mother's story about her daughter's problems. *She's Too Young* was part of the movement in that direction. *Homeless to Harvard* was an earlier movie that went that direction and did extremely well. Lifetime could have dismissed that movie as a fluke, but instead they allowed me to take the principal focus off of Marcia Gay Harden and put it onto the kids in *She's Too Young*. I was really honored to work with Marcia Gay Harden. Without her, the movie wouldn't have had the same dramatic weight. She was very supportive of my desire to put the emphasis on the teenage girls.

These scripts can be preachy, particularly in the scenes that focus on the parent's point of view. As a soon-to-be mother, Marcia understood the importance of reaching the teenage audience. When we were shooting, we trimmed back any preaching as much as we could. She was really a creative collaborator.

There's some really interesting character development in the movie. You seem to imply backstories for several of the supporting characters. You certainly gave Nick [Hannah's boyfriend] more depth than the story required.

I tried to do that with images. Nick takes Hannah home to this cavernous, empty house. There's no one there. He plays the phone message from his father, saying, "I'm not going to be home tonight, so use the credit card to order a pizza. Do whatever you want." I know from my own experience how I sometimes, as a parent, absent-mindedly used money to make up for feeling like I have not spent enough time with my kids. Nick was the kid who is basically raising himself. And not in a good way.

He was also somewhat inspired by a real person. There was a great documentary on PBS about an outbreak of syphilis at a high school in the South. The school had something like eighty cases that broke out and the parents and administrators were all saying, "What the hell is going on? How can this happen here?!"

It turned out that the kids were organizing sex parties. If you participated, you were in the cool group. I put that idea into a scene in *She's Too Young*. I purposely shot it handheld with night vision, so that greenish color makes everything even creepier. It adds to the "ick factor." So does the fact that everyone except Marcia Gay Harden is totally blasé about what's going on.

The documentary was a huge help. I could draw on the interviews with some of the young girls who were being coldly rational about what they had done and how many guys they had done it with. I used those influences when I was directing the actors. The note that I gave over and over again was "Just the facts." The more casual their delivery, the more horrifying their stories sounded. Especially if you're a parent.

I thought Miriam McDonald, who played Dawn, did an amazing job in the scene where she's talking to the social worker. The social worker asks, "How many boys were you with?" The entire time she's explaining, she tries not to cry. But then it happens anyway. Miriam kept trying to wipe the tears away from her face while talking. I knew she could do that, because she did it in the audition. Things like that really grounded the movie in truth, for me.

That's an interesting technique. It's reverse psychology—you tell the actors "try not to be scared, try not to cry" and it makes it more realistic when they show fear or remorse.

I also tried to make the camera movement look more realistic. My son Shane was going to Providence High School at the time, and they had an incredible filmmaking class. His film teacher Mr. Durkin put together a program where the kids were shooting their own little films and editing them. When I was starting *She's Too Young*, I went to speak to the class and watched some of their films . . . and what struck me was that those films had no rules. The teacher kept trying to emphasize structure and discipline in their storytelling, but the kids were just doing what they thought was cool. They were making movies based purely on their own instincts. Every so often, I would see something that was far more interesting and innovative than anything I'd ever seen from professional filmmakers. That was a real revelation.

That inspired me to bring a handheld consumer camera onto the set of *She's Too Young*. When my son was on the high school set, I'd give him the camera and say, "Just go shoot whatever you think looks cool." We shot a lot of the scenes revolving around the teenage characters—like the one where they are singing in the car—with consumer cameras. I felt that added a sense of realism, because it seemed as if one of the characters was recording what was happening. I kept telling my camera man, "Don't worry about the rules. I just want color, energy, excitement and unpredictability. Don't worry if it's not in focus. Find focus during the shot. I'll use those moments as cut points." The producers said, "Lifetime is *not* going to like this." But they did. They totally embraced it. In fact, they wanted more.

For me, it adds more than just energy. It gives you the feeling that you've been thrown into a world on the move. It adds a sense of unpredictability. Of course I had to be true to what each scene was trying to say. If it was a scene that was about the relationship between the characters—like the scene where Nick and Hannah are kissing on the couch, and in her mind it's like this old fashioned romance—then I let that play true without adding any conflicting camera movements. The goal is to get the viewer to identify with the emotion in the scene on a personal level.

When I was a student in Paris, I went to Rodin's Museum and I saw his sculpture "The Kiss." I could not stop staring. It triggered a memory of my first kiss. I was twelve years old and on the Peter Pan ride at Disneyland. That was also the first time a girl grabbed my hand on a date . . . The specifics of these moments aren't important. It's the *feeling*. I was overwhelmed that this piece of stone, sculpted by an artist a hundred years ago, could have such a profound effect on me. Certain images resonate in your subconscious mind and stick with you forever.

Odd Girl Out is another movie about a mother and daughter, but this one is even more narrowly focused on the daughter.

That was based on the book by Rachel Simmons. She interviewed high school girls and their parents, and their stories all deal with feeling like an outsider. The book was enormously popular—almost as popular as *Queen Bees and Wannabes*, which was the basis for the movie *Mean Girls*. Lifetime bought *Odd Girl Out* with the intention of doing their own version of *Mean Girls*. The first thing I did with the script was remove everything that resembled *Mean Girls*. I did not want the audience to feel that we were just recycling the same theme, ideas, or story. Also, *Odd Girl Out* was certainly not a comedy [like *Mean Girls*].

The second thing I did was remove the father figure from the story. What happened in *She's Too Young* was that the father became somebody for the mother to bounce ideas off of. That was his only function, because in the world of Lifetime the mother is the driving force. The father character had to offset her in certain respects—to be more open when she was more cautious, or more energetic when she would be more calm. I didn't want to do that again. So I took him out. I thought that added another undercurrent of pain. I remember in *E.T.*, when Elliot brought up his dad at the dinner table and everyone got quiet. There's a scene later where he smells his dad's cologne on a shirt he left behind. You never see the father, but his presence is strong in that movie.

Right up until we went into photography, we still had one scene in *Odd Girl Out* where the dad shows up in the hospital, after Vanessa attempts suicide. We cut that but kept a line of dialogue saying that he'd been there. I wanted the audience to feel that the father has nothing to do with the story's outcome.

It helps the mother-daughter dynamic because they're both on their own. Once they realize that, it strengthens their relationship. The lasting bond is between the mother and the daughter—as in *She's Too Young*.

Richard Kletter wrote some really good dialogue that made the mother seem vulnerable—like when Vanessa asks her mom if she still has any friends from high school. Mom says, regretfully, "Not really." I think that gave Vanessa more insight into her mom really humanized her and brought them closer together.

But to me, *She's Too Young* and *Odd Girl Out* are worlds apart. In *She's Too Young*, Marcia Gay Harden was actively trying to solve her daughter's problems. In *Odd Girl Out*, the mother wants to be able to solve her daughter's problems, but Vanessa really has to do it on her own. The movie was originally supposed to end with a big graduation sequence that I took out. I think it was so much stronger to end on the scene where Vanessa stands up for herself and tells her friend to fuck off. That unquestionably demonstrates the growth of her character. Viewers really responded to that scene because it's one of those moments that doesn't always happen in life, but you wish it would. Another example of movies as wish fulfillment.

Tell me about casting *Odd Girl Out*.

Alexa Vega was a child actress. She had done many things,

Tom and Alexa Vega on the set of *Odd Girl Out*

including Robert Rodriguez's *Spy Kids*. She's a terrific actress and as sweet as can be. All of her sisters are actresses too, and their mother brings all the girls on location whenever one of them gets a movie. They're all there as a supportive family group. They're home schooled and they take day trips together on the days off. When the next one of them gets booked on another gig, off they go. They have the most incredible childhood. Her mother also acts as a kind of acting coach, so she was on set all the time, going over scenes with Alexa.

I also had some other fantastic young actors in that movie. Leah Pipes is amazing. Elizabeth Rice had played Natalie Wood in a TV movie directed by Peter Bogdanovich [*The Mystery of Natalie Wood*]. There is something about her eyes that is utterly captivating. Alicia Morton, the little blonde girl who played Tiffany, was a Broadway star from "Annie." Tiffany's sidekick was my daughter. Hannah was in a number of scenes throughout the movie. And as her father, I was amazed to see her make acting choices that were completely different than what I would expect from knowing my daughter. I thought she has very unique, totally honest instincts.

Leah Pipes, Tom McLoughlin, Elizabeth Rice, Alexa Vega and Hannah McLoughlin in *Odd Girl Out*

It's easy to dismiss the guys in Lifetime movies, but they had some great moments. Chad Biagini was the boy who played the love interest and the one that the girls use as their reason for being pissed off at each other. I allowed him to improvise the scene with Alexa at the beginning of the movie. It was great!

The scene where he admits to liking "chick flicks"?

Yeah. We kicked around various ideas about what they could say. I thought that really added something to the scene—the fact he admitted that. I loved this sense of two people exploring each other. Elizabeth Rice's character sees them flirting and says, "Oh look who thinks she's all that." Some great teen girl moments. In many instances, all they needed was a look. For those girls, staring was a weapon.

One of the most interesting things for me about making that movie was I learned the importance of telling a perfect lie. To some extent, the better you lie the easier it will be for you to get through some of the harder situations in life. You have to be a good actor. More importantly, you have to somehow believe your own lies—because if you totally commit and believe them, then other people will tend to believe them too. It's scary how much we all lie in situations where we feel we have to.

On this point, I worked particularly hard with Leah Pipes, who played Vanessa's best friend. I made her convince me that she believed her own lies. What her character wants is to make sure her friend doesn't think she would ever do anything wrong, so she has to be extremely intimate when they talk. I would get the camera as close to her as I possibly could, so you could see that she was being absolutely honest. You'd never suspect that she was lying . . . if you hadn't just seen what she did in the previous scene! As a viewer, you think: *Whoa! What a bitch!* But at the same time, you have to think: *I do that too, don't I?* We all do it to get out of certain situations without having to deal with a conflict or a confrontation.

To avoid being the bad guy.

That's it exactly. That's what it gets down to—nobody wants to be found out, punished, or feel unloved.

There's a scene where Leah's dad makes the joke, "Son, this is the way girls work." I think maybe there's some truth in that. Guys will exchange words or punch each other and then it's over. Later, you can't even remember what you were fighting about. Women often remember the year, the month, the day, the song that was playing, the perfume they were wearing, the dress she was in, what the other woman's hair looked like when she said *this* to me . . . It's burned into the hard drive in their brain and does not go away. Sometimes I thought: *Are we going too far with this? Am I making these encounters too brutal?* When I saw the feedback for the movie on the Internet, I realized we could have gone even further. A lot of people's true stories were far worse than ours.

Alexa Vega gives a harrowing performance.

She did. I remember two scenes where I was really pushing Alexa. One was the scene where she completely freaks out on her bed, after learning that she's been betrayed by her friends, and her mom is trying to calm her down. I wanted a gut-wrenching scream at her mom. And there seemed to be nothing in Alexa's life that she could draw on for that. Very few of us ever get to that point in life (thankfully), but I kept pushing and pushing until finally she screamed and it had this chilling crack. It's funny how a little touch like that can make all the difference. She pushed herself so hard that her voice cracked. She also had a completely insane look in her eye. I went, "That's it." And kissed her on the top of the head.

The other scene was the last scene in the movie. She had to be completely grounded in what she was saying. It's not just the words that convince Leah Pipes's character that her friend doesn't need her around anymore—it's the fact that Alexa says it with total conviction and complete confidence. It sounds simple enough, but it's not that simple to do—especially take after take, when you're repeating the same material again and again, trying to make it sound fresh and at the same time filled with 100% confidence.

I think we did the highest number of takes that I've ever done on a scene. We were going into overtime. That's not what you want to do with a sixteen-year-old actress, because not only are you costing the company money but you are also breaking the law. The only thing that made me comfortable with it was the fact that Alexa's mother was right there, being an active part of the process. She understood what I was trying to do. Most importantly, Alexa wanted to get to the point where I was happy with the performance. After every take, we'd talk about what else we needed and then try again. All the while, the producers and crew were watching the clock.

Finally, Alexa nailed the scene—as I knew she could—and we got her off the clock. Then I had to shoot the mom's reaction. I needed Lisa Vidal to react to Alexa and Leah's performances without Alexa and Leah being there. I went to her and apologized profusely. I said, "I'm really sorry about this, but I'm going to have to get the script supervisor or one of the extras to read Alexa's part, and I'm so sorry but you'll to react to that." She said, "I'm really not comfortable with that." I said, "I understand, but we need to try because we're behind schedule." We had two extras deliver the lines, while the camera was pushing in on her face. At first she seemed like she was doing okay, but at a certain point I saw her eyes glaze over. She said, "Tom, I can't do this. This is impossible without the other actress." I felt horrible. She was right that I *was* asking too much—especially at the end of a long day, for the end of the movie, and such an important scene. I have to give Lisa credit for trying. She's a pro. But this was ridiculous.

So I scrapped her reaction and came back the next day and shot her reaction when we had Alexa and Leah on set. Thank God the line producer was supportive of that. And luckily we were still shooting at the school location. You never want to go back and re-light if you don't have to. But Lisa was right. This was a big, big moment for her character. She's seeing her daughter now as a stronger person. We had to get it right, and she was 100% correct to say, "I can't make this moment honest without seeing it unfold in front of me and letting myself react." It was one of those situations where art and commerce—show and business—conflict. For me, art has to win.

At least you'd done enough films to recognize that she didn't have what she needed in order to do justice to the scene.

I'm sure that if you talked to 100 different actors, you'd get various opinions about what's needed to perform a scene like that. One might say that the editing could play a big role in it. That's Eisenstein's theory that if you show a close-up of a face, cut to a shot of what they're seeing, and then cut back to the exact same shot of that person, the audience will swear that they're reacting to what they're seeing, even though it's the exact same close-up.

Another actor might say, "I understand the time restrictions. How about I give you a series of reactions? You pick the one you like best." That might work in editing, or it might not. Actors have to do casting auditions all the time, where they're reacting to a casting director or script reader who isn't connected to the scene at all. We somehow expect them to be not only good, but so good that they nail the role. But as a director on a movie, I don't want to put my actors in that position. I don't want them to walk away from a scene feeling like they didn't connect. It alienates them from the process, and it can affect their overall performance. I think I learned that from Nancy. I have learned a lot about acting by being married to an actress. Nancy has great insight.

You talked about using handheld cameras to add realism to *She's Too Young*? What were your aesthetic plans for *Odd Girl Out*?

After seeing the movie, a few people said to me, "Why was it so dark at the school?" I intentionally made it dark because I was going for a film noir look. I had an amazing Director of Photography, John Bartley, who created the look of *The X-Files*.

The scariest thing for me and John technically was that it was the first time I shot on HD, using those big-ass cameras. I'm used to having the freedom of 35mm, 16mm, or smaller video cameras. John had never shot HD before either, so it was the blind leading the blind. We both went in with the same attitude: *Let's make the movie we want to make, shoot it the way we want to shoot it, and figure it out in post.* We had a digital imaging person on set that was constantly telling us what to do and what not to do. He was always trying to get us to register the image right down the center so that it wasn't too bright or too dark. As a filmmaker, I'd look at the monitor and think, "That doesn't look dramatic," so we were constantly changing things to get the look we wanted, and driving this poor guy crazy.

In the end, you have to embrace the possibility of being hated. It's not easy when the people who are paying you are saying, "This just is not going to work." But you need to fight to put the film first and do what you know is right. Then pray that you *are* right. Unfortunately when we got to color timing, we were assigned to a guy who believed that the network would reject the movie if the bright white colors were blasted out or there wasn't enough detail in the black. So now at this part of the process everything we had tried to do became a quality control problem. Since that time the standards have loosened up, but I found myself at that moment regretting our rebellious nature. Ultimately, with compromises from both sides, we got the look we wanted. But it took a lot of work.

How did you get involved with *Cyber Seduction*?

Richard Kletter wrote that one as well. I actually recruited him into the project. At that point we had done *She's Too Young* and *Odd Girl Out* together and the script for *Cyber Seduction* needed a page-one rewrite. The original script was horrible. I had my agent saying, "Lifetime really wants you to tell them what to do with this." And I was thinking: *Throw it in the trash.* I remember pulling off the road one day, to talk to the head of Lifetime movies and saying, "I don't know what I can do with this. I understand the story you want to tell, but it's just not there." I convinced him to hire Richard Kletter to do a total rewrite. I said if he could make it work, I'd do it.

One of the best things about *Cyber Seduction* was casting Jeremy Sumpter. My daughter, and countless other teenage girls, fell madly in love with this kid in *Peter Pan* (2003). He's terrific—he has this wild energy and spirit. I knew that if Lifetime publicized the movie correctly, and really got his face out there, it would draw a huge teenage audience. Unfortunately, a new network administration came in when we were in post-production, and they backed away from the movie. The new execs thought the subject was too slimy.

What made you want to tell this story?

The original title of the movie was *Addiction*. I kind of liked the drama of that. At one point, Kelly Lynch explodes at her son, "Justin, you're addicted!" *Addicted to porn?* The truth is, yeah, you can be addicted. There are a lot of people addicted to porn. I wanted to show—and this is the message of the movie that I stand by—that porn can be dangerous for a particular personality type. Internet porn is not a very dramatic story, but it becomes a problem for *this* kid because he has an addictive personality. He has this constant need for something that excites him. The only time he has access to the Net is at night, so he starts Red Bulling to stay awake. It doesn't make him want to go out and molest or rape girls, but it does affect the more important things in his life—his school work, his involvement in sports and his

Michael Seater, Lyndsy Fonseca and Jeremy Sumpter in *Cyber Seduction: His Secret Life* (Lifetime, 2005)

relationship with his girlfriend. And his lack of sleep has serious ramifications.

In retrospect, I realize that it was a big mistake to try and show anything on the computer screen [representing Internet porn]. Since this was Lifetime, we had to restrict ourselves to Frederick's of Hollywood-type images, which was laughable. I should have just had him staring at something on the computer that we never saw. Let his reaction tell us that what he was looking at was far worse than anything we could show. The network censors kept cutting down the images until they became so tame that it looked like a joke. But the truth is that there is something in this story that can affect your life. In making the film, I really understood how guys can start looking at females as body parts instead of seeing who they are. It's wrong, but we do it all the time.

To the mother, porn is an addiction. To the kid, it's an obsession . . . at least until he gets so absorbed in that fantasy world that he starts losing his connections to the real world. That's a recurring theme in a lot of your movies: the main character is

Cyber Siren

put in a position where he has to make a choice between the real world and the fantasy world. My favorite scene in the movie is the scene in the pool. It looks like something out of a Hammer movie about Dracula's brides, and it conveys the sense that the main character's fantasy world is just as alluring as it is dangerous.

That was a scene I added that production really objected to. It required underwater gear and more time to shoot, so the producers were saying, "Do you really need this scene?" I said yes. I wanted a scene that had that dreamlike, sensual fantasy quality to it. I wanted a type of female who were attractive enough to be Sirens. Obviously they should have been naked. But since we couldn't show nudity on TV, I was hoping that the poetry of the image would be sensual enough. But you bring up an interesting point about the difference between addiction and obsession. What are the differences to you?

I think of "addicted" as a kind of judgment call—"you've got a problem." I don't think "obsession" necessarily has the same negative connotations.

I think that's an excellent distinction, because here you're getting at the basic component of drama, which is conflict. Is obsession as scary as addiction? If you're physically attacking a woman because you're obsessed with her, that's pretty scary. But if you just can't stop thinking about her, is that obsession or addiction? Have you really lost control? To me, an obsession is an intense love for a particular movie or person or whatever. But you don't necessarily think about it 24-7.

I think what we were trying to do with this movie was show an addiction. He was certainly more interested in porn than he was in getting into college. Everything in his life was suffering because of it. If it had been just an obsession, where he was able to get it out of his head and go to sleep at night, then it wouldn't have been a major conflict. Certain types of individuals just aren't able to stop. Their need becomes too strong.

The people who slammed the movie were mainly young guys. There were parents who saw this movie and emailed Lifetime, saying thank you. One woman wrote, "As soon as that movie was over, I went up into my son's room and I found a bunch of porn on his computer. Thank you, because I had no idea he was hiding this from me. I sensed something was going on with him." I'm sure her son sent a pissed-off email to Lifetime.

The main focus of *She's Too Young* and *Cyber Seduction* is responsible parenting. Both say that you have to be very aware of what your kids are doing. You have to trust them, but you can't blindly trust them.

Right.

So, naturally, any kid who wants to get away with anything is going to hate a film that prompts their parents to start going through the files on their computer.

Yes, but I'm thinking like a parent. That's our responsibility. To protect our children. For me, porn is sort of like horror movies . . . Critics say that horror movies cause violence in society. I don't believe that, but I do believe they can throw gasoline on fires that

Kelly Lynch and Jeremy Sumpter on the set of *Cyber Seduction*

are already burning. We're so Puritanical about sex in our country, to the point that we sometimes suppress the beautiful aspects of it, and that is part of the problem. Making something forbidden only makes it more attractive. (I know that from being raised Irish Catholic.) Setting boundaries for your kids can also mean that they might only want to break them. The hardest thing in parenting is establishing boundaries that you believe in and can maintain.

I grew up saying to my parents, "What do you mean? Why can't I do that?" I have that same fight with my kids. My daughter says, "I'm eighteen . . ." My son says, "I'm twenty-one . . ." And I think: *God, I wish I'd had somebody giving me strict advice in black or white terms when I was that age.* It doesn't mean I would have always taken the advice. But I think it would have helped me to consider both sides and make better decisions. I know my kids are going to fuck up and make wrong choices, as I did. I know there will be repercussions—if not now, then down the line. I'm not trying to make their decisions for them. But I know there's value in setting boundaries and telling them how their mother and I see things.

Of all your films dealing with twenty-first century teenagers, my favorite is *Not Like Everyone Else*. In a way, it starts where *Odd Girl Out* leaves off—the main character, Brandi Blackburn, has already embraced the role of outsider.

You know, the real Brandi loved reading Stephen King. The day she visited the set and she said to me, "All I wanted to do when I was growing up was write horror movies." She actively tried to stand out—adopting the punk look, dying her hair black. I could understand why people in a Bible-Belt Oklahoma high school were picking on her. She looked like a runaway druggie on Sunset Boulevard. Since she stayed to herself, she was considered very suspicious. After Columbine, those outsider qualities were now perceived as threatening. Brandi was deemed guilty because she was different.

One of the things I kept thinking of while I was watching the movie was King's early novel *Rage*, which is about a teenager who brings a gun to school and takes his class hostage. I kept expecting Brandi to turn violent—to act like a monster because everyone was treating her like a monster. But she turned out to be much more grounded than that . . .

We were working completely off of the true story. Brandi didn't lash out and there are always limits to our artistic license. The real story was an ongoing conflict with the school authorities that didn't end until she graduated. I don't know what the real principal was like, but I opted for casting a little guy with a Napoleon complex.

Tom and Alia Shawkat on the set of *Not Like Everyone Else*

I also played up the witchcraft thing. When the movie was first pitched to me, I was told it was about teenage witchcraft. When I read it, I was surprised. She's not a witch. It's about being different in a society that doesn't like anything outside of the accepted norm. It's a story about a witch hunt, not a girl who's a witch. It had a bit of that Stephen King / *Carrie* quality to it. She fights back, but not to the extreme that Carrie did. In fact, at the end, she doesn't tell off the bitchy girls.

The thing is, Brandi didn't really *want* to belong. That's what was cool about her. Her mother encouraged her outsider mentality. She would look at her daughter's crazy drawings and joke, "Who are you? You can't be my daughter." But you could tell her mom was proud. She thought her daughter was really cool. I love the actress who played that part—Illeana Douglas. I was extremely excited to work with her because she just lights up the screen. She's so committed to whatever she's doing, and she was 200% committed on this film.

Tom and Ileana Douglas on the set of *Not Like Everyone Else*

In real life, Brandi's father was the opposite of the character in the movie. He did fight for his daughter, but it wasn't because he had a personal agenda. He just felt that his daughter was being singled out unfairly. Ironically, at home, she was not allowed to take part in some of the cultural traditions that her brother took part in—like going to see a medicine man. I wanted to expand on the distance between the father and daughter for dramatic purposes. I felt like I needed more conflict, so I added that subplot. And I think that, just like in the movie, the real father and daughter were closer after the experience of this movie.

At the end of the movie, Brandi's father wakes her up one morning, and she thinks he's just asking her to make breakfast like she usually does. Instead, he takes her to see the medicine man. We actually shot that at the end of one of our shooting days. We had a very small window of opportunity to get the scene before nightfall. Our casting director had gone to New Orleans the previous weekend and found a real Native American medicine man. We paid him to come and teach the actor how to say the lines in native dialect, and to play the role of the medicine man at the end of the movie. My favorite experience on that shoot was the ride back from that location after we shot the medicine man's scene. I got to talk to him about his life and his travels. He, his wife and kids basically lived in their car. They were so grateful that we were putting them up in a hotel for the night. I managed to get them an additional night at the hotel. He really looked at this experience as a great blessing. His gratitude was overwhelming.

Not Like Everyone Else seems to me like your first distinctly post-9/11 film. D.C. Sniper was obviously rooted in our collective fear of terrorism, but Not Like Everyone Else seems more political. It really says something about American culture during the Bush administration . . .

For parents, Columbine was just as frightening as 9/11. It demonstrated how much the world had changed for our children. I remember in the sixties not getting served in restaurants and being spit on after the Manson murders, because my hair was long and hippies had become a scary thing. After Columbine, teenage loners became a scary thing.

That paranoid attitude is the real monster in *Not Like Everyone Else*. That monster is the way people allow themselves to be controlled by fear, and the way other people use that fear to manipulate. That never stops. What we're dealing with right now [2008] with the stock market is all about fear. Yesterday, the critics reluctantly said that the stock market was rebounding. Reluctantly. They don't want people to get too comfortable. It was the same thing with the recent hurricane. The news said, "It's coming, it's coming, everybody get the hell out of New Orleans." They were replaying these images of the levee rising, trying to make it look as horrific as they could. Then it didn't happen and they moved on to the next crisis.

In *Not Like Everyone Else*, it's the metal detectors and the daily shakedown at the entrance of the school. Suddenly these kids are in a whole new world, run by a new fear. When we got to that scene, the producers said, "Do you really need more than one metal detector?" I insisted that it had to look like an airport. Everyone has to be inconvenienced, unsettled and tense. That's what it was like in many schools. It's such a weird image. These kids are just going to get an education, and they're being shaken down like they are criminals. It was the best way to tell the story visually. I also had tons of cameras in the school, so Brandi was constantly looking up at them and knowing she was being watched. They actually did have cameras in the school we filmed at, and I really wanted that Big Brother aspect.

There are a few other details I homed-in on. We were prepping and I saw all of the buses pull up to the school. The kids piled in and then there was this incredible parade of buses leaving all at once. It all happened within about a three minute time period. I said, "We've got to get this on film." So we got there early one day and set up about seven cameras. We didn't have enough crew members to run all of them, so we had to have unmanned cameras. I felt it was important to show this huge, almost robotic system at work.

Not Like Everyone Else asks the timely question of how much invasion of privacy we're willing to accept in order to feel protected.

I usually avoid the speeches at the end of movies. If it's needed, I really try to downplay them as much as I can. In this case, I didn't want to say that the people who are persecuting her are bad people. Instead, I wanted to convey a sense that it's the times we live in that makes people want to throw the baby out with the bath water. I wanted Brandi to simply express that basic truth about accepting people for who they are. Stop being afraid and condemning people just because they're different. As you know, it's what the classic monster movies were all about. The monsters were defined by the society that rejected them.

Your next movie, *The Staircase Murders*, was also based on a true story—one that had already inspired a lengthy documentary. How did you get involved in a dramatization?

The thing that fascinated me most about *Staircase* was the role of documentary or reality television. Michael Peterson was a

Tom with the cast of *Not Like Everyone Else*

suspected murderer who had the arrogance to allow an Oscar-winning documentary team to come in and make a film asserting his innocence [*The Staircase*]. I wanted *The Staircase Murders* to be a movie about making a documentary about this guy. People already knew the story, but I was interested in doing a film about our desire to craft the truth in the media. There's a scene in the movie where Michael Peterson is unhappy with his response to one interview question and he says, "Can we do that again?" And the documentarian says, "Yeah, let's shoot it again." It was so carefully orchestrated. To me, things like that were the more unique aspects of the film.

In the movie, Michael Peterson is very unsympathetic. Was the real guy that sleazy?

I really studied the documentary. I was right up against the screen, watching his eyes and looking for little "tells" that would reveal he was lying. I was trying to figure out if he really, 100% believed what he was saying. He looked completely comfortable

Treat Williams (left) as Michael Peterson in *The Staircase Murders* (Lifetime, 2007)

when he was telling his version of what happened. But the facts of the case told a different story.

I didn't want Treat [Williams, who plays Michael Peterson in *The Staircase Murders*] to mimic the real guy, but to convey his apparently genuine belief that he is the real victim. When the documentary crew took him out by the pool where the murder took place, he told his story in a tone that said: *It hurts me to think that you could even think that I killed her.* Every now and then, he'd launch into a bit of poetry or something that seemed completely disconnected from what an innocent man would be saying or thinking in that situation. That's when he's grasping. Trying to show how someone as intelligent and poetic as him could do something so horrible.

Assuming he's guilty, do you think he believes his own lies?

I think if you tell yourself something long enough, it can become a truth in your mind. You can maybe even pass a lie detector test because you are so comfortable with it. I think Michael Peterson has that ability, as a lot of people do, to convince others of the lie, despite all the facts to the contrary.

Occasionally I've seen this sort of thing with children. They drop and break something. I say, "Why did you drop that?" And they say, "Drop what?" They can look at it and, in a very convincing manner, say, "I didn't drop that." "I just saw you drop it." Then they act confused, "You saw me drop something? What do you mean? I don't understand. How could you have seen me do something I didn't do?" At a certain point, you start to feel like you're going crazy. "I just *saw* you drop that. Why won't you admit that you dropped it?" "Because I didn't. If I did drop it, I would say I dropped it. It's not a big deal. I just didn't do it."

This is an example I give actors all the time. Especially if we know their character is lying. You have to convince the other person to believe that they're wrong, and you sometimes do that by being unemotional, rational and matter of fact. That's what Michael Peterson did, and that's what made him such a frightening villain. There were times when I was watching the actual documentary that I started to believe him, because what he was saying made sense. I'd think, "That's true . . . Why *would* he want to kill her? What does he get out of it?" Then I'd have to remind myself of the facts. *If she had fallen down those stairs, would the blood be spattered so high on the wall?* Those questions he just shrugged off. He said, "I can't explain it. All I know is that I didn't kill my wife."

It's too bad that the real story was public knowledge, or you could have played it as more of a mystery, and forced the audience to have that same internal debate.

Believe it or not, many did. The documentary filmmaker, at least up until the time that the documentary aired in Britain, claimed that he didn't believe Michael Peterson was guilty. He stuck by that, and the documentary presented this as a case of injustice. After I watched it a few times, I started to see the filmmaker at work—choosing particular shots, taking certain scenes out of context, and setting the whole thing to this wonderfully emotional and tragic musical score. The documentary really is a finely crafted example of cinematic art. I was very hesitant about doing *The Staircase Murders* because I knew critics and viewers would compare the two. What made me want to do the movie was examining the art of a documentary, and how it can manipulate "reality."

In the movie, it seems like the truth doesn't even matter to Michael Peterson's kids. With one exception, they were determined to take his side no matter how much evidence indicated that he had killed their mother.

They were 100% willing to defend him, despite everything telling them not to. They just flat-out refused to accept the facts. Maybe because their father was the only parent they had left, they refused to give him up.

After *The Staircase Murders*, you went back to high school for *Fab Five: The Texas Cheerleader Scandal*—another ripped-from-the-headlines story. How did you get involved with this one?

As I've said, I find myself drawn to projects where children are empowered in some way. Sometimes that's a good thing, like in *Fairy Tale*, and sometimes it's a bad thing, like in *Turn of the Screw*. My intention was to show how certain kids of that generation can behave when they are given too much power. They develop an unbelievable sense of entitlement, and become insanely demanding. They're so used to getting what they want that they feel unstoppable and have no respect for authority. Their view of the world is so skewed that they have no qualms about doing anything that crosses the line.

During editing, I started becoming concerned that there's no central character that takes you through the whole movie. The lead actress, Jenna Dewan, plays the wide eyed coach who comes into a high school and has to—almost like *Mr. Smith Goes to Washington*—deal with the corruption. (In this case, a squad of cheerleaders.) As good as Jenna was in the part, her character wasn't that interesting to me because she fell into the clichés of "Mrs. Smith Goes to High School." She comes in very innocent and naïve, but you know that by the end she's going to somehow

The cast of *Fab Five: The Texas Cheerleader Scandal* (Lifetime, 2008)

turn the kids around. The only thing I could change was that she didn't turn *all* of the kids around. The main reason I wanted to make *Fab Five* was because the Brooke character intrigued me. Maybe I should have been focusing on the coach or the mother, but I was most interested in Brooke.

She was this gorgeous girl that seemed to have everything, but she was constantly fighting with her mother and she had issues with her father because he had wanted a son. I wanted to make people realize that this was a kid who was just crying out to be loved, but also to be properly disciplined. She's a very strong personality, so somebody's going to have to work incredibly hard to get through to her. In the end we don't see her change, because she's too set in her ways to change overnight. But every now and then, there are moments where you can see the vulnerable little girl.

You say you were concerned about losing narrative focus, but I really like the choppy narrative of *Fab Five*—especially the way you transition from scene to scene using freeze frame. It looks like the Lifetime version of a grindhouse movie.

I made a conscious choice that I was going to pay homage to

Aimee Spring Fortier, Tom, Ashley Benson, Jessica Heap, Ashlynn Ross and Jenna Dewan on the set of *Fab Five* (Lifetime, 2008)

that genre, and try not to let Lifetime catch me. There's a scene where the girls are going to buy booze, and I purposely added surf music to give it that grindhouse quality. One of the network execs said, "What's that old '60s music doing in there?" I said, "It's my way of saying that this sort of thing has been going on with teenagers for decades . . . you know?" Somehow I got away with that explanation.

When I started doing the teen movies, I've tried with each film to find some kind of music that is representative of that particular world—because teenagers today have such diverse taste in music. On *She's Too Young* and *Odd Girl Out*, my editors and I spent an enormous amount of time going through library tracks and cherry-picking the songs. By the time I got to *Fab Five*, I was searching for some kind of music I hadn't used. I didn't want to do *Bring It On*. I wanted the music to have a darker edge, because the girls were darker and tougher.

I started exploring rave music, using my son as my guide. One weekend, I went to a rave in downtown L.A. I was overwhelmed, because there must have been ten thousand kids there, and I was at least thirty-five years older than everybody else in there. Interestingly, most of the kids didn't pay attention to me at all. I was just some invisible entity walking around, observing. It was like I had died and gone back to my teen days. I was thinking: *This is just like the Love-ins and outdoor music festivals of the mid-'60s. I remember that guy. I remember them.* It seemed all these young faces sort of looked like people I had known. It was amazing.

I stayed from eight o'clock until four in the morning, just walking around, mesmerized. Kids kept coming up to me, offering me ecstasy and saying, "Dude, how old are you?" I'd say, "Old enough to be your father." And they'd say, "Man, I hope when I'm your age, I'm still doing this too." Some asked what it's like to see all of this, and I'd say, "I hate to tell you, but it's pretty much the same thing we did at love-ins in the sixties." The rave music created the atmosphere and, if you were there, they assumed you were cool.

On Monday, I started putting rave music into the movie. Then I immediately realized that it wasn't going to work because of all the emotional changes that happen in the story. The music needed more variety to match the storytelling, so then I started searching for additional types of music. The first cut that I showed to Lifetime had a very eclectic soundtrack. It was still a work in progress. I told them, "I'm still trying to get a handle on the music." They came back and said, "Why are you putting disco music in some scenes. *Disco?*" That's when I realized that rave music sounds like disco to the older generation. I knew this was never gonna fly with Lifetime.

I worked intensely with a music editor to pick the songs. We ended up going back to more of an electric guitar sound because I wanted a slightly masculine edge to this movie. I thought it was a nice homage to the juvenile delinquent movies of the '50s and '60s. Later, the teens I spoke with who saw the movie didn't even seem to notice the music. They accepted the eclectic variety. It seemed natural.

What have people responded to most about *Fab Five*? I guess it's not the music...

I think it's the performances. I think people don't expect to like it, and they're surprised when they do. I was really careful to not

Tommy's Angels

exploit the girls, even though this is a movie about girls who are purposely exploiting themselves. I was hoping that people would like them . . . or at least like watching them. I wanted people to walk away from it saying, "I just hated them, but I couldn't stop watching." The ladies' performances are the thing that people bring up again and again.

Do you tell actors not to come in to rehearsals with preconceived ideas about their characters? I think that was something that Capra did.

I've learned over the years that every actor works a little differently. Some really do come in and they just *want* to be directed. It's wonderful when actors have the freedom and trust in their own ability to do whatever it is that you ask. And if you cast the right people—and again, this is what Capra said: "Ninety-five percent of directing is casting"—they come in and they bring whatever you need with them.

With *Fab Five*, I had all the girls create character journals, so that they really felt like their characters had a history. Some actors like to do a lot of work in advance, to feel comfortable enough to come onto the set and be told what to do. The hard thing is when they've learned their lines and gotten into a particular rhythm and cadence, and their performance starts to become mannered. I'm always saying to actors, "Please don't restrict the character any more than you would restrict yourself in life."

I assume that, with so much focus on the hot young cheerleaders, *Fab Five* got an unusual amount of attention from male viewers.

When we were editing, I wrote an impassioned letter to the president of Lifetime, saying, "Everybody thinks I'm crazy for bring this up, but have you ever actually tried to target a male demographic?" There wasn't one guy in the post production department who didn't wander into our edit bay and say, "You know, I'd sit and watch this movie because the girls are hot." They could have advertised *Fab Five* on ESPN or Spike, and males would have taken note. Guys don't give a crap that it's on Lifetime if it's something they want to watch. But Lifetime didn't want to go beyond their tried and true demographic. I'm sure they were also concerned that women were going to get turned off if I went too far.

The network asked me not to make the fights too violent . . . but I made them very violent. One reviewer said that *Fab Five* was like a western. All we were missing was a shootout at the end. We had to follow the facts of the real story, or I would have had a hell of a catfight at the end. I would have really loved to have staged something like that.

I fought the happy ending, because at the end of the day the real cheerleaders pretty much just walked away from the situation. The coach got her story out and was vindicated, but it wasn't any great victory for her. I wanted to end the movie after she saw the news report and said, "What difference did I really make?" Then we'd fade to black. As far as I'm concerned, you can turn the show off right there and that's it. Of course the network didn't want to end on that note, so there's the scene where the coach goes back for a cheerleader competition at the school and a few of the younger girls on the squad say thank you. Begrudgingly, I admit it did add that Capra-esque quality—one person can make a difference.

Now you've got me thinking of *Fab Five* as Western. The revisionist Western is pretty cynical, but the classic Western is about how the loner can save the community. At the end of the film, there's always sense of community that wasn't there at the beginning of the film.

Ultimately, I think that story, and I know I've said this a gazillion times already, but I truly believe that it all comes down to connecting with the characters and the actors playing the characters, and believing that they are connecting with each other. When that happens, the viewer is magically a part of the storytelling process. You're constantly wondering: *What are they going to do next? What is he going to do when she does this? What is she going to do when she finds out that he's . . .?*

Behind the scenes, those answers come from a lot of different places. Many times the writer doesn't have every answer. The actors don't have every answer. Sometimes the D.P. changes the lighting and suddenly the whole tone of the scene changes, and now maybe the audience is more engaged than they were if both characters were equally lit. The smallest things can make a huge difference. As a director, you hope that you can catch all that—that you can come up with the right ideas, or that your cast and crew will be supportive and in tune with what you're trying to achieve artistically and can contribute to the process. I find that I'm the most happy when people are collaborating on the set of a movie I'm directing. I love being part of something bigger—the group, the film, the family. It's not just about me. The entire experience is more real when I'm sharing it with other people.

There are so few, if any, feature directors who have complete creative freedom. No movie is ever completely ours, especially at the end of the process. Making movies is sort of like raising kids. When you bring them into the world, your responsibility is to mold them the best you can. At a certain point, their teachers and friends start pulling them in different directions. When the kid takes over completely, sometimes before becoming an adult, you suddenly have no control. Your hope is that they'll take all the best influences and make them their own. That's kind of what making a good movie is like to me. You exert as much influence as you can, and others contribute positively, and it becomes something really worthwhile. Of course, sometimes you give the wrong advice, or the wrong influences take over and completely fuck things up. Your baby ends up with a bad reputation or in jail.

At the end of the day, you seem pretty comfortable with the idea that your movies are created by all these different forces. I think the parenting comparison is brilliant, because it's possible to destroy a story by not letting the characters go where they need to go.

I was just reading something this week about how a movie is different every time somebody watches it. The movie itself doesn't change, but the perception of it changes. Theater performers are very aware of this, because they know what it's like to have an audience in the palm of your hand one night, and then everything is completely dead the next night. Comedians have this experience more than anyone else. A crowd seems to either love you or hate you. One night, the audience gets the joke and the next night they don't, and you think: *Did I change my timing on the delivery? Is there something going on in the news that makes it not funny tonight? What happened?* You examine every possible reason. Sometimes things just don't come together. Other times, all of the right elements merge and you have a perfect night.

VII: LOOKING AHEAD

This interview took place on May 26, 2009, between the editing of "The Wronged Man" and the shooting of "At Risk."

FILMOGRAPHY

THE WRONGED MAN (LIFETIME, 2010)
DIRECTED BY TOM MCLOUGHLIN
TELEPLAY BY TEENA BOOTH. BASED ON A MAGAZINE ARTICLE BY ANDREW CORSELLO.
STARRING JULIA ORMOND, MAHERSHALALHASHBAZ ALI, LISA ARRINDELL ANDERSON

A lawyer devotes twenty years of her life to seeking justice for a wrongly-convicted man.

AT RISK / THE FRONT (LIFETIME, 2010)
DIRECTED BY TOM MCLOUGHLIN
TELEPLAY BY JOHN PIELMEIER. BASED ON A PAIR OF NOVELS BY PATRICIA CORNWELL
STARRING ANDIE MACDOWELL, DANIEL SUNJATA, ANNABETH GISH, ASHLEY WILLIAMS

A cold-blooded district attorney and her protégé investigate a decades-old Massachusetts murder, then turn their attention to the Boston Strangler.

Tell me about *The Wronged Man*.

It's the true story of Calvin Willis, who is in jail for a crime he did not commit. Early in the movie, his grandmother meets a lawyer named Prissy, and she says, "Can you get my boy out? He didn't do what they say he did." There's something about her plea that touches Prissy deeply and keeps her going on this case for twenty-two years.

I remember when you first got involved with the project, you said you were picturing Holly Hunter as Prissy. Then you ended up getting Julia Ormond, who has a very different screen persona. Did you have to rethink the character?

First of all, I never met the real Prissy. The screenwriter did, and she described her as a short, feisty, outspoken Southern woman. Based on that, I thought Holly Hunter would be perfect casting. Casting Julia Ormond—who in my mind is an ethereal, classy, British, staid woman—made absolutely no sense to me. The first thing I thought about was altering the character, to make her quiet, grounded and determined instead of wild and feisty. It turned out that Julia is such a consummate professional that she can do anything. She has so many aspects to her personality. Plus she's so intellectual, and she understands character and story extremely well.

Julia was in complete agreement with the idea that we needed to dress down her character. I thought Prissy would buy clothes because they're comfortable, not because they fit well. Julia loved that. We decided her character would wear the same coat or dress for years. In fact, when we were screening the movie for one of the execs, they said, "Wasn't she wearing that same blouse earlier?" And I said yes. "Why?" Because that's what people do. Not everyone can afford to go out and buy new clothes whenever they want. When they go into their closet in the morning, it's about finding something that covers their body and keeps them warm or keeps them cool. Prissy's life isn't a fashion show—which is what we're used to seeing in movies. Julia really wanted to embody the honesty of that.

In real life, Julia's causes are key to her. She actively campaigns against international slavery and human trafficking. That told me a lot about who she really is. When Prissy realizes what's happened to Calvin, she responds very strongly to the injustice. That

Julia Ormond and Tom on the set of *The Wronged Man* (Lifetime, 2010)

becomes her cause, and she is very strong-willed and determined to fight for him. Her story really reflected who Julia is.

What about Calvin? The title suggests that he's going to be the main focus—like in Alfred Hitchcock's *The Wrong Man*.

We were working off of a GQ story called "The Wronged Man," and the reason this movie is called *The Wronged Man* is because of that magazine article and the idea that this is a story about a righteous man wronged by a corrupt system. [Producer] Gale Anne Hurd was interested in making a movie about importance of righting this particular wrong in society—using DNA evidence to clear Calvin Willis and others who are wrongly convicted. I was interested in making a movie about this woman Prissy's drive to accomplish something that was important to her, even while everything else in her life keeps going wrong. Whatever it takes, she's going to find a way to get Calvin out of prison because she's committed to finding justice. Gale and I both felt strongly about these perspectives.

In editing, I kept thinking that this is really a movie more about Prissy than about the wronged man. Prissy proved that one person can make a difference. People kept telling her that what she was trying to do was impossible—"the system won't allow it." But she didn't give up. I felt like her story deserved more focus, so I shifted the focus. When Gale saw how I had changed the structure, she was not pleased. She had my editor, Charles, create a "producer's cut" that started with the wronged man instead of Prissy's life, as in the script. I was ultimately happy with it. In the end, the only thing that was a frustration to both Gale and I was the fact that these films are only 88 minutes. We lost a lot of wonderful moments of Julia's performance.

Did you steer the story away from Calvin because he's not as sympathetic?

Calvin is sympathetic because of the circumstances of his conviction. Whatever he may have done wrong in his life, he apparently was not the kind of man who would do the horrible thing that he was convicted of. But he wasn't exactly a saint either, and that's why nobody would fight for him in the beginning. The consensus on his conviction seemed to be: *He may not be guilty of this particular crime, but he's not innocent of some other things.* That's what Prissy knew was so horrible. She couldn't change those other aspects of Calvin's case, but she wanted justice.

The casting of [Mahershalalhashbaz] Ali was very fortunate because he's very sympathetic. In life, Ali really is a grounded, incredibly spiritual person, and he brought a lot of strength to the later scenes—after Calvin has been in prison for a long time, and that experience has transformed him into a more spiritual person. To me, the only way that an innocent person can go through an experience like that and not become corrupted by their surroundings is through prayer and belief in God. So we showed him reading the Bible in about four different scenes. That may not be exactly how it happened to Calvin Willis, but from a dramatic storytelling point of view, that was important.

It sounds like you consciously chose not to make this a character study instead of a "message movie" about prejudice in the justice system.

I chose to put more emphasis on Prissy's determination. That, to me, was the most fascinating element. She was like Erin Brockovich, Norma Rae, Karen Silkwood—all these woman who operate outside of the system, but who are determined to get inside it in order to improve things. They're willing to do whatever it takes to make some kind of change, even if it's minor.

I did four polishes of the script and during that period, *The Wronged Man* became more of a personal movie. Once the actors got involved, I shared creative power so we could tackle the story one scene at a time. I wanted to give the actors the freedom to change dialogue and other elements within the scenes, to make the moments more authentic. Those changes took some of the emphasis away from the "message" and made the movie more about the characters, and the emotions between characters.

The other really great thing about doing this film was working with an amazing crew. I got to re-team with some of my best collaborators from previous films: production designer Craig Stearns (from *One Dark Night* and *Date with an Angel*), cinematographer Shelly Johnson (from *The Fire Next Time, Murder of Innocence* and *The Yarn Princess*) and producer Bob Wilson, who was my A.D. for years. And my A.D. on this film was the grandson of my mentor, Frank Capra III.

Looking at the finished piece now, I see a lot of things I could have done better. But on the second lowest budget I've ever had (*One Dark Night* being the lowest) and with a fifteen day / twelve hours-a-day schedule, I'm very pleased. It does have the feel of an independent film that's all about the characters. My next project [two adaptations of Patricia Cornwell's detective novels *At Risk* and *The Front*] is going to play out on a much bigger canvas because it's about a city and fictional characters that are bigger than life. That's going to be a challenge for me since I've been doing nonfiction stories for so long.

Tell me about *At Risk* and *The Front*. How far along are you in pre-production?

I've almost finished with my director notes on the first one, *At Risk*. It's strange prepping for two movies at the same time.

Tom and Daniel Sunjata on the set of At *Risk* (Lifetime, 2010)

Usually I get the script, the book and all the research materials, and it takes me weeks to sort everything out. Once I do that with *At Risk*, I start all over again with *The Front*. Then I'll start watching movies that have the kind of visual style I want. I like to go into pre-production with a visual shorthand in mind for the Director of Photography. On these two films, I want to set some scenes in high rises with glass windows, to give this world a wider scope. Having just done small, everyday locations on *The Wronged Man*, I want to play these stories out on a much bigger palette.

I imagine you'll also be trying to add more emotional depth to the main characters, Win Garano and Monique Lamont. In Cornwell's books, both of these characters are pretty aloof.

Yeah, there's not a lot of emotional depth here—although there is a genuine loneliness about them. Win is a good guy who is very tortured within. He lost his parents when he was quite young, and he needs a sense of love and intimacy that he never got growing up. His only source of guidance was his grandmother, who loves him dearly but who is a bit of a kook. He listens to her because

Andie MacDowell and Tom on the set of *The Front* (Lifetime, 2010)

she is his only family. She's his touchstone. But he's also got to protect her, because she can be like a child at times. In a way, she's his strength *and* his Achilles heel.

The Monique Lamont character has the same loneliness. She comes from a rich family and her father has not really been involved in her life. There's a scene in the movie where he comes to visit her and they don't really have much to say to each other. I want to have them speak in French in front of Win, so that he doesn't know what they're saying. He assumes that it's a good relationship. When he and Monique go into the next room, she says, "I have no relationship with him. And now he comes to tell me that he's dying." Then she quickly moves on to another subject. She doesn't want to ever be vulnerable. I want to show her in her glass house and office because that's who she is. Dazzling and seemingly transparent, but really vacant and feeling hollow inside. She's all about maintaining this appearance—the perfectly groomed D.A.

That's what she and Win have in common. They both look incredible on the outside, but they're painfully vulnerable on the inside. At the end of the first movie, we see him break down and cry. That's not in the Cornwell book—the screenwriter put that in. I'm trying to figure out if we should really show that side or if we should we make this more like a traditional film noir, where the audience wonders how these tough characters can remain so tough.

It's interesting that you're finally making a film noir, since you said that's the kind of movie your father would have made.

I hadn't thought about that. Hope I can make a good one. Actually, two.

Do you think that's the direction your career might go—toward darker, more adult-oriented films? Now that your own kids are grown up and out of high school, do you feel like you've "graduated" from movies about teenagers?

I've always said the great thing about teen movies is that all of the emotions are fresh and new and so intense. When you're a teenager, every situation is life or death. Because you don't have the life experience to predict how things could go, you jump into everything without any hesitation. It's like: *I'm in love I'm in love I'm in love, I'm never going to be in love with anybody else. I will die before I lose this relationship.* Classic Romeo and Juliet. It's the same thing with drugs and other forms of experimentation. With everything, really. You need to see for yourself what is good and what is bad.

Have you talked to your kids about your own rebellious youth?

Anytime I tried to relate past experiences where I screwed up—to try and share some kind of life lesson—Nancy would say, "You shouldn't have told them that." Nine times out of ten, she was right. Well, maybe eight times out of ten . . . Those confessions came back to haunt me as counter-arguments. "If you did these things, why can't I?" The big secret that I kept from my kids, all the way up until Hannah just graduated from high school, was that I didn't graduate. I told them I'd taken some college classes, which was true, but I didn't tell them that I was auditing those classes.

When my kids were going through those times where they were not doing well in school, I was terrified that they would do what I did and just drop out. Thank God they were not as rebellious as I was. Even if they go into show business, where a high school diploma doesn't necessarily mean much, they'll still have that feeling of personal accomplishment. I look back on dropping out with a lot of regret . . . but at that time I was 100% sure of what I was doing with my life, and high school just didn't fit into my rock star life. My bullheadedness allowed me to pursue other dreams as crazy as mime, and going into the extremely competitive arena of writing and directing feature films. Remember I was the clown in the bear suit saying, "Mr. Frankenheimer, I'm going to direct one day." In my heart and mind, I was so sure that I was going to make it. And it wasn't that I thought I could bulldoze my way through. It really was about persistence. I thought maybe I won't be a filmmaker until I'm sixty, but I'm going to make it.

Honestly, I'm still not at the point where I have made the movie that I want to make. I don't even really know what that movie is, but I know I haven't made it yet. I haven't had that feeling of total accomplishment. I'd love to leave behind something like *It's a Wonderful Life*, or *E.T.*, or *Rocky*, or *The Exorcist*. Something that affects and changes people the way those movies affected me. I promise you that neither fear nor age are going to stop me from pushing towards that goal until the coffin lid closes.

You've said that *One Dark Night* and *Date with an Angel* are the films that feel the most personal to you . . . and yet you didn't have final cut on either one. To me, *Sometimes They Come Back* and *The Fire Next Time* seem more like expressions of your view on life—because, in the final reel, they come down to hard choices between Heaven and Earth, idyllic fantasy and harsh reality. The main characters get to glimpse a more peaceful world, and yet they choose to walk back into the storm—to fight another day. But you haven't yet made the movie where the lead character decides that he can let go—that he or she has done what they came to do, and can move on to that better place . . .

Wow. I never thought about that. You know, originally, I wanted to end *Date with an Angel* with the embrace and the whiteout indicating that she had taken him to Heaven. For me it was like the end of *Close Encounters of the Third Kind*, where Richard Dreyfus walks in [to the spaceship]. We *wanted* to see him do that. He looks back at Melinda Dillon and she smiles and Truffaut says, "Go on." And we're sitting there in the audience, saying, "Yes!" We so want to be him and go.

That was the ending I wanted in *Date with an Angel*. I was in my early twenties when I originally wrote that screenplay, and I knew someone whose friend had died from a brain tumor. He had headaches all the time and when he finally learned what was causing them, the tumor was so big that it was inoperable. And then he was gone. All I could think was how unfair that was. But maybe if God, in His goodness, sent down somebody as beautiful as Emmanuelle Béart to take you . . . it wouldn't be such a bad way to go.

Of course, to most people, getting on a flying saucer and dying are two very different experiences. Not to me. Who can say if you're ever going to come back from either of those adventures? And the Jim Saunders character would be getting out of a great deal of pain . . . So I'm back to my favorite Peter Pan quote. "To die will be an awfully big adventure."

The alternative is to keep fighting. Keep making movies until the coffin lid closes . . .

And be ready to keep getting hurt. If you really want to make movies, you better accept the pain because that's all it's about at certain points. Thankfully, there are also times when things are so wonderful that you totally forget all the hurt. Then the process starts over again. Every time you begin a new project, you've got to say to yourself, "Am I willing to go through this all over again?" For me, the answer is always yes.

I still tell aspiring actors, musicians, writers and directors that the trick is learning to endure the flame. Fire is attractive and compelling, but stick your hand in it and see how long you can hold it there. Most people have to give up. Success comes to those who keep trying—those who keep building up scar tissue and enduring the pain a bit longer each time. You have to convince yourself that you don't mind getting burned, that it's better than giving up. You stay in show business because there is no way you could accept doing something else. You can't *not* do it. So you *have* to succeed on some level.

Every time I finish a project, I feel like that's it. *It's over.* I feel like I'll never get another job. I really, honestly feel like that. Last night, I dreamed I got onto a new film and I was running around, trying to find the locations, trying to figure out my relationship with the producer . . . For a filmmaker, it's always a scary thing at the beginning because you don't know the sensibilities of the other people you're working with, and you're praying that somehow you'll all see eye-to-eye. At a certain point in this dream, I'm arguing with someone about what I want to do. I finally say, "You know what? I don't even have the script!" And the producers look at each other, confused. Then one of them said, "You haven't read the script?" Suddenly I'm thinking I shouldn't be saying this. *Why have I agreed to take this project before I've read the script? Have I become so desperate that I've agreed to make a movie and I don't even know what it is?* It was the worst feeling—knowing that I'm supposed to be the guy in charge, and yet I don't have a clue what I'm doing. What does it mean? I don't know. Maybe inside I should trust that I've been making movies long enough that I can get the script and figure out a way to connect with it and make it work. I know I've still got more work to do.

If I died today, I wouldn't be ready to go. I'd be arguing with the man in the clouds that there's been a mistake. "You've got to send me back. I haven't accomplished all of my missions." Like Warren Beatty in *Heaven Can Wait*: "It's not my time, Mr. Jordan." Will I ever make that film that defines me? Will I ever make a film that contains all the elements to become a classic? God only knows. But the desire is what keeps me going.

VIII: TOMMY LIVES!

This interview took place on August 28, 2013.

In the spring of 2009, you flew to Toronto to shoot *At Risk* and *The Front* back to back. I know you aren't happy with how those movies turned out. What went wrong?

They offered me those Patricia Cornwell movies a year before I did *The Wronged Man*. I read them and dismissed them. I just couldn't find the humanity in them, or anything I could relate to. I said, "I can't say yes to two scripts that I think just don't work." And it wasn't just the scripts. If you go onto the Patricia Cornwell websites, you'll see that her fans overall didn't like those books. I kept looking at that and thinking, *If her fans don't even like these stories, is this really a good idea?*

When Lifetime was ready to greenlight the movies a year later, they came back to me with the same scripts. So I said "no" again. At that point, there were some difficult things that were going on within my family and I felt like I really should be home at that time. But my representation and my family were encouraging me to go—because "this how you make a living and this is what you love to do." Part of me thought that maybe once I started the movie, I would be able to escape into a fictional world . . . but I also felt guilty about that, because I felt like I was abandoning my family. And there was also a part of me that said, "How am I going to escape into a world I don't care about?"

The bottom line was financial. It had taken so long to get *The Wronged Man* made, and I hadn't been working during that period.

Our home needed major repairs and I had two kids in college at the time, so money was going out but not much was coming in. Now suddenly I'm being offered two movies simultaneously. And the producers are saying that they want these movies to feel *big*. They want them to have feature film scope. And now I start rationalizing: *Well, if I can make these movies look big and spectacular, that might be interesting* . . . I made a choice that I swore I would never make, and I paid for it.

The second I arrived in Toronto, I had this feeling that I had sold out. Sold my soul for money. Abandoned my family during an important time. To me, it was the darkest hour. I can't say it was the darkest hour of my life, but it was my darkest hour *creatively*, because I lost my desire to do the very thing that was in my blood since birth. I didn't even want to *watch* movies during that period. It completely shut me down.

And then during prep, I learned that the budget had been severely cut, and we had to reduce the scope of everything. Key scenes had to be cut due to budget and time restraints. It turned out to be *the* most miserable filmmaking experience of my life. Every morning I woke up thinking, *I should just call and say I can't continue, that I have personal issues at home and I've got to go home.* As much as I wanted to say "I'm the wrong guy for this job," I could not quit. I've never quit anything once I committed to it. I had this image of tying myself to the helm of the ship. *Whether we crash or not, I'm going to stay at the helm.* My family eventually came to Toronto, but I was still couldn't get away from the feeling that I was doing something that I had no passion for.

You've said that this was a reality check for you—that, in hindsight, you see your experience on those two movies as a kind of life lesson. What did you learn?

I have never taken a movie that I didn't have some kind of passion for. I knew better, but I did it anyway. In hindsight, I ask myself: *Did I take those movies because I knew it was time for a change?* Because it definitely forced me to change. I was sent to movie jail and couldn't figure out how to get out. I had to stop for a while, and really think about what was next.

Tom among the *Masters of Horror*

I was excited because your manager seemed to be pushing you back toward the horror genre at that point. As a horror fan, I was very curious to see what you'd come up with.

I think that was the easiest way for someone to re-market me. *One Dark Night, Jason Lives!* and *Sometimes They Come Back* were some of the bigger successes of my career. And I love doing horror. But I haven't done it in a long time, so now the question becomes: Can I go back to horror and create something new?

My manager sent me a script that I thought had a lot of promise, called *Imitation*. The thing I really liked about it was that it was completely surreal. I've added touches of surrealism in stuff I've done over the years, but this was just a wild ride into a dead man's fantasy life and I found that incredibly cool. I saw it as an attempt to do a full-on, pedal-to-the-metal mindfuck—sort of a Mario Bava / Dario Argento-type thing, but revolving around a very relatable character. When I was collaborating with the writer, that was my main contribution: trying to humanize [the main character] enough that the audience would accept all the crazy stuff that happens around him.

Screen Gems was interested in the project, and then Intrepid, the company that did *The Strangers* (2011). Intrepid seemed really gung ho and I thought it was going to happen, but they decided to wait and see how their movie *The Raven* (2012) did before moving forward. And *The Raven* didn't do very well. The company eventually shut down.

At the same time, my manager and I were trying to develop the book series *Generation Dead*—about a group of zombies in high school—into a TV series. To me, that series was about empathy for the outsider. It taps into that experience all teenagers go through. The zombie kids are the freaks that get made fun of in high school, because they're "brain dead" and not as physically capable. It's obviously a little bit tongue-in-cheek, but to me the outsider theme was cool enough to make it work.

We went around and pitched *Generation Dead* to all the major networks, but nobody wanted to do zombies for television. This was before *The Walking Dead*[23] [and *Warm Bodies*].[24]

This must have been around the time that your wife Nancy threw you a sixtieth birthday party at Hollywood Forever Cemetery. What was it like being back there, thirty years after you shot *One Dark Night* in the Cathedral Mausoleum, and then being toasted by so many people that you've worked with over the years?

I remember thinking, *Holy shit, is my career over? Is this the equivalent of someone's AFI tribute? After this, I'm going to go home and sit in front of the television for the rest of my life, waiting for my old movies to come on. Like the scene at the end of The Comic* (1969) with Dick Van Dyke.

That last scene always scared me. Dick plays this old silent movie star named Billy Bright, who wakes up at four in the morning and turns on the TV. It's the morning show and the host is saying "Here's something from way, way, WAY back. An old Billy Bright movie." The final image is this sad old comic at five in the morning watching his epic film. That has always stuck in the back of my mind. Especially when I was doing physical comedy. *Could that be where it all ends? What do you do when you get old and you can't do what you loved doing the most?*

---

[23] The AMC series premiered in October 2010 and went on to become one of the highest rated shows on television.

[24] The zombie rom-com was released in early 2013 to the tune of over $100 million in box office receipts.

Cathedral Mausoleum at Hollywood Forever

Nancy, Tom, Shane and Hannah McLoughlin at Tom's sixtieth birthday party.
Photo credit: Bern Agency

The day after the party, I went back to the cemetery to thank them. I started talking to Theodore Hovey, one of the administrators there, not just about the party but about my long relationship with Hollywood Forever. How I shot *One Dark Night* there in the Cathedral Mausoleum, how I wrote my *Friday the 13th* movie there. Across the street was the Pierce Brothers Mortuary where I saw Peter Lorre. And on the other side of the fence was the Paramount studio, where I met Nancy, and where I had an actual studio job as a story editor on *Friday the 13th: The Series*. I said, "This place has meant so much to me. If I were ever going to choose a burial place, it would be Cathedral Mausoleum. But I was told while making *One Dark Night* that there aren't any more spaces left."

And he goes, "Well, it's interesting you should say that." When the new management took over the cemetery [in 1998], they found out that there were actually some crypts in the mausoleum that had *not* been sold. And he said, "Would you like to see them?" And I got this tingling sensation in my spine. I had this overwhelmingly positive feeling: *This is something you're supposed to do.*

So we got in a little golf cart and cruised over. The first two crypts that he showed me were way up at the top, and I wasn't interested in those. Then he said, "There's one other one that I think you might like better." And there it was . . . I don't know how to explain it except to say that it just had this feeling that this was going to be my final home. My heart started racing and I'm thinking, *I don't know why the hell I'm so excited about a crypt* . . . but the part of me that is so intrigued about what happens on "the other side" was incredibly excited. For me, this was a calling.

My wife Nancy wasn't very happy about it at all. Especially because I did it without asking her about it first. She obviously didn't think that throwing me a birthday party was going to turn into planning for my death. But then neither did I!

Suddenly here was a chance to do something that I never even thought about, much less planned for. I felt like this really was the setup for my third act. I wasn't quite sure what that was, but I knew it had something to do with the subject matter of my first four movies. *One Dark Night* was about using bio-energy to reanimate the dead. *Jason Lives* was about bringing Jason back with a lightning bolt, so he's now a walking corpse that cannot be killed. *Date with an Angel* was about a guy dying and an angel coming to take him away, but she falls in love and stays on earth instead. And then *Sometimes They Come Back* . . . The title says it all.

On top of all of my personal connections to the place, there's also a "strange idea of entertainment" aspect to Hollywood Forever. There are guided tours, conducted by "the woman in black," Karie Bible.[25] She takes people around the cemetery and tells them all the Hollywood legends. I've always loved that kind of stuff—cemetery tours and ghost walks—and I'm thrilled to think that maybe one day I might be a part of that. Cinespia has movie screenings and concerts there on summer nights. People bring picnics and sit on the lawn. And during the Day of the Dead celebration, they bring art and decorate the mausoleums. I'll get to be a part of all that! To me, that's like continuing to entertain people after I'm dead . . . but not actually gone.

Most people think that when you die, it's over. For me it's not over. That's the real third act. I can't tell you much more because I don't know any more about it. I have to get there first.

Do you have a plan—like Raymar—to come back?

Not exactly. I'm mostly thinking in terms of bio-energy. We know that we all emit energy, and my belief is that sometimes that energy exists in the form of ghosts and spirits. My thought is that if I can put enough of my own energy into that space [inside the mausoleum] over the next few decades, then very possibly my "presence" could remain there after I'm gone . . . and be experienced by certain individuals who believe and are open to it.

I'm not talking about coming back from the dead, or about becoming a ghost who can't move on. I'm talking about leaving

---

[25] The "woman in black" is a Hollywood legend. Every year, on the anniversary of Rudolf Valentino's death, a mysterious woman in a black veil visits the star's final resting place and places roses on his tomb.

Tom and his fake crypt on the set of *One Dark Night*

Tom and his real crypt at Hollywood Forever

something behind that other people might sense, feel, hear, or see. It's like leaving behind a reel of film. You could call this my contribution to Hollywood Forever.

In 2011, you were involved with a few other film projects that didn't work out. What happened?

Lucky Christmas was a Hallmark Channel movie—a light but well-written Christmas comedy. I thought it would be a lot of fun for me to do comedy again, so I committed to it. The producers and I put together a crew and we were going to shoot it in Michigan. Then the new governor of Michigan decided that there would be no new tax incentives for filmmaking in Michigan, and they couldn't make the movie on the budget we had without those tax incentives. They hired another producer, who knew that the only affordable way to make the movie was to shoot it in Canada. In the end, there wasn't enough money to bring me to Canada as the director. Despite three months of work, time and dedication—all unpaid—it was over.

When I got the news, I sat there in shock and anger for about ten minutes. Then I got up, went to my computer and started searching for producers in Ireland. I just decided, *I'm an American director with an Irish passport and I would love to make a movie in Ireland.* For some reason, that became my next big goal. I felt like I needed to make a some kind of major change like that. I must have sent out fifty letters of inquiry. Basically what came back was: "You're overqualified, but we don't have enough work for our own directors. If you can find a project and a producer . . ." And then I was right back to needing to find a project. So I turned my focus to script writing.

For years, I had carried around this desire to tell a story about the rodeo. I wanted it to have a sense of the family mentality that is part of a rodeo world and when I pitched that idea to my friend Nancy Miller, she said well let me bring it to my agent at William Morris. Her agent said we represent the Professional Bull Riders association (PBR), and I can set up a meeting with their CEO. So that motivated me to produce a pilot script.

When I started doing research on the PBR, I realized these guys are like the Oscar winners, an elite group. And they want to be perceived as squeaky clean, all-American athletes. Not dirty cowboys. In fact, they work very hard to get away from the cowboy image. They do their shows in arenas, not in rodeos. Which was less appealing to me . . . I thought, *You can do a movie about Hollywood royalty or you can do* Rocky. I wanted to do *Rocky*. And when I added the darker elements, the CEO of PBR basically said, "We can't endorse this. It's just not the way we present ourselves." So that hasn't gone anywhere yet.

My friend Peter Desberg and I developed an eight-part cable series idea about nineteenth century Italian composer Niccolò Paganini. You could say he was the first Elvis or Hendrix. People clambered to see him; women fainted. He did all these mysterious things like rehearse in cemeteries at night, and stare down the audience before he started playing. Rumor was that he had made a pact with the devil. In the end, he became a victim of his own publicity. At the time of his death, the Catholic Church refused him the last sacraments and refused to bury him. Our story was about his son trying to learn who his father really was. So it was a very unusual biopic.

This was around the time you started singing in a band called The Sloths. Were you making a conscious attempt to refocus on music?

Not exactly. What happened was an attorney named Jeff Briskin, who played with me in a band called The May Wines back in 1966, hired a private detective to track down his old bandmates. I was the easiest to find, because I had an agent and a show business profile.

Before he was in The May Wines, Jeff had been in a band called The Sloths. They got together in 1965, recorded one song ("Makin' Love") and then disbanded. Jeff and some of the other members formed The May Wines. I joined them and, for a while, we played the exact same songs and opened for a lot of the same bands. Then Jeff left and The May Wines morphed into TNT. That was the end of The Sloths until 2011, when a copy of "Makin' Love" sold for $6,500 on eBay.

The May Wines in 1966

At the same time, this guy named Mike Stax—who runs a '60s music magazine called *Ugly Things*—was looking for The Sloths. He tracked down Mike Rummens, who had played rhythm guitar in The Sloths and The May Wines. One of The May Wines was never found. Two of The Sloths had passed away. The rest of us got together at IHOP one historic night.

It was surreal to suddenly see these guys again after almost forty-five years! We did the interview for *Ugly Things* and I said, "Well, wouldn't it be cool to get together in a garage someday, just for the fun of it, and see what happens?" For a while, we kind of let it go at that. Then one day I got a call from the drummer Bob Krasnow, who said, "Do you guys want to do this or not?" Jeff and I really did!

We got together in Bob's garage and started playing the songs that we had played when we were sixteen years old on the Sunset Strip. Old Rolling Stones songs. Yardbirds songs. Animals songs. Jeff hadn't really played in forty-five years. I had not sung in just as long. Thank God we didn't make a tape of it because it probably sounded like shit—but it was amazing how many songs we remembered. We kept getting together for a while, again just for fun, but I really didn't expect it to lead anywhere. I thought it was the equivalent of a Wednesday night poker game.

Your first concert was on October 1, 2011, at a club called Eleven in San Diego. What was it like performing on stage again, after so many years of being behind the camera?

That was an experience that, if I put it in a movie, the reviewers would go, "This is just too unbelievably corny." A guy in his sixties getting up on stage with a bunch of other guys in their sixties, playing the music they were playing when they were sixteen. I never thought I'd get back on stage again, much less be performing like some Mick Jagger-esque punk. But there I was, looking out into the audience and seeing Nancy, Shane and Hannah . . . and the looks on their faces made it all worthwhile. None of them had ever seen that side of me, because that part of my life happened so long ago. To our amazement, the audience reception to the reborn Sloths was phenomenal.

When it was over, I figured: *That's a once in a lifetime experience.* But from that show, another offer came. And then another one. Which shocked all of us. Ever since then we've been playing gigs whenever and wherever we can get them—whether it's for fifty people or 500 people. We even went back to the Sunset Strip. We've played On the Rox, The Echo and The Vex. We've also played in San Francisco and Oakland, and we just did a big music festival in Reno. And we have two festivals coming up in New Orleans and Spain later this year. Being in an unsigned band that's going to Europe—especially at a time when so many young bands can't even get into a local club without paying for their own tickets and selling them to family and friends—is overwhelming.

So why is this happening? Who knows. It's just sort of happening and we're going along with it. Around the time we did our sixtieth show, I had to accept that this is not just a passing thing. By then I had decided take up the harmonica, which is an instrument that I started to learn when I was a teenager. Then I started taking flamenco dancing lessons. Most people don't start flamenco dancing at sixty-one, but I wanted to incorporate certain moves into my performance during our shows. I also learned how to play the castanets. I also started taking singing lessons. If I'm going to do this, I want to be as good as I can be. I recently reconnected with Wenndy MacKenzie, my vocal coach, through Facebook. I was

The Sloths reunited, 2012.
Photo credit: Cheryl Zeichik

The Sloths play The Stork Club in Oakland, May 2012.
Photo credit: Tiger Lily.

very close friends with her back in the '60s. She's a phenomenal singer and teacher.

Then I've always wanted to play an Irish instrument, so I started learning how to play the bodhran—the Irish drum. I found I had a natural aptitude for it, and that was an incredible revelation. I'd always believed that musicianship was one talent I didn't have, so

I never really pursued it. I am still far from a good musician on any of these things, but the more I practice and play, the more confident I become. These discoveries have been extremely exciting for me.

At this point in your life, are you now thinking of yourself more as a musician than a filmmaker?

No. No way. I never for a second will let go of filmmaking . . . I'm still writing, and trying to develop and discover something new. The problem is that the TV movie business has really changed in the last few years. When A&E took over Lifetime [in 2009], they made it very clear that they did not want to keep making the same type of movies with the same people. That was a big door that closed on me. I had to move on. Then, last year, a new Lifetime project came out of left field—a biopic about Stephanie Lazarus, the L.A. policewoman who was convicted of murder. I thought that was a really interesting project, but it just seemed like something kept holding it back. I spent about five months working with the producers and Lifetime on the script. We went into what's called "soft prep." But by the end of 2012, Lifetime passed.

I met with the executives at ABC Family Channel about a couple of movies they wanted to do with me. That led to a long, long, long wait, only to find out that ABC Family has gone the route of most other TV networks, which is they only want to do one or two movies a year and otherwise concentrate on series, because there's more longevity and more money in a series.

I then spent the first half of 2013 developing a very unique take on the [Boston mobster] Whitey Bulger story, but that fell apart as well. So I continue in this transitional phase, wondering what's next. My feeling is that I'll be back in the feature film world.

In December 2012, you reunited with the L.A. Mime Company for one night at The Magic Castle in Hollywood. Was that like reuniting with the band?

No. Completely different. For one thing, I was once married to Katee. And the group was really like my extended family.

Over the years I've stayed in touch with everyone. Tina and her husband Mike Caveny are friends with magician Rob Zabrecky, who was booking shows for The Magic Castle in 2012. One day he said, "What do you guys think about doing an L.A. Mime Company tribute?" Tina looked at me and said, "What do you think?" I said, "Well, I'm performing again. You and Mitchel never stopped. It's a question of whether Katee and Albert would want to do this." I figured the least we could do was ask. As it turned out, they loved the idea of a reunion.

Months later, when the great day finally came, it was pretty surreal. It felt like we all just totally picked up right where we left off decades ago. The only difference was hair colors . . . and the amount of hair . . . and wrinkles. Mitchel is still the exact same character. Katee still has her same energy and spunk. Tina is basically the same, but much more confident than she had been in the old days. Albert is still the boy who refuses to grow up, which is why I love him. We all got together at Tina's house, had dinner, and started putting a show together. We voted on a skit that we could do at the end of the tribute. It had a bit of a magic trick involved in it, so it was perfect for the Magic Castle and the occasion.

When the night was over, it was like the end of making a movie. Everyone is looking at each other, going, "It's over? We have to stay in touch . . ." And, just like after a movie shoot, we did that for a couple of weeks. Then everybody slowly disappeared back into their lives. But it was an incredible experience. I really love them.

You've talked about the Hollywood Forever birthday party as the setup for your third act, and so far the third act seems to keep bringing you back to where you started . . .

Just proves that God has the final draft and the final cut, right? When The Sloths reunited, it really was a lark and I didn't expect it to last at all. But it did. It's only getting bigger. I'm realizing everybody secretly wants some kind of second shot, but we don't dare to say it out loud. It's an impossible dream. In the big scheme of things, how can we possibly succeed? But The Sloths

L.A. Mime Company in the 1970s

L.A. Mime Company in 2012.

keep moving on. We just recorded two new songs and I listen to them and I think, *They're not bad. But are they any good? Who knows?*

One of the songs is called "Lust." It's a classic hard rocker with a rebellious attitude. What we called "rebel rock" is now called "punk rock." The other one is "Wanna New Life." It's about the idea that your future was once filled with all these opportunities and possibilities, but somewhere along the line somebody changed the game and now you want a second chance, a new and better life. I tried to write it so that it sort of speaks to you whether you're sixteen or sixty.

Guitarist Mike Rummens came up with a new blues riff called "Before I Die." He said, "People used to say they wanted to die before they got old. Right now, I've got all this shit I wanna do before I die." It's a reversal on The Who. I took that and created the lyrics, which are about how people of our generation do not want to let go. *I'm not slowing down. I'm speeding up.* There's so many new challenges out there that I still want to go for. I keep doing things that I never dreamed I would ever do. That's my life now. In a way, the movie I'm making right now is *me*.

I just took a job as an adjunct film professor at Chapman University. I never thought I would be *teaching* cinema, but the truth is I'm really excited about working with the next generation of filmmakers—not just as a teacher, but as a student. In my first class, looking at this eclectic group of future filmmakers, the first thing I said was, "I'm still a student too. We're gonna teach each other." I know that's how it will be, because I genuinely believe what Chaplin said in *Limelight*. "We're all amateurs. We don't live long enough to be anything else."

"To die will be an awfully big adventure" —Peter Pan

FILMOGRAPHY

Sleeper (theatrical feature, 1973)—actor
The Incredible Machine (documentary, 1975)—actor
"Van Dyke and Company" (TV series, 1976)—actor / writer
Prophecy (theatrical feature, 1979)—actor
The Black Hole (theatrical feature, 1979)—actor
The Incredible Shrinking Woman (theatrical feature, 1981)—actor
One Dark Night (theatrical feature, completed 1981, released 1983)—writer / director
Alice in Wonderland (TV miniseries, 1985)—actor
Friday the 13th Part VI: Jason Lives! (theatrical feature, 1986)—writer / director
"Amazing Stories"—"Go to the Head of the Class" (TV series, 1986)—writer
"Amazing Stories"—"Such Interesting Neighbors" (TV series, 1987)—writer
Date with an Angel (theatrical feature, 1987)—writer / director
"Freddy's Nightmares"—"It's A Miserable Life" (TV series, 1988)—director
"Friday the 13th"—"Master of Disguise" (TV series, 1988)—director
"Friday the 13th"—"The Playhouse" (TV series, 1989)—writer / director
"Friday the 13th"—"The Prophecies" (TV series, 1989)—writer / director
"The Steven Banks Show: Home Entertainment Center" (Showtime special, 1989)—director

"They Came from Outer Space"—"Malibu or Bust!" (TV series, 1990)—Creator/Writer
"She-Wolf of London"—"She-Wolf of London" (TV series, 1990)—Creator/Writer
Steven King's Sometimes They Come Back (Theatrical Feature, 1991)—Director
In a Child's Name (TV miniseries, 1991)—Director
Something to Live for: The Alison Gertz Story (TV movie, 1991)—Director
The Fire Next Time (TV miniseries, 1993)—Director
Murder of Innocence (TV movie, 1993)—Producer/Director
The Yarn Princess (TV movie, 1994)—Director
Leave of Absence (TV movie, 1994)—Director
The Lies Boys Tell (TV movie, 1994)—Director
Journey (TV movie, 1994)—Director
The Turn of the Screw (TV movie, 1995)—Director / Producer
A Different Kind of Christmas (TV movie, 1996)—Director / Producer
Fairy Tale: A True Story (Theatrical, 1997)—Writer / Producer
The Third Twin (TV movie, 1997)—Director
"Leaving L.A." (pilot entitled "Intermission," 1997)—Director / Producer
Behind the Mask (TV movie, 1999)—Director
Anya's Bell (TV movie, 1999)—Director
"The Others"—"Theta" (TV, 2000)—Director
The Unsaid (Theatrical, 2001)—Director
"Fiona"—pilot (Sony Pictures TV, 2001)—Director
"Any Day Now"—"The Real Thing" (Lifetime, 2002)—Director
"Any Day Now"—"Truth Hurts" (Lifetime, 2002)—Director
Murder in Greenwich (USA Network, 2002)—Director
"Without a Trace"—"Underground Railroad" (CBS, 2003)—Director
D.C. Sniper: 23 Days of Fear (USA Network, 2003)—Director
A Very Married Christmas (CBS, 2004)—Director

SHE'S TOO YOUNG (LIFETIME, 2004)—DIRECTOR
ODD GIRL OUT (LIFETIME, 2005)—DIRECTOR
CYBER SEDUCTION: HIS SECRET LIFE (LIFETIME, 2005)—
    DIRECTOR / PRODUCER
NOT LIKE EVERYONE ELSE (LIFETIME, 2006)—
    DIRECTOR / PRODUCER
THE STAIRCASE MURDERS (LIFETIME, 2007)—DIRECTOR
"SAVING GRACE"—"THIS IS WAY TOO NORMAL FOR YOU"
    (TNT, 2007)—DIRECTOR
FAB FIVE: THE TEXAS CHEERLEADER SCANDAL (LIFETIME, 2008)—
    DIRECTOR
THE WRONGED MAN (LIFETIME, 2009)—DIRECTOR
AT RISK (LIFETIME, 2010)—DIRECTOR
THE FRONT (LIFETIME, 2010)—DIRECTOR

APPENDIX: JASON LIVES!

Here's a little something extra for *Friday the 13th* fans . . . Tom McLoughlin's original treatment for *Jason Lives!*

Darcy DeMoss, Thom Matthews, Nancy and Tom McLoughlin at a signing for the documentary *Crystal Lake Memories* (2013)

```
              FRIDAY THE 13TH - PART 6

                 "JASON HAS RISEN"

              Treatment for a Screenplay

                         by

                   Tom McLoughlin
```

```
                                          Rick Jaffa
                                          William Morris Agency
                                          151 El Camino Drive
             W.G.A. Reg.                  Beverly Hills, CA 90212
                                          (213) 859-4142
```

Ominous black clouds creep across the full summer moon. We tilt down to the quiet forest road below. Suddenly a car ROARS around the bend like a bat out of hell! TOMMY, a good looking 18 year old boy, races like a mad man toward a terrifing destination. As we move into his cold, determined eyes, we see flashes of his horrid past (Friday 13th - Parts 4 and 5). In the final moments of Part 5, a doctor rushes in and restrains the goalie masked Tommy. Another quick flashback shows us Tommy in a psychiatric session pleading he has to be sure that Jason is truly dead. The boy vows to destroy Jason, body and soul, forever. Back to the present, we see on the seat next to Tommy a steel spear, a shovel, gas can, and the infamous goalie mask. Thunder and lightning detonate over the speeding car.

Tommy hurries across the small town cemetery. His flashlight searches the tombstones. He stops frozen before two side by side. Jason Voorhees and his mother. As storm clouds continue to rage above, Tommy begins to exhume Jason's body. Opening the rotted casket, lightning illuminates the decaying cadavier of Jason. Wasting no time, Tommy plunges the long spear into its chest, again and again! Leaving it planted there, he then throws the goalie mask into the grave. As he prepares to douse the corpse with gasoline, the sky explodes hellishly. A bolt of electricity strikes the spear like a lightning rod. Jason's decomposed eyelids flash open! Unaware, Tommy goes to pull the spear out. JASON SPRINGS UP TO GRAB HIM. Panicking, the boy throws gasoline on the rising corpse. Tommy starts to light a match but is foiled as the clouds begin to rain! He runs for his life across the cemetery. Jason reaches down and once again dons his beloved mask. Grabing the spear that brought him back to life, he stalks Tommy to settle the score. Jason looks for the boy. He then turns and heads for us! Freeze. The credits proclaim 'Jason Has Risen'.

Later that night, Tommy's car SCREECHES into the quaint little town of Forest Green. He bursts into the Sheriff's office trying to explain what has just occurred. SHERIFF GARRIS is a macho, no nonsense type who informs Tommy that Forest Green used to be named Crystal Lake. The town has worked very hard to remove all reminders of the horror Jason had brought there. The Sheriff says with their new camp facility going so well, they don't need some crazy kid claiming Jason is back from the grave. Tommy screams why didn't they cremate Jason. Sheriff replies that they were, but some family member sent money to have Mrs. Voorhees and Jason buried. The frustrated Tommy yells, "Jason is coming back here. He wants me and he'll kill anything in his path. We've got to stop him!" Tommy grabs a shotgun. The Sheriff and his deputy, after quite a struggle with the strong teenager, jails him for the night. Tommy warns him of the consequences. The undead Jason is more unstopable than ever before.

A likable, young couple drive down the muddy back roads looking for the camp. Laughing, the new counselors are trying to read their map. Suddenly, the young man SLAMS on his breaks.

3

Standing in the middle of the road holding the spear is Jason! The boy tries to get the menacing stranger to move. His girlfriend pleads with him to just turn around. He decides he's gonna scare this weirdo. Taking a hand gun from the glove compartment, he threatens Jason. Jason retaliates by smashing the guy's headlight. The girl yells for them to just get out of there...now. But her pissed boyfriend fires a warning shot over Jason's head. Slowly, the masked killer stalks him. Frightened, he fires at Jason. The bullets are seen exiting his back! JASON KEEPS COMING. He IMPALES the boy, lifts him up and tosses him aside. The girl goes hysterical. She attempts to drive away. The spear SMASHES through the window. She exits out the other side, slips and twists her ankle. Crawling through the mud as Jason stalks her, she offers him her money and credit cards. Jason seems to hesitate, looking at the currency in her trembling hand. Then without warning, he raises the spear and DRIVES IT DOWN! Her lifeless hand falls releasing the money to float in a muddy puddle. Jason continues down the road toward his objective...Tommy.

    The next morning, Tommy is awoken in his cell by the Sheriff's spunky and attractive daughter, MEGAN. She and her three friends, CORT, SISSY and PAULA are all counselors at Camp Forest Green. They want the Sheriff to check the roads for two missing counselors who may have had car problems due to the storm. Tommy tells them he fears the worst with Jason out there. The Sheriff shuts him up. The teens are curious about the so-called

4

'Jason legend'. Megan approaches Tommy. There's an immediate attraction between them. He implores Megan to convince her father to go to the cemetery and check his story. Irritated, the Sheriff ushers the kids out. He then tells Tommy he is going to escourt him to the outskirts of his jurisdiction and never wants to see him again. Tommy warns him that the town's former nightmare is begining again.

Deep in the woods, four Rambo-esque hunters prepare themselves and their weapons. Straping on guerilla artillery, the intensely macho guys move out toward their prey.

Camp Forest Green is a beautifully renovated cabin retreat on the site of old Camp Crystal. Everything is freshly painted and well groomed. Megan and her friends drive up and are joking around about Tommy. Megan defends him and is teased by her colleagues. A big yellow school bus pulls up filled with screaming youngsters. The four counselors sigh in dread. Cort comments that the 'Jason character' is probably a pussy next to these monsters. The children charge wildly out of the bus.

A gentle deer is seen through a rifle scope. Then another angle of the animal through another scope. And another. All the Rambo-clone hunters have it sighted. On a signal from their leader all open fire. Proudly, they go to claim their prey. But the bewildered men can't find it. They hear a noise, turn, and see the deer running away. Chagrined, they turn back around. JASON STANDS BEFORE THEM. They get macho with the stoic killer. Jason suddenly GRABS the leader by the throat! They attack Jason but

5

they're no match for this unbeatable villian. He brutally destroys all but one who runs shrieking through the forest. Jason looks down at all the artillery before him.

At the cemetery, MARTIN the old alcoholic caretaker finds Jason's open grave. He is terrified that he'll be held responsible for not preventing this body snatching. Quickly, he starts filling in the muddy hole mumbling something about, "He'll never understand. He'll kill me. Never get no more money." The hung-over caretaker shovels as fast as he can.

Sheriff Garris and his deputy follow Tommy's car out of town. They discuss the boy being badly traumatized from the past and in need of more psychiatric treatment. Suddenly, Tommy's car turns and speeds up the road toward the cemetery. Angered, the Sheriff pursues him.

Tommy screeches to a halt in front of the old graveyard. As the Sheriff arrives, Tommy dashes across the muddy cemetery yelling he'll prove his story. Needless to say, the boy is shocked to find Jason's grave looking undisturbed. The Sheriff apprehends him but Tommy still insists his story is true. Sheriff sees the old caretaker and calls him over. Martin adamently insists he was on duty all night and nothing unusual occurred. Sheriff drags Tommy away as the boy pleads for them to dig up Jason's coffin.

Megan, Sissy and Paula have a series of comic encounters with the young campers. Cort meanwhile tries desperately to teach the young boys the joys of wilderness sports. The kids just stare at him bored and unimpressed. One of the youngsters comments to another, "If this is as exciting as it gets, we're in trouble".

Jason's feet are seen coming toward us. As we tilt up, we see he has a Uzi-machine gun, ammunition belt, and other guerilla weapons straped around him. Jason has become a one man Army!

The Sheriff's car pulls over on a main interstate road. Tommy's car, driven by the deputy, pulls up behind it. Sheriff Garris releases Tommy and tells him if he <u>ever</u> finds him in his jurisdiction again, he'll shoot first, <u>then</u> ask questions. "You're a sick boy. You need help." Tommy argues it's Camp Crystal Lake that needs help. "Jason is returning to where it all began."

That evening, it's very quiet and peaceful on the camp grounds. The children are asleep in their cabins. Paula and Sissy are playing a board game. They discuss Megan going back to visit her '<u>new</u> heart-throb' in the jail. Suddenly, a child's horrified SCREAMS echo through the camp. The girls rush into the children's cabin. A little girl NANCY has awoken from a bad nightmare. She tearfully reveals that a big, scary man was chasing her. Paula and Sissy reassure her it was only a bad dream. After getting the other children back to bed, Paula notices Cort is missing. Sissy says he's probably with Miss rich bitch.

An R.V. is seen bouncing in the moonlight to the beat of loud rock music within. Cort and his girlfriend JILL are getting it on in her daddy's expensive mobile home. Jason emerges from the shadows of the forest. He stares at the noisey R.V. Their

7

wild love making is suddenly cut short when all the electricity goes out. Jason has torn the cord out of the outdoor plug-in outlet. Nervously, the couple go out to investigate. Finding the cord destroyed and no one around, they decide they better get out of there. Cort and Jill re-enter the R.V. and drive away. Laughing again, Jill goes to the closet toilet to clean up. JASON EXPLODES OUT OF THE DOOR. Like a crazed soldier, Jason opens fire blasting the teens and the mobile home to bits! The swirving R.V. finally drives off the road and overturns. Jason throws open the door and exits unharmed. He continues down the road toward the camp in his search for Tommy.

Megan arrives at the Sheriff's station. Her father is surprised and pleased to see her. That is until he hears it's Tommy she's interested in. As he lectures her, a call comes in from his deputy. He's found the bodies of the murdered camp counselors. Also he's got this crazed hunter who claims there is a bizarre super killer in a hockey mask who attacked him and his buddies. Leaving, Sheriff tells Megan to stay there. He's sure Tommy is responsible.

Moving down the aisle of an old library, we find Tommy seated alone at a huge table. He is surrounded by books dealing with the occult, witchcraft, zombies, and evil powers. As he reads he seems to have found what he needs to know. Tommy slams the book closed and exits.

Megan sits alone in the station. A large window is right behind her. Bored, she is balancing herself on the back legs of

8

the chair. Tension builds as we slowly move toward her. Suddenly, the phone RINGS LOUDLY. Startled, she screams as she falls backwards in the chair. Megan answers the phone laughing at herself. Tommy is at a phone booth. He needs to talk to the Sheriff. Megan tells him about the murders and that her father thinks it's him. Tommy says he's found <u>the only way</u> to stop Jason's reign of terror. But he needs help. Megan doesn't think it's safe for him to drive into town. She volunteers to pick him up and help him. Before he can argue, she's on her way.

Out of the darkness of the woods a figure steps into the moonlight. Jason stops and stares. Laying peacefully before him...Camp Forest Green. Jason is at first confused by it. He then pulls a razor sharp machete from his commando belt. Jason proceeds into the new camp.

A very bloody, sheet-covered body is lifted into an ambulance. Sheriff Garris and two other cops are at the scene of the over turned R.V. One of the cops holds the Uzi-machine gun Jason used. He tells the Sheriff it belonged to those hunters who were attacked. The Sheriff orders an all points bulletin on that wacko kid Tommy. From the backseat of the Sheriff's car, the arrested hunter JAKE, yells, "That's no <u>kid</u> out there. That's a damn zombie!" The Sheriff pays no attention to the hysterical man. He orders road blocks set up throughout the area. As Cort's bullet riddled body is pulled from the R.V., one of the cops shakes his head. "All this is enough to turn you superstitious." Sheriff asks what does he mean. He shrugs, "You know, this being Friday the thirteenth". An icy chill goes through the Sheriff.

WHACK. The machete cuts the phone line. We then follow Jason as he heads for a lit and open window. Inside the counselors cabin Paula is sound asleep. Sissy is paging through Playgirl magazine ogling over the sexy guys. She hears footsteps and sticks her head out the window to look. She doesn't see anyone. Thinking it was just a squirrel or something she returns to her magazine. She hears it again. Sissy calls out "Cort?" Paula stirs and half awake asks what's going on. Sissy says she thinks Cort is trying to sneak back and scare them. Paula tells her to teach him a lesson and she falls back asleep. Hearing him right outside the window, Sissy grabs an open bottle of Coke. Putting her thumb over the top, she shakes it and aims it out the window. She knows she got him but he didn't respond. Laughing, she sticks her head out the window to check. A FLASH OF STEEL SWOOPS DOWN. SISSY IS INSTANTLY DECAPITATED. Her body falls limp across the window ledge. Paula stirs again and looks, "Oh, that'll scare him. Just go _out_ there after "him". Her heavy eyelids close again. Sissy's body is violently yanked through the window! Paula looks, snickers at her friend, then falls back asleep.

Megan's car ROARS UP in front of the phone booth where Tommy waits. He runs to the car carrying a heavy satchel. As they drive Tommy fears Megan's safety being with him. She says, "You can't be a cop's daughter and not know how to handle trouble". She inquires about the contents of the satchel. Tommy says according to his research it's what's needed to stop Jason. Megan looks in and is shocked. "That's it? You are crazy", Tommy tells her, "It's gotta work". Hurry, we have to reach the camp before Jason does". Megan steps on it and blasts down the highway.

Inside, a moonlit cabin rows of bunk beds filled with sleeping children are seen. Jason's silouette carrying Sissy's headless corpse passes by the windows. His evil shadow moves across little Nancy who sits up wide-eyed in fear.

Zooming around a curve, Megan's car screeches to a halt. A police road block waits before them! Tommy asks her what she's gonna do. She pulls his surprised face down on her lap and whips the car around. She knows another route. Seeing this, one of the officers takes off after them. A high speed chase ensues. The officer radios in the car. The Sheriff immediately recognizes it as his daughters. He has other units close in. Megan is forced to pull over. Tommy is arrested.

Paula rolls over in her sleep. Her cabin door is heard opening. Slowly, we creep toward the sleeping girl. A shadow falls across her face. Paula senses something and opens her eyes. SHE GASPS. Little Nancy stands over her. She tells Paula she can't sleep, she's afraid, she saw someone outside. Paula tells her it's Sissy playing a joke on Cort. Taking Nancy's hand Paula says, "Let's go out and find them, okay?"

Paula and Nancy exit the cabin and slowly walk the grounds searching for the counselors. Waiting in the darkness, Jason watches their every move.

Back at the Sheriff's station, Tommy is once again behind

11

bars. Megan and her father scream at each other over his involvement in the murders. The jailed hunter Jake joins in the debate saying it wasn't Tommy. Megan pleads with her father to take them to the camp before it's too late. The Sheriff says he's been calling out there to tell the others about Cort but no one's answering. He'll drive out there to check on things. But he's leaving them here with his deputy. Tommy and Megan beg him to listen. As he exits, the sheriff grabs his shot gun. The crazed hunter yells, "That won't do you no good with that dude. It'll just make him madder!"

Trying to be quiet so as to not awaken the other little girls Paula and Nancy tiptoe back into the cabin. She tucks the sweet child in her bed and whispers that Sissy and Cort are probably back in their own beds sleeping. Paula tells her whenever she gets scared just say a little prayer and everything will be fine. Neither one of them sees JASON GLARING THROUGH THE WINDOW AT THEM. As Paula walks through the cabin, Jason follows her from window to window. She exits and looks around. She's very confused over the whereabouts of her friends. A long tense moment. Hearing something, she turns to look. No one is around her. JASON SLAMS DOWN BEFORE HER from the branch above. His powerful hands seize her throat and squeeze before she can even scream. Paula crumbles at his feet. Jason's gaze goes from the dead girl up to the children's cabin.

At the station, the deputy is filling out forms. Tommy motions for Megan to come over to his cell. He whispers a plan

12

and she nods. Suddenly, Tommy pulls Megan to him! He holds her against the bars as he passionately kisses her. She pretends to struggle. Jake is whooping it up. The deputy goes over to help pull her away from Tommy. In the struggle, Megan secretly grabs his gun and holds it on him. She orders the deputy to release Tommy and they put him in the cell. Grabbing the satchel, they race for her car. Megan comments on how impressed she was with his kissing. Tommy says they'll discuss it later as he jumps behind the wheel. They tear out down the road.

Jason is in the children's cabin! He walks slow and menacingly through the boy's section. The youngsters sleep peacefully unaware of this monster at the very edge of their beds. Jason opens a door and enters the girls' side. All of them are asleep as well. All but...Nancy. Her horrified eyes are peeking over the sheet. Jason scans the cabin. His eyes then connect with the childs. He heads toward her.

Sheriff Garris' car pulls into the camp followed by another police car. The Sheriff and the two officers survey the camp site. A strong wind is beginning to whip through the trees.

Jason stands over Nancy's bed! The child is too terrified to move. As his masked face slowly descends toward her, she begins to pray aloud. At that moment, Jason hears the Sheriff's voice outside. He turns and heads towards it. With her tiny eyes squeezed shut, Nancy continues to pray unaware that Jason has gone.

The Sheriff orders the officers to take a look around while he talks to the counselors. They ask him what they are looking for. The Sheriff, sensing trouble, says, "Anything unusual. And be careful not to wake the kids." The two cops spread out, searching the area with their flashlights. The wind now rages causing everything to whistle and move.

Checking the counselor's cabins, the Sheriff is <u>very</u> concerned to find them empty. He rushes towards the childrens dormitory.

One of the cops is checking the landing area and the boats. Jason stalks him from behind. He pulls out a long Devil's Dart from his commando belt. The unsuspecting officer turns around. His flashlight illuminates the approaching killer! Before he can pull his gun, <u>Jason fires the razor sharp dart at him</u>. IT IMPALES ITSELF DEEP INTO HIS SKULL. The cop falls backward into a small boat.

The door of the boy's dormitory slowly opens. Sheriff Garris looks in fearfully. All the kids are sleeping soundly. He is relieved. Quietly, he tiptoes to the other open door. Looking in on the girls he finds them also in dreamland. But one of the unmade beds is empty. Little Nancy is nowhere to be found.

Tommy and Megan are racing toward camp. Megan pulls out the heavy chains in the satchel. Tommy tries to explain that Jason's body has to return to its <u>original</u> resting place for this nightmare to finally end. That is, the bottom of Lake Crystal where he drown in 1957. Megan wonders how can that be done. Tommy says he's got a plan that he hopes will work. Unless Jason

14

gets him first.

The other cop is getting frustrated looking around for God-knows-what. He suddenly sees someone move through the bushes! Or was it just the wind? Cautiously, he approaches. He calls out. No reply. The officer draws his revolver as he gets closer. <u>The tension builds</u>. SUDDENLY HIS LEG IS ATTACKED. It's Nancy holding on to him for dear life. He catches his breath and asks her what's wrong. She tells him about the scary man. He laughs kindly and says, "What scary man?" JASON EXPLODES OUT OF THE BUSHES. Nancy runs shrieking. The officer fires at Jason but the bullet has no affect on the undead fiend. JASON GRABS THE COP'S FACE AND LITERALLY RIPS HIS SKIN OFF HIS SKULL. A bloody grinning skull stares at us for a moment, then drops from view.

Sheriff Garris is taking his shot gun from the police car. He sprints toward where he heard the shot. Nancy comes screaming around the corner. He grabs the child and tries to comfort her. All the children are now staring out the windows awoken by gunshots. The Sheriff quickly puts Nancy in the cabin. He orders all the kids to lay on the floor and not to get up until he comes back. Terrified, they hit the deck. Some hide under their beds.

Sheriff pumps the shotgun and moves in with great vigilance. He finds the horribly mutilated officer. Jason, of course, is gone. The wind continues to whip the bushes and trees and the Sheriff twitches at every movement. Slowly, he heads between the cabins searching for the murderer. Suddenly, he <u>trips</u> on something

15

and falls. Sheriff finds himself laying on Paula's corpse! HER CONTORTED FACE IS PRESSED AGAINST HIS. Quickly, he scrambles to his feet. He turns and JASON IS RIGHT THERE. The Sheriff backs away from this motionless figure of evil. A long wait. Suddenly, Jason steps toward him! Involuntarily the Sheriff blasts him with both barrels! A huge hole is bored in Jason's side. BUT JASON KEEPS ON COMING. Horrified, the Sheriff pulls his .357 and empties the chamber at the stalking ghoul. The bullets pass right through Jason angering him even more. Sheriff Garris has one choice...run for it.

Megan's car arrives at the camp. She and Tommy leap out and nervously survey the area. Finding the cabins empty, Megan panics and runs to the children's dormitories. Tommy is lugging the heavy satchel toward the lake.

Jason relentlessly pursues the Sheriff through the savagely windy forest. The macho law man has never experienced this kind of nightmare. He runs for his life!

Megan bursts into the children's cabin. The startled kids SCREAM. Megan assures them everything will be okay. She hugs two of the quivering children.

Meanwhile, Tommy prepares one of the docked rowboats. He recoils in horror to find a murdered cop. Quickly, he goes to another more rickety rowboat. Taking out the chains, he arranges them in the boat. Tommy then looks along the shore for something.

Jason's feet stop. He begins to retrace his steps. It

16

seems he has lost his prey. Carefully, he scans the wind blown bushes. Hiding in the thick brush, the Sheriff's face is drenched in sweat. He holds his breath as Jason passes.

Megan instructs the children to stay in the cabin. She goes outside to look for her father. Tommy is rolling a very heavy rock toward the boat. He tells Megan to use her father's C.B. to radio for more help. As Megan opens the police car door, SISSY'S HEAD ROLLS OUT. It's dead eyes stare up at Megan who screams! She starts calling out for her father fearing that he too has been killed.

The Sheriff hears his daughter's distant cry. So does Jason. The Sheriff peeks out of his hiding place. He is even more terrified than ever to see Jason heading in the direction of his daughter's voice. Without thought, his fatherly instincts cause him to leap out and protect his daughter. He attacks Jason from behind and rages, "Not her, you bastard!" The Sheriff lays into Jason with an almost super strength, pounding him into the ground. For a moment, you think he might kill the monster. But only for a moment. Jason rolls over. His hands grasp the Sheriff's arms. JASON TEARS THEM OUT OF THEIR SOCKETS. Throwing the arms aside, Jason grabs the Sheriff's head and bends his body all the way back. HIS SPINE IS SNAPPED IN HALF. Jason gets up enraged. He picks up the lifeless Sheriff and throws him aside like a rag doll. Megan's voice calls out again. Jason heads toward it with deadly intent!

Tommy has the terrified Megan help him get the large

17

boulder onto the chains in the boat. It cracks a bit from the weight. He then gathers the chains around the rock and secures them with a strong padlock.

Jason stomps through the forest heading for them!

Tommy straightens out the rest of the long chain and fashions a noose. Megan continues to call for her father. The children are seen peeking out of the windows in fear.

Jason is getting closer!

Tommy has Megan push him out onto the windy churning lake. He tells her to hide in the cabin with the kids. She fears for his life. Tommy yells at her to get to the cabin before it's too late.

JASON EXPLODES THROUGH THE DOOR OF THE CHILDREN'S CABIN. The kids go shrieking toward the other door.

Megan runs like hell toward the cabin as the kids stream out. Tommy watches helplessly from the boat. Just as Megan reaches the kids, JASON BURSTS OUT THE WINDOW. The children run helter skelter. Megan is grabbed by Jason! His other hand grips her face. She is about to share the same horrific facial fate as the cop. Tommy's voice yells, "Jason!" Jason turns to look. "It's me, you want, Jason. Come and get me!" Realizing who it is, Jason drops Megan. He heads for Tommy in the middle of the lake.

Holding the chain noose in his sweating hands, Tommy watches Jason coming for him.

The children gather around Megan. They all stare in fearful

18

anticipation.

Jason is focused on one thing as he wades into the churning waters... <u>kill Tommy</u>. The boy sits waiting, trying to mask the terror he feels. Jason is getting closer and closer to the boat.

Megan can't stand it. She screams, "Tommy, don't! Get out of there!"

Jason looks back at her. Tommy, quickly calls out to him. "Hey asshole. It's me you want, remember? Come on!" Jason swims like a hungry shark toward the boy. Keeping the noose down low, Tommy slides it open. As he shifts, the floor of the boat cracks a little more.

Jason is almost to him!

Tommy grits his teeth and readies the noose.

JASON SUDDENLY SUBMERGES, DISAPPEARING INTO THE DARK WATERS.

Tommy goes crazy looking from one side to the other for where Jason will reappear. <u>A long tense wait</u>. Bubbles rise and Tommy holds the noose over them, prepared. Without warning, JASON POPS UP from the other side. Tommy falls and drops the noose in the boat. His fall causes the bottom to crack even more! Water leaks in.

Jason tries to grab Tommy and pull him out. Tommy struggles to reach the noose. Megan is going crazy watching from the shore.

Jason succeeds in grabbing Tommy who fights him off. As the boat rocks back and forth, it splits open even wider.

Tommy tries to snag the noose with his foot.

Jason gets a stronger hold on the boy.

Tommy's foot catches the chain and he pulls it to his outstretched fingers. The boy then swings around and manages to get the noose over Jason's head. Enraged, <u>Jason lunges at him</u>.

The boat bursts in half! <u>Both are dragged under</u>.

Megan screams hysterically.

Underwater, the large boulder falls to the bottom of the lake. As Tommy struggles to free himself from Jason's grasp, the noose is yanked tightly around Jason's neck. He lets go of one hand off Tommy as he tries to pull off the choke chain.

Megan and the kids are petrified.

Tommy struggles to hold his breath and fight off Jason. Angry, but weakening, Jason tries again to strangle Tommy.

On the top of the lake, bubbles continue to appear. Suddenly, they cease.

Megan covers her mouth in dread.

After a moment, Tommy's limp body rises to the surface. Megan tells the kids to stay there. She runs and dives into the water. Swimming to her man, she grabs him and treads back to shore

Underwater, HER LEG IS GRABBED BY JASON'S HAND. She struggles to not be pulled down to her death. Her foot kicks at Jason's throat! A stream of bubbles rush from his mask. His hand lets go of her leg. <u>Jason's body hangs underwater lifeless at last</u>.

Megan pulls Tommy's body to shore. The concerned children surround them as she gives him mouth to mouth. He doesn't respond.

Megan starts to cry as she pushes on his abdomen. Little Nancy closes her eyes and begins to whisper a quiet prayer. Megan keeps trying to revive him. Finally, Tommy coughs. He's alright. She embraces him thankfully. Nancy smiles warmly at them. Looking over at the lake, Tommy tells them the nightmare is over. Jason has gone home. Fade out.

We fade up into the next morning at the cemetery. Martin, the old caretaker, is bent over pulling weeds. Slowly, we move toward him. He senses something and turns <u>startled</u>! From over the shoulder of a dark suited, grey haired STRANGER, we see Martin turn <u>overly</u> friendly. In fact, he seems to be hiding true terror. "Oh, morning, Mr. Voorhees. Haven't seen you for quite a few months." There is a deathly silence from the mysterious man. Martin points nervously, "I've been taking <u>real</u> good care of your wife and son's graves. Go look". Mr. Voorhees hands him a small wad of money. Martin is very grateful as he backs away. The strange father of Jason slowly approaches the graves of his son and wife. He stands menancingly over them. Watching. Waiting. We finally see him. But only his eyes. Dark. Evil. Demonic. Then the worst occurs. Slowly they look <u>right at us</u>.

We dissolve over his spine chilling eyes to the sunlit and serene lake. We glide tranquilly over the blue water to the middle of the lake. Then moving closer to the water, we wait. JASON EMERGES AT US. No, it's only his infamous mask. Freed from its owner, it floats peacefully along old Crystal Lake...for now.

The End

INDEX

Alice in Wonderland (TV miniseries) 52-53
Allen, Woody 6, 33, 39-40, 227
Anya's Bell 180, 215-217
Ash, Albert 2, 36, 44, 185-186, 189, 191, 317
Amazing Stories 75, 76, 101
At Risk 291, 295-297, 303
Ball, Lucille 6, 42-43
Banks, Steven 1-3, 77, 82, 113-115
Behind the Mask 180, 204-215
Bertinelli, Valerie 125, 126, 129-130, 134, 137-138, 154-158, 179, 181, 184
Black Hole, The 2, 57-58
Brando, Marlon 4, 179, 204-209, 215
Burman, Tom 50, 62, 67, 81
Burnett, Carol 6, 42-43
Caesar, Sid 42-43
Capra, Frank 1, 6, 7, 33, 47-49, 75, 81, 90, 92, 96, 100, 101, 127, 135, 148, 168, 183, 286, 288
Chaplin, Charlie 1, 6, 9, 16-17, 34, 36, 37, 38, 39, 147, 207, 319
Cyber Seduction: His Secret Life 7, 230, 254, 269-274

D.C. Sniper: 23 Days of Fear 7, 230, 247-251, 277
Date with an Angel 76, 91-102, 103, 133, 255, 295, 299-300, 309
DeLaurentiis, Dino 78, 92, 95, 96, 97, 98, 99, 101, 107, 113, 114, 116, 138
Different Kind of Christmas, A 179, 194-197
Doors, The 2, 6, 9, 25, 26-28
Exorcist, The 57, 59, 103, 105, 138, 179, 216-221, 226, 237, 299
Fab Five: The Texas Cheerleader Scandal 5, 7, 231, 254, 282-289
Fairy Tale: A True Story 7, 179, 184-192, 282
Famous Monsters of Filmland 6, 51-52
Fire Next Time, The 125, 138-152, 198, 295, 299
Frankenheimer, John 6, 50, 53-55, 219-220, 240, 299
Freddy's Nightmares 76, 105-106, 238
Friday the 13th (TV series) 76-77, 102-105, 308

Friday the 13th Part 6: Jason Lives! 5, 6, 75, 83-91, 92, 96, 98, 131, 133, 148, 255, 308, 325-346
Front, The 291, 295-298, 303
Halmi, Robert 138-139, 145, 189
Hawes, Michael 61-66, 70, 75, 80
Hendrix, Jimi 2, 22, 23, 29, 312
Hitchcock, Alfred 1, 9, 87, 122, 134, 224, 293
Hollywood Forever Cemetery 1, 3, 16, 223, 306-311, 317
Home Entertainment Center 3, 77, 113, 115
Houdini, Harry 1, 13, 179, 189-191
In a Child's Name 125, 129-138, 148, 156, 162, 167, 175, 200
Incredible Machine, The 40
Incredible Shrinking Woman, The 40
It's a Wonderful Life 3, 47-49, 111, 196, 253, 299
Jagger, Mick 1, 9, 26, 314
Journey 7, 127, 171-174
Keaton, Buster 1, 34-37, 252
L.A. Mime Company, The 36, 41-45, 48, 96, 185, 316-317
Langdon, Harry 47-48
Leave of Absence 126, 163-165
Leaving L.A. 180, 199-201
Lies Boys Tell, The 7, 126, 149, 151, 165-171
Lloyd, Harold 34-36, 37-38
Lorre, Peter 3, 9, 13, 15-16, 308
Mancini, Chris 22, 28
Mancuso, Frank Jr. 83, 90, 96, 102-103, 105
Marceau, Marcel 1, 6, 31, 33-34, 60, 185
May Wines, The 24, 27, 312-313

McLoughlin, Ethel 12, 18-21
McLoughlin, Hannah 2, 7, 113-114, 175-177, 194, 195, 196-197, 254, 263, 264, 298, 307, 314
McLoughlin, Maurice "Navarre" 12-15, 16-18, 113-115
McLoughlin, Nancy 2, 7, 37-38, 55-57, 82, 85, 86, 87, 90, 91, 101, 138, 141, 151, 159, 160, 168, 175-176, 182, 192, 199, 200, 201, 221, 239, 254, 268, 298, 306, 307, 308, 314, 325
McLoughlin, Shane 2, 7, 112, 159-160, 175, 192-198, 254, 260, 307, 314
Miller, Nancy 180, 199-200, 227, 311
Monterey Pop Festival 2, 9, 22-23, 29
Murder in Greenwich 7, 229, 239-247, 250
Murder of Innocence, A 7, 20, 126, 137, 153-160, 162, 295
Nelson, Craig T. 126, 142-145, 149, 153, 167, 171, 198
Not Like Everyone Else 7, 201, 231, 254, 274-279
Odd Girl Out 7, 201, 230, 254, 261-268, 269, 274, 284
One Dark Night 2, 5, 60-71, 75, 78-83, 87, 88, 133, 222-224, 255, 295, 299, 305, 306, 308-310
Others, The (TV series) 180, 221-222
Prophecy (1979 film) 49-55, 62, 220
Rocky 46, 49, 111, 299, 312

Rolling Stones, The 24, 28, 30, 313
Scorsese, Martin 1, 46, 101, 132
She's Too Young 7, 230, 254-262, 268, 269, 272, 284
She-Wolf of London (TV series) 77, 113
Sherwood Oaks Experimental College 33, 46-47, 57
Sleeper 39-40
Sloths, The 312-315, 317
Smart, Jean 126, 159-161, 187, 230, 252
Something to Live For: The Alison Gertz Story 125, 138-141, 145, 162, 200
Spielberg, Steven 82, 101-102, 221-222, 240
Staircase Murders, The 7, 231, 245, 247, 278-282
Stearns, Craig 61, 81, 295
Stephen King's Sometimes They Come Back 6, 78, 106-110, 112-121, 127, 133, 152, 198, 216, 299, 305, 309

Tati, Jacques 1, 36
They Came from Outer Space (TV series) 77, 113
Third Twin, The 180, 201-204
Tilly, Meg 66, 68-69, 75, 80, 81, 127, 173-174
TNT (band) 23-24, 312
Turn of the Screw, The (film) 7, 179, 181-185, 188, 189, 282
Unsaid, The 7, 229, 231-239
Van Dyke, Dick 6, 33, 41-45, 306
Van Dyke and Company 41-45
Very Married Christmas, A 230, 251-254
Welles, Orson 1, 37, 45, 206
Who, The 23, 35, 319
Woman Under the Influence, A 20, 46
Wronged Man, The 7, 291-296, 303, 304
Yarn Princess, The 7, 126, 159-162, 187, 295

www.ingramcontent.com/pod-product-compliance
Lightning Source LLC
Chambersburg PA
CBHW050332230426
43663CB00010B/1824